AMERICAN WOMEN

images and realities

AMERICAN WOMEN
Images and Realities

Advisory Editors
ANNETTE K. BAXTER
LEON STEIN

A Note About This Volume

New Englander Anna Carpenter Garlin Spencer (1851-1931) early revealed a talent for public speaking. In 1891 she became the first female ordained minister in Rhode Island. In later years she was associated with the New York Society for Ethical Culture, the New York School of Philanthropy (Social Work), the University of Wisconsin, the University of Chicago and Columbia University. She was concerned with factory laws, child labor and, as head of the Family Relations Division of the American Social Hygiene Association, with prostitution. This collection of her articles analyzes the dilemmas of women in such roles as lady, genius, spinster, worker, and post-graduate mother.

WOMAN'S SHARE
IN SOCIAL CULTURE

BY

ANNA GARLIN SPENCER

ARNO PRESS

A New York Times Company

New York • 1972

Reprint Edition 1972 by Arno Press Inc.

Reprinted from a copy in The Wesleyan
University Library

American Women: Images and Realities
ISBN for complete set: 0-405-04445-3
See last pages of this volume for titles.

Manufactured in the United States of America

- - - - - - - - - - - - -

Library of Congress Cataloging in Publication Data

Spencer, Anna (Garlin) 1851-1931.
    Woman's share in social culture.

    (American women: images and realities)
    1. Woman--Social and moral questions. 2. Woman--
History and conditions of women. I. Title.
II. Series.
HQ1399.S5 1972   301.41'2   72-2623
ISBN 0-405-04479-8

WOMAN'S SHARE IN SOCIAL CULTURE

WOMAN'S SHARE
IN SOCIAL CULTURE

BY

ANNA GARLIN SPENCER

NEW YORK AND LONDON
MITCHELL KENNERLEY
MCMXIII

Press of J. J. Little & Ives Company
East Twenty-fourth Street
New York

DEDICATION

To the memory of Lucretia Mott, who prophesied in life and in work the Womanhood of the Future, not neglectful of least or oldest duty, not loath to assume largest and newest service, linking the past and present to coming ideals.

CONTENTS

NOTE

These chapters have appeared in THE FORUM *as monthly articles in a series. They are here reproduced for the most part in original form, any repetition occurring by reason of this previous use being justified, it is thought, as giving special emphasis to each sub-topic. The analytical Table of Contents is introduced not only to show succinctly the main argument advanced, but also in the hope that it may prove of service in class-work should the book be honored by use in sociological study.*

INTRODUCTION

EVERY problem of environmental change becomes
more acute as it works inward toward the family.
Every element of social unrest intensifies both in stress
and in difficulty, as it relates itself to the home and
to the position of women who constitute the centre of
the home. Every awkwardness of adjustment of our
still adolescent democracy is shown in higher light
as it touches the life and labor of women. Every demand upon personal character for new types of excellence to match the new forms of social organization
acquires a more imperious force as it appeals to the
changing feminine ideal. Every obstacle to human
progress toward justice and the common weal as
against the privilege of caste, of custom and of wealth,
shows a more tragic quality where the selfishness or
shallowness or coquetry or low-mindedness of women
blocks the upward way. Every question of the sociologist cuts, like the etcher's tool, more deeply as it
approaches that most subtle and most fundamental of
all problems: . . . What is the nature and function of Woman? Every moral devotion that strives
to attain and to preserve a human personality equally
strong and fine in Being and in Doing fibres upon its
deepest root as it engages in its newest spiritual adven-

i

ture, namely, a Womanhood justly balanced in individual achievement and in social service.

What wonder, then, that the "woman movement" has become more complex and confusing as it has advanced from point to point? That women should own their own souls and be morally responsible for their own acts seemed clear long ago. That women should own their own persons to the extent of being secured by law against cruelty and outrage has seemed evident for a considerable period. That women should own their own property by inheritance, and the fruit of their own labor as earnings, began to seem clear to our civilization early in the last century. That women should own their own "influence," should "make up their own minds," should be accountable for their own share in social control and in social uplift, is newly perceived. That women for their own sake, and for the extension of a truer democracy, should be steadied and sobered by equal political responsibility with men in the State, is fast coming to wide acceptance. That women have a right to the utmost reach of educational, professional, artistic, commercial and industrial opportunity as a basis for capacity for that self-support which is an essential to feminine as to masculine dignity of character, is approaching perception. That society needs the full liberation of all potential possibilities of feminine contribution to the thought and the labor of the world, is on its way to belief. That the distinct and specialized genius of womanhood, as the outgrowth of unique functional discipline in the experience of life, has in it a gift to human growth which shall yet add peculiar value to every sphere of mental and moral endeavor, is dimly appearing as a truth of the future. That these principles, and their relation to the evolution of the race, may be seen a little clearer, is the purpose of this book. The fruit of many years of thought, of study and of observation, these inadequate but serious essays of interpretative and appreciative criticism aim to give some clarifying help in this vital crisis in the individuation of woman. The keynote of this study is that while "new occasions teach new duties" and the call to-day is for women to assume with courage and with gladness the new life of the new time, new duties do not abrogate old responsibilities, but rather enlarge, spiritualize and transform them.

In a time when so many believe that all that mankind needs for its perfection is new and more clever mechanisms of economics, statecraft and statute law, it is peculiarly difficult for women, as newcomers into the world of public affairs, to keep their old deep-bedded faith in the worth and power of the individual choice. In a time when all the inherited ethical standards and religious sanctions are radically changing in the crucibles of scientific laboratories, it is especially hard for women, as newly claiming the moral and intellectual initiative, to bear testimony to the inner trusts and aspirations upon which their souls have fed. Newly arrived, as a partially accepted and slightly modifying factor in the organized church, school, shop, market-place, State and social order, which man has arranged for his own development and his own self-expression, women hesitate to voice their mental questionings or moral hesitations concerning these established institutions, lest they be thought still childish and untrained and their chance "to do what men do" be taken away or made too difficult for success. Eager women students in college and university take the man-made ideals and civilization they find there outlined as a fixed intellectual and ethical mould, to which they must fit themselves or fail in their new ambition to become complete and effective human beings, each on her own account. Women, as well as men, have for the most part a far clearer realization of the one-sidedness of woman's functional development, than of the equal one-sidedness of man's discipline of life. Men and women alike take what they find as already developed out of the segregation of the sexes in all the deeper and higher areas of human experience and achievement, and assume that what men have thought and written and lived and done is the measure of human power. Slowly, however, the truth is dawning upon women, and still more slowly upon men, that woman is no stepchild of nature, no Cinderella of fate to be dowered only by fairies and the Prince; but that for her and in her, as truly as for and in man, life has wrought its great experiences, its master attainments, its supreme human revelations of the stuff of which worlds are made. That woman has been but a "silent partner" in the building of the outer temples of thought and action during the ages when she has been denied the tools of self-expression in art and science, in literature and politics, is no proof that her contribution has been small even in these lines. It is an old error of man to forget to put quotation marks where he borrows from a woman's brain!

Margaret Fuller, the American sibyl, declared in her prophetic book *Woman in the Nineteenth Century,* "What woman asks for is not equal power, for of that omnipotent nature will never allow her to be defrauded, but a chartered right too fully recognized to be abused." That chartered right women are fast gaining in every field and in every land: the chartered right to legal protection from abuse, to legal property-holding and contract power; the chartered right to freedom of decision in the vital choices of life; to educational opportunities in which compulsory school laws include girls with boys; the chartered right to full citizenship, too long delayed after the eighteenth century struggle for the rights of man, but coming fast, at last, in all enlightened nations; the chartered right to reform the world if she can, to feel the pain of thought and know the joy of creative work, to drink the cup of mingled bitter and sweet which is pressed to the lips of those who lead their fellows in the upward march.

Even progressive women, however, are not as a rule fully emancipated from the fear of scorn if they magnify their own office, or the dread of indifference or even contempt from their elder brothers in the larger life if they stand for their own order. They have not yet become so sure of themselves as to reverence their own natures and take counsel of their own instincts while they traverse the highways that man has built. This is the main reason for the ethical mistakes

some most conscientious women are making; they are
testing their new activities by man's idealism rather
than by their own spiritual sanctions. If man has
gained a right, or overcome an obstacle, or attained a
goal, in a certain manner, it is natural for women to
think that man's way is the only way of attaining the
same human advantage when they come to see that it
is right and necessary to seek such for themselves.
This is the explanation of the sad ethical blunder of
the militant suffragists of England. They want the
rights men have gained for themselves, and know
they should have them for their own and their country's good. Failing receipt of justice on peaceful demand, and aware of the signal inconsistency of statesmen in this matter, they nerve themselves against the
age-long tendency of womanhood to depend upon
spiritual weapons alone, and with pale faces and
trembling hands take up the weapons of lawless revolt and anarchistic violence (weapons that man in
his highest estate has already discarded) in order to
force the issue of political justice. The fact that even
progressive women are not yet fully emancipated from
the effect of their long subjection to men is shown again
in the bitter sex-antagonism expressed by some reformers who are leading in the crusade against the
traffic in womanhood. There is a growing sex-solidarity among women which can no longer abide the
monstrous horror which casts its black shadow over
marriage and the home. This sex-solidarity of women
is the great, new asset of human fellowship, and is
destined to work miracles in socializing our still crude

democracy. Men have had their groups and fraternities and guilds, and have thrived socially within these firm bonds of allegiance to a partial brotherhood. Women have lacked these apprentice-disciplines in "team work"; having, until recently, been held strictly to their household sympathies. Even now, when women have entered the professions and higher occupations, they are not made fully free of the guild comradeship of the groups they enter. Perhaps this is in part owing to the fact that the time for most vital companionship in these ancestral groups of thought and of service seems past even for men. Each partial fellowship, however revered and prized, is becoming socialized; and the call is now for a world fraternity in a universal order of common service. However that may be, women are not yet, and may never be, full sharers in the guilds and fraternities that have played such a part in the world leadership of men. Instead, there is growing rapidly a guild of all womankind, a sisterhood of the mother-sex, a free-masonry of the feminine. This is making the trade union movement among women not a class grouping, but rather a mingling of rich and poor, wise and ignorant, strong and weak women for the benefit of the woman wage-earner. This sex-solidarity is making a union of professional women, lawyers, doctors, ministers, artists, business women, etc., more at one with each other than is either group with the men of like training and work. This sex-solidarity, crude and unlovely in some of its expressions, silly and sentimental in others, is yet binding women in a conscious loyalty of each to all and all to each which is giving even small-natured women a new sense of honor and a new power of coöperative action. This sex-solidarity of women has already built a mighty bridge to close the chasm between the "good" woman and the prostitute, and to hold in one common outreach of sympathy the honored mother and the woman of the street. This it is which sometimes creates sex-antagonism of a new sort. Pure and noble women, stung to the quick by the new and near view of the enormities of the social evil, often abhor the common manhood which consents to this abomination and has made fast the link between greed and lust, on the one side, and weakness, ignorance, even innocence and helplessness, on the other. When they have out-grown the passionate revolt of a new experience, these women will see more justly how many-sided conditions have bound men and women alike in evil chains which only men and women together can break.

The effect of the claim of the progressive and radical among women for equal power with men to protect and help, to reform and to advance, to discipline and to direct, on equal terms with men, themselves and all humanity, by voice and pen and daily task and vote, is to cause revolt on the part of timid and conservative women. Some of these who protest are only "anti-suffrage," all other sex-equalities being admitted by them as right and useful. Some are "anti-coeducational," sure that the age-long segregation in school secures the best training of the mind and heart. Some are anti-"economic-freedom," convinced that it is best for women to lean upon men and for men to be stif-

fened to duty by such dependence upon them. Some
are anti-outspoken "moral reform," feeling that "men
know best" and should be "let alone." All these protestants against the movement for equality of rights
and duties between the sexes are alike moved, however,
with a common fear lest the "new woman" prove less
lovely, less winning, less the happy custodian of the
idealism of men, less the devoted mother, less the inspirer of genius, less the embodiment of the sacred
reserves and intimate affections of life. The spiritual
significance of the revolution in the position of the
average womanhood, as coextensive with the rise and
growth of modern democracy, has not yet dawned
upon the mind of such doubters. The basic fact that
women must be democratized in order that democracy
may be socialized is not yet accepted by their consciousness. The deeper social reasons for the development of distinctive womanhood along its own lines, in
freedom and by means of absolute equality of opportunity in education and in activity, has not yet even appealed to their perception. Hence any departure by
radical women from the established feminine codes of
"morality of habits" and ethics of manners, strikes
terror to the souls of these protestants and makes them
shiver with apprehension lest women lose their rightful place in human relationship. The reckless speech
and undisciplined behavior and ungracious attitude
of a few leaders in the "woman movement" give some
reason for such fear. The fact, however, that the
position of woman has been so radically changed in
so short a time as a single century, from status to con-

tract in law, from passive to active in education, from
mass to personality in social life, and with so little
domestic friction and so little revolutionary struggle,
is proof that the interrelation of men and women in
the home has enabled them to keep step so nearly
that comradeship in the school and the State and the
industrial order has been comparatively easy to gain.

The explanation of these changes, however, and
their full significance in ethical advance have not yet
been embodied in educational guidance. This is the
reason for the many books about women and the
many activities by and for women which mark the
present day. This is especially the excuse for this small
contribution to the story of woman's share in race
culture.

What Emerson called "certificates of advance out
of fate into freedom" are held to-day by women's
hands; what he meant by "new perceptions which open
toward the Better and the Best" are grasped to-day
by women's insight. In the Hindoo fable Vishnu assumes one masculine form after another, from the
lowest to the highest, to mate with Maya as she as-
cends the stair of life from reptile to woman to become
at last a goddess, to woo him to become a god. So in
the new incarnation of the old spirit and purpose of
womanhood, if but that reincarnation becomes complete, we shall attain new uplift to man and new enticement onward for the race. Happily there is ample
prophecy of this outcome of the ferment and confusion
of the "woman movement" in the lives and achievements of many free and consecrated women of our

own day. Indeed, for the most part the womanhood of our time is moving along new pathways swiftly and with native power of instantaneous adjustment to difficult claims. To the highest leadership among women it is given to hold steadily in one hand the sacred vessels that hold the ancient sanctities of life, and in the other a flaming torch to light the way for oncoming generations.

Woman's Share in Social Culture

I

THE PRIMITIVE WORKING-WOMAN

REGULAR industry is rather an acquired habit than a natural tendency in the human race; and women rather than men seem first to have attained the discipline of a "steady job." The biologic hints of the busy bee, the industrious beaver, the ant, to whose example the human sluggard was long ago commended, all seem to have been taken lightly by the primitive man. Primitive woman, however, in a past too remote for any present trace of its earliest social processes, was harnessed to definite tasks which began with each morning. [1] Ward shows that although modern economists often talk as though "labor was natural to man and as though the main question was how to give men work enough to do" (and we may add of the right sort and under right conditions) "the original problem was how to make men work." He tells us

[1] Lester F. Ward, *Pure Sociology*, Chap. 13.

I

that in the primitive state, "Only the work of women in caring for the men and the children and in performing the drudgery of the camp approaches the character of labor" as we understand the term.

To be sure, primitive man had occasional activities of a strenuous and often dangerous sort. They are indicated by the saying of the Australian Kurnai:[2] "A man hunts, spears fish, fights and sits about; the rest is woman's work." Professor Haddon, writing interestingly about the primitive people of the Torres Straits, says: "The men fished, fought, built houses, did a little gardening, made fish-lines and fish-hooks, spears and other implements, constructed dance-masks, head-dresses and all the paraphernalia for the various ceremonies. They performed all the rites and the dances, and in addition did a good deal of strutting up and down, loafing and 'yarning.' The women cooked and prepared the food, did most of the gardening, collected and speared the fish, made clothing, baskets and mats." [3] Macdonald tells us that throughout Central Africa, "The work is done chiefly by the women. They hoe the fields, sow the seed and reap the harvest. They build the houses, grind the corn, brew the beer, cook, wash and care for all the material interests of the community. The men tend the cattle, hunt and go to war; they also do the tailoring, and spend much time sitting in council over the conduct of affairs."

These hints of conditions among undeveloped peoples give a reminiscent picture of the beginning of in-

[2] Fison and Howitt, *Kamilaroi and Kurnai.*
[3] James Macdonald, *East-Central African Customs.*

dustrial order in all primitive life. In apportioning sex-gifts women are generally denied the possession to any considerable extent of "inventive genius"; and from the point of view that "inventive genius loses sight of the practical and yields wholly to the spur of anticipated success residing in the mind" the denial is surely just. All the essential processes of peaceful industry, however, all those severely practical activities which led directly toward care for the individual life and comfort, and the start of the primitive home toward social well-being, were, as all students agree, initiated by women in the dim past. Hence, if woman is not markedly the inventor of the race she is the mother of inventions as well as of inventors. In the picturesque summary by [4] Mason of the life of the North American Indians, he describes the primitive woman as the first cutler, butcher, currier, tanner, tailor, dressmaker, milliner, hatter, toymaker, upholsterer, cook, spinner, weaver, sail-maker, decorative artist ("inventing the chevrons, herring-bones, frets and scrolls of all future art"), the first pack-animal and burden-bearer, the first miller, agriculturist, nursery-man and florist. As he declares: "All the peaceful arts of to-day were once woman's peculiar province."

Markham pictures the man-drudge—

> " Bowed with the weight of centuries he leans
> Upon his hoe, and gazes on the ground;
> The emptiness of ages in his face
> And on his back the burden of the world."

Otis T. Mason, *Woman's Share in Primitive Culture.*

But long before the centuries were counted, or the prehistoric ages set in their order, when even the rude hoe of Millet's peasant was undreamed of, the woman-drudge scraped the light soil with her sharp-edged stone or shell, made holes with her pointed "digging-stick" and planted the treasured seed preserved, perhaps by stealth, from one harvest to start another. And "in her face," however coarse-featured and un-lovely, the "emptiness" is touched with human purpose, as in patient service she binds upon her "back the burden" of the child, and goes about her unceasing toil. Wherever man's power of achievement has proudly made its mark upon the labor processes that have builded civilization, there, could he but trace them, are the prophetic signs of the handicraft of women in their crude but heroic beginnings of manual arts.

The reason for this priority of women in useful labor is of course obvious. Woman, from the first, enjoyed the special tutoring of that most persistent and effective trainer in industrial education which the world of nature has yet produced, the human infant. Any family of children, any single child, even, can provide the four prime essentials of discipline to reg-ular work—namely, an incentive to labor which can-not be ignored, an obvious suggestion of things to be done, a time-schedule (including a self-winding alarm clock), and a satisfying reward for duty well done! The woman and the child constituted, it is clear, the first social group. [5] "Mother and child," says Lippert,

[5] Julius Lippert, *Kulturgeschichte.*

"were the simplest elements of the earliest organization."

The biologic foundation for motherhood was so securely laid before the human was reached that our race started with this relationship as its most important and well-known social asset. Therefore woman long before man received the training of offspring in the capacity of inciter and director of labor. It is a recent decision of pedagogy that "no child should be obliged to employ an incompetent mother"; but the human race started with a clear conception that every child had a right to the service of some sort of a mother. And, as in primitive society all women are married, and all who can are required to have children, the first "female industrial school" is very ancient. Woman, as a human being of the mother-sex, found her job already waiting for her when she arrived upon the scene, and she has never been allowed to become an industrial "tramp" seeking her work afar. For the same reasons, woman has never had at her command those convenient "fictions" which have served man as ways of escaping irksome labor, and as means for procuring better opportunities for easier self-support. In short, woman, from the primitive mother to the modern housewife, has seldom, if ever, had a chance to "go a-fishing" at housecleaning time, or to plead "urgent business down-town" in domestic crises.

Pressed to her special tasks by the biologic push itself, primitive woman began at once to minister to the primal necessities of the race. In previous incarnations of the mother-spirit she had been drilled to suckle young with tenderness; to postpone for their comfort her own rest and play; to pick up food for offspring and feed them before her own hunger was appeased; to build nests for brooding and caretaking of the helpless; to develop courage and cunning for the protection of infant life; to engage in valiant essays into unknown fields of labor and of education, in order to train her little ones for independent life, and in this manner was made ready for the first experimentation of human existence in the region of social culture. Primitive woman thus carried over from the lower animal life into the human sphere a larger treasure than man had yet acquired of that pre-human tendency toward unselfish service to one's kin which has builded the family, and later the State. In that precedence of unselfish service the primitive woman implanted at the very centre of human progress that principle of "mutual aid" which [6] Kropotkin shows has from the beginning of sentient life modified and chastened the selfish strife for individual ends. In this was the first great contribution of earliest womanhood to social culture.

How and when man was first consciously and adequately harnessed to constant and peaceful labor is still matter of dispute among sociologists; but all agree that among the social forces that pressed him into the industrial yoke was the need of the human child for two parents and that both should serve the child and society from one common family impulse. In that

[6] **Prince Kropotkin,** *Mutual Aid.*

"prolongation of human infancy" which [7] Fiske regards as the "chief agency toward civilization," the mother could not do it all. Whether or not we hold with [8] Morgan, [9] McLennan, [10] Bachofen, and others to the theories of "Horde" and of "Mother-right" which affirm a period of woman's supremacy in social order at the start, we must believe (and from evidence adduced by both the followers and opponents of these theories) that, in the sphere of family rule and that private law of custom which antedated political and legal forms of control, the primitive woman had precedence and power. On the other hand, whether or not we hold with [11] Westermarck and others that "pairing was from the first the rule among the human race," and that the human father did not allow the birds and higher beasts to outdo him in conjugal affection and in the aid rendered the mother in care of offspring, and that he took his toll of power as family "head" from the first in payment for his coöperation, we must still believe that a father who comes and goes at will, and who at best rarely elects to stay for life with one mate and her young, is a less sure support to the growing family than the mother who is fastened to the infant from the hidden beginnings of its life until special care is no longer needed. All theories of primitive social groupings seem alike to indicate that for a longer or shorter period, in a more or less com-

[7] John Fiske, *The Destiny of Man.*
[8] Lewis H. Morgan, *Systems of Consanguinity.*
[9] J. F. McLennan, *The Patriarchal Theory.*
[10] J. J. Bachofen, *Das Mutterrecht.*
[11] Edward Westermarck, *The History of Human Marriage.*

plete irresponsibility, and under every form of early
marriage and family autonomy, man enjoyed privileges
of roaming at will and of temporary sojourn with wife
and children as a "paying guest," which made his apprenticeship to family obligations a rather difficult
matter.

That grotesque expression of man's undisciplined
imagination the [12] *couvade,* so widely extended as a custom, and so clearly testifying to conscious assertion by
man of his paternity, and consequent headship of the
household, shows that in some way and time man began to think it well to proclaim his relationship to offspring by a formal ceremony. The practical genius of
woman would never have initiated a form of ceremonial so extravagantly troublesome as the pretended
illness of the man of the house at the moment when a
new baby claimed attention! And, judging from the
general habit of primitive man in respect to steady
labor, he would hardly have "taken to bed" at such a
time, "with simulated pains and weakness and atten-
dant care of neighbors and friends," had he fully
realized that such proclamation of fatherhood must
finally put him into industrial bondage to what he then
despised as "woman's work." Had he but known it,
not make-believe "labor pains," but actual drudgery
of daily life as "head of the family" was prophetically
symbolized by this ceremonial nonsense. How the
primitive woman must have laughed at the absurd
custom in the privacy of her own consciousness—however solemn and deferential she may have been out-

[12] See Ch. Letourneau, *The Evolution of Marriage.*

wardly in the presence of her lord and master; as women of later date have had their secret fun over many man-devised methods of asserting masculine superiority at the very crises of domestic experience when men are most helpless, and often most in the way.

Meanwhile, as woman went about her daily tasks, and infant society was getting used to peaceful ways of living with one's kind, man was accomplishing great things along the line of specialization of labor processes. His special tasks of fighting and hunting, his habit of moving about and "talking over affairs," had given him at once his massive bone structure and great muscular development, and his growth in the rational quality. Although often a mere "casual laborer," his particular tasks required tremendous spurts of energy, and also gave him a fine turn toward that pride of achievement which constitutes the soil in which genius is grown. War, man's earliest and latest monopoly, has always greatly stimulated invention, and has developed that deceptive capacity which furnishes so much raw material of intellectual power. Moreover, the catching of wary fish, the trapping and killing of shy animals, the taming of wild beasts for purposes of transportation, burden-bearing and agriculture, all gave man a decided bent toward making his brains serve his desires. In the language of the modern factory system, man's early tasks were in the nature of "piece-work," while woman always had to "work by the day." Man could "speed up" for a definite achievement and afterwards rest until another crisis of effort—in itself a distinct industrial advantage. It

is in the nature of "piece-work," to make individual
capacity conscious and manifest, to increase the skill
and rapidity of operations, and to give a keen sense
of interest in the process, as well as in the ends, of
labor. In this manner, and by these means, man early
acquired a persistent bent toward specialization and
toward perfection in his work, which has stood him
and the world in good stead. As producer of distinctive and increasingly appreciated economic values, and
as leader in that mastery of physical forces for human
use that has resulted in modern civilization, man was
aided industrially toward his legal control of social
relationships, and his preëminence in the formal culture of the schools.

One by one, man's specializing capacity took over
the multifarious occupations of women, which women
could never develop to their utmost reaches of skill
because of the necessity of serving as Jack-at-all-trades
which the demands of the family have unto this day
laid upon them. One by one, man assumed as his own,
and often shut woman out from pursuing, the tasks
that he found made ready to his hand by her efforts.
This is not the place for a recital of "the invasion" of
man into "woman's sphere," but it furnishes interesting
reading. Woman's priority in the industrial field,
however, enabled her to prepare all the processes of
peaceful labor for the more specialized genius of man,
and slowly induct him, through the crippled and aged
who could not fight, and by the training of young boys,
into the ways of industrial progress ordained for his
travel. This was the second great contribution of

primitive woman to social culture. Nor did woman's path-finding for the family and the social good end here; primitive woman took the first steps on that dark path which led toward the higher industrial organization of later societies, the path in which she was driven to incredible exertions, from without, by cruelty and oppression.

It is claimed by most sociologists that man was tamed to the labor harness chiefly by the institution of human slavery: that only such an economic "despotism" could have "set the mould" of masculine industry. If that is so, then here, as elsewhere in the world of labor, women led the way along the path to future civilization. [13] Bebel says: "Woman was the first creature to taste the bitter fruit of bondage." Somewhere along the line of woman's experience and discipline of life (there is still much disagreement as to the precise point) her natural impulse to work for the benefit of the child and all the weak and needy of her kind was rudely accentuated by man's forcible use of her as a slave laborer, the "thing" of service for himself and the family that he had captured or purchased, stolen or begged. The story of man's oppression of woman is confessed by all students of human society to constitute the blackest page of human slavery. Happily we are not obliged, in view of all the testimony so far gathered, to accept the unmitigated horrors of this enslavement of women as summed up by. [14] Letourneau and others. There is evidence to show that even

---

[13] August Bebel, *Woman and Socialism.*
[14] Ch. Letourneau, *The Evolution of Marriage.*

in savage life the intimacies of sex-relationship made some appeal to affection and to consideration, even, that tended to soften the bond; and there is more evidence to show that woman's inherent power in the family circle, her never wholly violated control of some domestic customs and rites, her influence as teacher of all girls and of all little boys, her power to make man uncomfortable in underhand ways when he was "bad," and her more subtle power to give him unexpected joy when he was "good," have all modified the slavery of woman to man as no other type of slavery has been modified. This, however, gives but a slight softening to what was the greatest social crime ever committed, and the most stupid of social mistakes ever stumbled into—the subjection of the mothers of the race.

The great puzzle of sociology has been to explain that enslavement of women. How was it accomplished? By brute force, say some. But the savage woman is too nearly the physical equal of her mate for that to be the sole solution. By religious doctrines and customs, say others. But how did religion come to take that turn? By reason of the burden of the child which kept woman from self-assertion and self-defence and allowed her to be overcome half unconsciously, say others. But how did it come about that man should generally desire to use that supreme proof of woman's usefulness to the race as the weapon by which to subdue and ill-use her, when many beasts and birds before him had learned to "love and cherish" their mothering mates? By the rise of the institution of private property, by which man came to claim as his sole possession the marital rights and power over womanhood which had been before a horde or communal ownership, say others. But proof is lacking of the universality of this "collective marriage," and even inheritance by the female line does not always, if ever, indicate a true "matriarchate" at all corresponding to the male headship of the family by which woman was enslaved. By the change from familial to political organization, with the military bases of the State in which woman was counted out, say others. But the patriarchal family itself is the central element in woman's bondage, and that developed far earlier than the feudal state of military order. [15] Ward's now famous explanation, namely, that "life begins as female and that the male sex is an afterthought of nature"; that human life begins with an established "gynecocracy" or woman rule as shown in primitive hordes; that the origin of masculine supremacy is in the sexual selection by all females of male strength, cunning and power of every sort; that in the development of the rational faculty of man, by this process, woman finally became the slave of the intellectual powers her own sex had evolved, the victim of a Frankenstein master for whose ability to destroy her freedom and her dignity of choice in mating, the eager activity of her side of the house of life was responsible—this explanation, although suggestive of broad outlines of development, is altogether too simple and partial to cover all the ground. This theory

[15] Lester F. Ward, *Pure Sociology*, Chap. 14.

makes the final step by which man assumed entire do-
minion over the sex which had created him one following his belated discovery of his own paternity, and
marked by a violent crisis in human relationship. We
have not sufficient proof on the one hand of a condition of human existence in which primitive woman
was the free and honored creature this theory seems
to presuppose; nor, on the other hand, have we sufficient proof that in any special era was there, for the
race in general, one such conscious and tragic struggle
between men and women for social supremacy, from
which all men emerged triumphant and all women
hopelessly captive. The antithesis of "woman-rule"
and "man-rule" suggests that often misleading tendency of the philosophic mind to "evolve from the inner
consciousness" a theory so symmetrical and commanding that it tolerates no contrary "ifs and buts," and
masses all facts for its sole service. It is a bit safer
to mix common sense with social facts reported by
differing observers; as with medical prescriptions
when doctors disagree. It is sensible to conclude from
the diverse evidence that the disciplines of sex relationship have been varied, that the male creature had
attained much power to grab more than his share of
good things before he became human, that women were
always weighted by motherhood's demands too heavily
to keep a sharp eye out for their own advantage, that
sexual selection was but one of many agencies by
which Nature built up the rational faculty and put
brains in the saddle, and that there was hardly likely
to be so great an exception to the slowly evolving

changes in human development as a "landing," part
way up the ladder, on which all men definitely gained
from bloody contest a wholly new control of all
women.

It is true that the *couvade* of primitive custom has
its more advanced counterpart in the tragedy of *The
Furies*, in which [16] Æschylus pictures a conscious
change from the reckoning and duty of relationship
solely on the mother's side, to the doctrine announced
by Apollo that "the male is the generative source, the
mother but the nurse of the newly sown offspring."
The Furies, rising from the underworld to defend
the "blood-claim" of motherhood, excuse Clytemnes-
tra's murder of her husband because she "was not the
kindred of the man she slew," and call upon Minerva
and the citizens of Athens asked in to settle the dispute, not to "ride down the ancient laws" and let Orestes, the slayer of his mother, "to whom he was bound
in blood," escape their vengeance. Orestes, justified
at last by Minerva herself for slaying her "who gave
him birth," because his "dark-souled mother slew his
dearest father," ushers in that "revolution of new
laws" which the Erinnys so fearfully bewail.

Probably the Græco-Roman civilization developed
unique self-consciousness in changes of sex-relationship
and family order, as it also gave to patriarchal claims
unexampled legal and religious definiteness. But even
in this case, preserved in its spirit by literary genius,
in the change from the maternal to the paternal relationship, the maternal side was not left wholly bereft

[16] Æschylus, *The Furies*, T. A. Buckley, translator.

of privilege and power. As Æschylus makes Minerva
declare, woman has always had and must ever have
"some first-fruits of sacrifice for children and the rites
of marriage," even in temples in which she was bought
and sold. To her has been ever intrusted the "safety
of mortal seed," even when man's greedy power has
denied her all right in offspring. She has been enabled
to "render joyful offices with thoughts of common
weal," even when man-made laws have defrauded her
of the simplest rights of humanity. We must believe,
therefore, that no one line of evolution in marriage
and the family, and hence no one explanation of the
cause, the methods and the forms of the enslavement
of women, can be accepted as complete. The old nursery rhyme that tells of the stately wife "who had a
little husband no bigger than her thumb, she put him
in a pint pot and there she bid him drum," may indeed
hark back to some Amazonian reminiscence of the
insects that carry their male companions in pockets
provided by Nature! And, on the other hand, the
woman of the East who must not sit or eat before her
lord, or the savage slave who carries on her person
the scars of her master's daily chastisement, may find
their progenitors in equally remote vagaries of
Nature.

In many ways, through darker or lighter paths,
through many mixed conditions, women and men have
attained the relative positions which the earlier and
more despotic forms of political organization fixed
in unjust laws. In any event the "brutal treatment of
women" which Spencer says was "constant and uni-

versal" has not prevented women from acquiring refinement of feeling, some measure of moral excellence,
and many self-protecting charms, even in the savage
state. Hence that brutality must have had some limits and many palliatives hard to discover from the
modern standpoint. Humboldt declared that "Nature
has woman in her special care." Certainly Nature
made woman exceeding tough of fibre and hard to
kill, in preparation for her manifold burdens and
the abuse she was destined to receive. But, in addition, Nature gave her some weapons of defence all
her own, and enlisted the very claim of masculine
ownership which wrought her deepest degradation in
behalf of her protection against indiscriminate outrage. Above all it must be remembered that although
women have seldom owned property they have very
generally been property, and thrift early learned to
take care of its own. Women were too valuable as
laborers in the beginnings of the industrial order for
the rudest and least instructed social sense to permit
them, permanently, or for any considerable period of
time, to be destroyed or hopelessly crippled in their
usefulness as at once mothers and servants. In this
slow amelioration of even the horrors of slavery
which women accomplished from their coign of vantage at the centre of human affection in the home, and
also through their early understood economic value,
they have made their third great contribution to social
culture.

We are but just beginning, however, to recognize
the full value of woman's early service to "the com-

mon weal." "It is all work, and forgotten work, this
many-peopled world," says Carlyle. How much
more deeply buried in oblivion has been the labor of
women than even the humblest toil of man, until this
later day! Poets and painters have sometimes pictured the value and the pathos of the peasant and the
artisan after man became a farmer and craftsman.
Not until the new sciences were born did the more
fundamental labor of women emerge to view. In that
greatest poem of the vocations yet written, the author
of *Ecclesiasticus,* although paying exclusive homage to
the sage and the ruler, as was the wont of ancient
writers, still does such justice to the manual laborers
as to declare:

> "These are they that maintain the fabric of the world,
> And without them is no city builded." [17]

It is this "fabric of the world," rather than any pattern wrought upon it by the genius of great persons,
in which the new psychology and the new sociology are
chiefly concerned. It is the contribution to social progress by the humbler mass of men and women, this
which has been so scornfully ignored by the older
writers of history, which to-day yields to social science
the truest answers to the riddles of human growth.
In this "fabric of the world" of common life woman
is the warp—the threads of her being "stretched on
the loom of time" from out the mystery of the past
on toward the mystery of the future without a break.

[17] The Apocrypha, Ecclesiasticus, Chap. 38.

Man is the woof—passed from pattern to pattern by the changing shuttles that weave the stuff of human progress and oft embroidering upon the endless web the splendid characters that inspire reverence and admiration. In the massive contribution of womanhood to the social fabric the part played by the primitive working-woman appears to-day, for the first time, in its true proportions. Rightly typified by the Eskimo woman who rises in the dim morning twilight of an arctic winter to set her rude hut in order and stir the fire for others' comfort, the ancient mothers of the race started the first steps of human endeavor on the paths of social order in the gray dawn of human existence. The primitive working-woman gave the "curtain-raiser" of prehistoric experience that prepared human consciousness for the epic of history. In the dream-like pantomime of her opening prologue, in which man passes back and forth in fleeting and inconsequent action, and in which not individual women but collective womanhood holds the stage, her cloud of witnesses show forth her mighty gifts. Silently she sets in place the four cornerstones of the house of life:

The treasury of pre-human motherhood to dower humanity.

The initiation of the race into useful and peaceful labor.

The softening of the rigors of slavery by a unique appeal to pity and affection.

The cultivation from within the home, even in captivity, of those coöperative impulses which make for social welfare.

In and through these gifts the primitive woman appears to-day more modern to the instructed sympathy than many of the "speaking characters" that follow her in the drama of historic times. The warring heroes who must die on the battlefield or be disgraced, the unsocial rulers who despoiled the people to make a bestial holiday for courts, the aberrant geniuses who overlaid simple human duty with vagaries of theology that instituted bloody inquisitions, even the philosophers who captured the idealism of the race for unworkable and often dangerous theories of human conduct—these all are less in harmony with our present and oncoming industrial and social order than is the womanhood that led the way toward social solidarity.

As the searchlight of science is turned from one dark corner to another of the stage whereon the kindergarten of the race held session, these simple everyday workers of the mother-sex become our familiar and well-beloved teachers. They are more and more perceived to be the real "prophetesses," symbolized by some religions as deities—those who in half-conscious response to the "vast soul that o'er them planned," in the dark and terror and suffering of the earliest time, "builded better than they knew" the foundations of the Temple of Humanity.

II

THE ANCIENT AND THE MODERN LADY

IT is recorded that Alfred of England, the Good and the Great, was illiterate until the age of twelve years, and that he was then incited to learning by his charming young stepmother, Judith, the granddaughter of Charlemagne and also of that earlier Judith who was in her day "the most accomplished woman in France." The pretty story runs, that the tactful stepmother showed the sons of Æthelwolf, of whom Alfred was the youngest, a book of Saxon poetry, beautifully illuminated, and promised it as a gift to the one who should earliest learn to read it. Whereupon Alfred spoke first and asked: "Will you really give that book to him who can first understand and repeat it?" At this, we are told, his stepmother "smiled with satisfaction" and confirmed the promise; upon which the boy took the book from her hand and "went to his master to read it and in due time brought it back to her and recited it."

If, as Professor Cook [1] suggests in the preface to his translation of the epic fragment—*Judith*—the

---

[1] Albert Stanborough Cook, *Judith; An Old English Epic Fragment.*

21

Saxon poem promised as a reward for learning to
read, was this same heroic song, which in subtle compliment by its author bore her name, we have in this
incident of Alfred's stepmother a complete illustration
of the social value of the lady at her best.   Inspiring
works of genius by her loveliness and sympathetic
appreciation, lifting and sweetening social intercourse
by the higher companionships of literature and art,
and handing on the fruits of learning and the gifts
of imagination to ardent youth, the lady of this type
is the fair link between the intellectual achievements
of the race and the social life of cultured leisure.

The lady is but the woman of the favored social
class; she is, however, more than a member of a special
class; she is the earliest of womanhood to attain individuality.   She is the first person singular of the
female sex.   She begins her career as a belle of some
savage tribe; some maiden of unusual beauty and attractiveness, according to the prevailing standards of
her time and place, who by the partiality of her elders
or by her own daring appeal succeeds in getting herself
made a "favorite," and in securing the service of less
desired women to ease for her the burden of feminine labor.   She is always, at first, young; generally
very young.   The "old lady" cannot be found in primitive society, save as she is transformed into a priest-
ess or a public counsellor in those early forms of social
organization which preserve most ancient ideals of
sacredness and power along the female line of descent.
She may be, as in Chinese society, the acknowledged
head of domestic concerns, custodian of never-disputed

customs, and in a sense therefore the lady in command. But for the mass of old women in less advanced civilizations the fear of their tendency toward "witchcraft," the dislike of their power as mothers-in-law and the complete ignorance of their possibilities of social use, combine to make them either ignored or so overworked as to destroy them prematurely.

As law supersedes custom, and history grows out of unwritten experience, the individual lady becomes more clearly one of a class, with certain distinctive caste markings. The power of the individual, even in the restricted sense possible to women of any era, is always manifested by the lady; but when she is no longer a rare exception and becomes one of many, her place and function are fixed, as in classic civilization. The Roman matron, at the head of her household, pure and high-minded, bred in a rigid puritanism that forbade frivolity and selfishness in women, comrade of her husband and his men-friends, dignified by certain noble relations to the State, and in later times winning great freedom of thought and movement, strong legal protection and economic power, is one type. The Greek wife, secluded within her home walls and a perpetual minor, unlearned and unfree, with whatever feeble "influence" she might have gained through her husband's affection largely neutralized by the brilliant women outside the family bond who alone shared the intellectual life of her country, is another type. The Greek wife, however, [2] "distinguished chiefly," as has been well said, "by the number of things she might

[2] Emily J. Putnam, *The Lady.*

not do," was a lady only in the strictly economic sense
of one who has slaves and servants to wait upon her;
she never attained the spiritual possibilities of the
privileged class of women.   The Feudal lady, although
busy with many cares and much restricted in law and
custom, yet had a recognized place of social command,
especially during the long absences of the lord of the
castle in his wars and his pleasures; and her power
over "her set," and over the dependants of her house,
was of the strongest.   She was able to surround herself with a home atmosphere of her own choosing and
with a crowd of artists, singers, writers and courtiers
who were my lady's knights, rather than my lord's
vassals.   The lady of the manor house, again, friend
of churchmen and intimate of statesmen, made it clear
amid the changing life of the Renaissance and at the
beginning of modern civilization that although man
may be the "master" of the house, woman is the mistress of its functions.   He may and still does rule all
the conditions of vital existence, but she controls the
realm of conventional society in its ethics, its æsthetics,
and its manifold customs.

In any case, in near or remote times, the lady stands
on a pedestal above the common life in privilege and
protection, raised to distinction of personal outline
and individual opportunity either by slave laborers or
serving attendants or at least by mechanisms that lessen her work for self or for family.   She is placed and
sustained there, for the most part, by some one man or
some small class of men of power and wealth.   In
early times she owes her escape from that complete

subordination of personal wish to family obligation
that marks the lot of the mass of women, to her personal charms, physical or mental, and to her good
fortune in securing the kind of husband who can afford
and appreciate a lady for a wife. As family autonomy
becomes more strictly outlined in historic periods, as
the patriarchal system, whether more or less perfect
in form, develops "noble blood," as the growth of
private property gives special power to the strong and
the favored, she becomes able to inherit "in her own
right" the chance to stand upon this pedestal and to
attain this opportunity. As, for example, this same
Judith, wife of Æthelwolf, was accounted "noble" before her marriage and afterward sat upon an equal
throne beside her royal husband.

The lady then, as daughter, wife or mother, is in
a social position elevated above the common life and
can therefore begin to show special gifts of quality
or faculty, although in a limited, "feminine" field of
thought and action. She may, as a primary distinction, differ in her way of life from the unmitigated usefulness demanded of the mass of her sex. She can
have things done for her instead of always doing
things for others. She may therefore have some
leisure to learn, and still more important, some chance
to find out what she would like to be and to do on
her own account. She can thus begin to develop that
"infinite variety" in womanliness which is the basis
of selective love. She can begin to make conscious and
to attach to herself that idealism in man of which she
is destined to become the custodian and guide. She

can lead the way toward that "play activity" of sex-attraction which gives the delicate touch of romance to the mating of men and women. She can, when risen to full self-consciousness, realize in sensitive temperamental reaction to the Time-Spirit of her day the essence of the intellectual life of man; even when still forbidden to share his formal learning. She can thus draw great and wise men to her intimate companionship by an appreciation untroubled by desire for self-expression. In this way she may become the special providence of artists and men of talent, inspire works of genius, and, incidentally, keep genius from starving to death before it has "verified its credentials." She can incite to noblest devotion to the State and stimulate activity to ends of personal and domestic, even ecclesiastical and civic, beauty. Emerson says: "Women stimulate production and finish literature and art in conversation." He means here, of course, the lady of the cultured circles of society, and she has often become all that this implies.

It took the lady a long time to emerge from the indistinguishable mass of merely useful womanhood. The "gentleman," in the sense of a man who is served by slave, vassal or inferior of some sort and who can order others to relieve him of disagreeable tasks, arrived first; and naturally, since he so early secured the constant service of woman, as the first slave, before he could settle down sufficiently to tame for servitude his alien captives or his own weaker brethren. The degraded condition of the high-caste Hindoo wife today shows how far the men of a race can go toward superior intellectual life, refinement of taste, high breeding in manners, freedom in choice of occupation, and the capacity for noble friendships among their own sex, and yet leave their women behind in the darkness of ignorance and domestic servitude.

Not until some women were raised above the necessity of unremitting drudgery, not until some wives were chosen for other than purely economic reasons or even those of family inheritance, could the lady appear. Not until the ideal of desirable womanhood included some sense of a social return from her leisure, and some perception of the advantage to man of sharing his pleasures with woman, could the class of the lady evolve. As members of such a class the lady has shown the special traits and functions of her order with well-defined outline. Certain things she must never do; certain others she must always do; and certain others she may attempt or should if possible accomplish—quite in the same fashion as other classes in society have been differentiated.

First, then, the lady must not work at the forms of labor demanded of the rest of her sex. At least she must not do so while the rules and practice of ladyhood are forming. After her social status is secure, and the ideal of the lady contains a character content as well as an economic differentiation, she may do many unusual things, and not imperil her caste. But, as in the case of all "climbers," she must obey conventional taboo to the letter while winning her prominence. On the other hand, the lady must be as responsible for the comfort of her family by securing it through the manual labor of others as the common run of women through their own effort. She must efficiently oversee and direct her slaves or servants to the required ends of family comfort and well-being at whatever personal cost. The fundamental definition of lady still stands as "a woman at the head of a household." Second, the lady must not earn money; she must not be a producer of any values not included in domestic and social occupations as outlined in the "theory of the leisure class." No one has ever been disturbed, it would seem, at the actual overwork of women; either of the multitude or of a special class. The lady may properly labor to nervous prostration in superintending incompetent or too numerous helpers in a too elaborate scheme of life; but she must not use power toward "self-support" in the accepted sense of that phrase. To become a wage-earner, or acquire a salary, even at congenial and comparatively easy work, has until very lately broken the caste of the lady. On the other hand, she may and should do all kinds of work that call for leisurely accomplishment and demand only personal or friendly standards of excellence. Fine needlework; decorative weaving; "arts and crafts" in reminiscent play-work; illuminating or binding books that only wealth can own or preserve; preparing for and managing the often arduous duties of the salon or the drawing-room; "entertaining," not only intimate friends, but in the stately and formal commerce of society; all these things belong to her as by common consent.

She is also associated with the cultivation of fruits

and flowers in the garden which forms her appropriate out-of-door setting, and the love and service of tamed beasts are hers at command. She is close-linked with many forms of recreation and she may rightfully exhaust herself in play activity, but not as a professional worker. Men, as well as women, have so emphasized this point—that the lady must not earn money or do things that servants do—that various customs, like the foot-binding of the Chinese women, have been adopted, which forcibly prevent the lady from being improperly useful. The reason for this on the part of men, as has been often shown, is their desire to demonstrate their wealth and power by having in the family idle, or seemingly idle women, to "show off," while they retain for themselves the really interesting and important activities. The other fact, however, that women's energy estopped from old paths of labor always has found and always will find for itself other channels of activity, is less often noted. And the more important fact that the self-found ways of interest and effort which have been used by the lady have potential social value as well as a possible social danger, has still less often been demonstrated.

What are the main forms of activity which the lady has developed and made peculiarly her own?

In the first place, women of leisure and social command have quite universally displayed a seemingly natural tendency toward the refinement of manners and the elaboration of a social code. This code tends to become as exact and binding for domestic and recreative life as laws and military rule for business and statecraft. The social dangers inhering in this activity of highly placed women are plainly to be seen. The conventional code often leads to extremes of conservatism, to superficial ethics divorced from the common life and to the substitution of canons of taste for laws of morality. The results have often made the reactions of domestic and "society" standards upon the larger life of education, religion, politics and economics, hurtful to human growth. The lady has always tended too much toward confounding pleasant manners with good character; and to confusing with ethical values of the vital sort, those expressions of refinement and culture in dress, modes of politeness, easy command of the elegant in personal accomplishment, which it has been her main business to secure. Many women's colleges, and some women's organizations, to-day show this tendency toward the small and superficial in moral judgment as a result of the "sequestration of the feminine intellect." On the other hand, the larger social value of regulated, gentle, thought-suggestive, artistic and cultural intercourse between men and women, age and youth, is definite and important. In the miscellaneous population of our own country it is coming to assume primary importance as the most difficult of social conditions to maintain. The modern tendency toward social progress is strikingly toward greater variety of relationship and associated effort among an increasingly diversified civic and national group. To-day, therefore, especially in the United States, we have the greatest need for expert guidance along most intricate social ways in carrying out collective regulations for the common good.

The tendency of man, outside of his noble personal friendships with his chosen few, has always been, and in general still is, toward a free and easy manner with the crowd when "off duty," which often degenerates into coarseness or curtness; while in serious relationships he tends as surely toward the positions of chief and subordinate. Both of these masculine tendencies result in extreme clumsiness in the adjustment of details of fraternal action in the mass. This is shown with painful clearness in the difficulty experienced in making democracy "work." What Ambassador Bryce justly called our "administrative awkwardness" keeps our technique of political advance woefully behind our accepted ideals. The average man, although a "good mixer" on the surface of things, has so far not attained the golden mean between command and intimacy in the more diffused but important social concerns. Especially is this true of the Anglo-Saxon man. He is not able to play the game of life "like a gentleman" except with his special cronies. Social democracy will demand of us all the manners of the noble of France, combined with the morals of the broader-minded puritan, and the skill of the great lady in keeping everyone in good humor. For social democracy, if it means anything at all, means a way of life which will include in social control, social adjustment and social provision a thousand things now left to private arrangement or neglect. If, as Bagehot says, "The ages of despotism were needed to set the mould of civilization,"—our present civilization of modified aristocracy with its coarse-fibred and partial political control—may it not be that the ages of conventional training in the artistic blending of personalities in polite society will presently justify themselves?

Woman's share in social culture, as the lady who can command courteous treatment, as the creator of a group atmosphere in which all must show their best and none must browbeat or bore another, as mistress of the art of bringing useful and pleasant things to pass without friction and by the appeal of gentleness and good cheer, is surely not a small one. If, as we now think, the gifts of economic mastery and political control are to be tempered more and more by consideration, sympathy and mutual aid to ends of universal sharing of best things, the lady's "diamond edition" object-lessons may well be copied in the large. The lady herself, however, will have to outgrow her narrow prejudices and her caste distinctions if she is to take part in the process. Meanwhile, the gentle breeding and orderly behavior which the lady displays and secures, her special sphere in which there is no coarse familiarity and no churlish avoidance, provide at least one small spot in the social organism in which compulsion becomes attraction and thought flowers to imagination and the commonplace itself becomes the rich soil of fair and happy living. In so far as the elaboration of a social code, and the "morality of personal habits," and the attention to details of individual adjustment have concerned themselves with normal forms of family life, and with cultural recreation, they have already enriched the larger social

life. If the socialization of political and economic
fields is to be extended, it must require an enlarged
use of the same art of living.

In the second place, the lady has succeeded in spir-
itualizing sex-attraction. "Man does the courting,"
says Professor [3] Thomas, "but woman controls the
process." The lady began early in her career to control the process to ends of romance, of intellectual
stimulus, of refined pleasure that made appeal to something higher in man than the merely physical. Chivalry was the formalized and fantastic expression of
the lady's assumption of control of the process of
courting. It was but a side-issue, it is true, in the business of human mating. It divorced "true love" from
marriage. In chivalry, and the reign of the lady's
chosen "courteous love," the husband was not expected to be the lover. How could he be, when he
chose the wife solely for State or family or property
reasons? The lady's knight, on the other hand, must
never mix the gold of his unselfish devotion with the
alloy of fleshly desire. Such an artificial separation
of courtship and love from marriage and the found-
ing of a home could, of course, have but a brief career
of influence. But, like the doll-play of the girl-child
that prophesies motherhood's function with amusing
variations, so chivalry showed, even in its extrava-
gances, the way women meant their lovers should
come to feel. Women thus wrought upon the only
malleable masculine material the rude times afforded—
the gentler scribes and clergy, teachers and artist-folk,

[3] W. J. Thomas, *Sex and Society.*

who served the social needs of the castle. We cannot
agree with Professor Thomas that [4] "Chivalry, chaperonage and modern convention are the persistence of
the old race-habit of contempt for women and of their
intellectual sequestration."   Many elements in these
forms of treatment of women are such survivals of sex-
aversion and contempt; but in chivalry, whatever else
was involved, woman "broke her taboo" in respect to
real comradeship with a selected class of men.   The
master of the house, absorbed in hunting, fighting,
drinking and the game of class politics, might despise
the sort of man the lady used for doorway, as it were,
into the masculine civilization from which she had been
so long excluded: but our age does not despise, it honors such.   The intellectual sequestration of woman began to open outward toward freedom and opportunity
when in the early days of our civilization the great
families taught the boy—"Richt well to back a steed,"
the girl—"As well to write and read."

In the third place, as has been already noted, it
is always the lady in every epoch in which she has appeared, who has helped the man of wealth to become
the discriminating patron of art and science, and on
her own initiative has advanced the cause of learning.
Moreover, as arbiter of taste she has largely determined many forms of thought-expression her time has
cherished.   As chief "consumer" of luxuries and de-
finer of "necessary comforts" she has largely directed
the course of craft and manufacture.   As specifically
the purchasing member of the household firm she has

[4] W. J. Thomas, *Sex and Society.*

led the way (often disastrously it must be confessed) in all changes of fashion and in all popularizing of the canons of the studio. In the sphere of the recreative vocations she has clearly dominated social standards. Her practical genius, however (her certificate of membership in her sex-guild), that unerring trend of the woman-nature toward that which directly concerns the well-being of individuals now living, has at once restricted and intensified the lady's power of intellectual stimulus. She has shown scant welcome for "naked thought," for the impersonally, ideally remote. Not infrequently, like the Rosamond pictured with such master-strokes by George Eliot, she has hung the burden of her selfish exactions about the neck of men, to strangle their highest ambitions. Oftener, however, such is her genius for sympathetic appreciation, she has nourished in man a sort of greatness foreign to her own sex-development, as embodied in one beloved friend whose personality she has understood more perfectly than his thought. The woman-friendships of great men have passed into biography, as a distinct social phenomenon; and the lady has often in such relationship become the mother of ideas, the stimulant to heroic effort, the inspirer of masterpieces treasured by the world. Tennyson makes King Arthur say:

> "I know of no more subtle master under heaven
> Than is the maiden passion for a maid;
> Not only to keep down the base in man,
> But teach high thought and the desire of fame,
> And love of truth, and all that makes a man."

This is true; but perhaps a still more subtle master is that diffused and less personal influence of the "ever womanly," shown often by the older woman the youth may never dare wish to possess, who challenges his utmost height of being at every meeting-point of sympathy.

So far as the lady has embodied this "ever womanly," and she has often embodied it in all-embracing appreciation and in all-prevailing charm, her past is secure. The women "to know whom is a liberal education" have been socially worth their keep, whatever agency has settled the bills!

The lady has now, however, fallen upon evil times. She is being pelted with bad names, the commonest and most stinging the epithet "parasite." And as she receives the blows of harsh criticism she is unable to preserve the splendid composure of Marie Antoinette among the rabble of the revolutionists, since she is no longer sustained by inner conviction of her own superiority. She often apologizes for herself, a sure confession of weakening self-esteem. Sometimes she confesses her unreality and seeks to transform herself to other patterns of womanly excellence.

It is worth while, nevertheless (as always when brickbats or harsh words are being thrown around), to examine more carefully than is the current custom, into the real significance of the modern indictment of the lady. True, she toils not, neither does she spin, and "Solomon in all his glory was not arrayed" like some of her! But is she grown not only obsolete but harmful?

Olive Schreiner gives a deadly grading of woman-hood from the worth-while to the socially injurious. At the head stands the woman who "bears children and at the same time labors in productive ways." Next comes the woman who bears children and personally superintends their care and her home, but depends upon the man or men of the household for her own pecuniary support. Third comes the woman who neither usefully labors nor bears children, but depends upon her husband for the material basis of life and gives him only a "sex-equivalent." At the bottom of the list, and not far from the third in her estimation, Olive Schreiner puts the prostitute who earns her living frankly by the sale of her body. The argument that makes the author of *Woman and Labor* declare the "fine lady" to be "the most deadly microbe which can make its appearance on the surface of any social organism," although well known, must be reiterated if serious attempt be made to answer the question: Is the non-earning woman a parasite? Women in the early days worked productively, had a recognized market-value, and also bore children and personally cared for them. As man has taken over from domestic crafts into shop and factory the industries that women founded they have lost the chance to do their old work in the old ways. They must therefore labor in new fashion or sink into uselessness. Women of a selected class, by the use of slaves and servants have become inactive, the mere recipients of values, no longer creators but "feeding on unearned wealth." This hurts their nature and debases the social fabric.

If a woman does no labor in her home which could properly make her self-supporting outside that home she is in duty bound to do something outside her home to justify her claim to support. The special social danger now apprehended by those who sum up the above indictments of the lady, is the possibility in modern times of having so many of her. In old times only a few at the top of favoring circumstance could be supported by the labor of men. Now the great middle class may successfully ape the fashions of nobility, and even the poor may imitate the customs that keep the married woman at least from entering "gainful occupations." Thus parasitism may spread to the very paupers! Thus proceeds the argument of Olive Schreiner.

Mrs. Perkins Gilman [5] outlines the way out of this social danger to be a wholesale movement of women into man's specialized industrial order, each woman to do for pay, whether single or married, with or without children, some work she has learned to do well; with women teachers, nurses, caretakers, and all whose specialties cover the home needs of children, housekeeping and the rest—to enable all women to make marriage and maternity an incident of experience rather than a vocation giving material support. Ellen Key,[6] on the opposite side, calls earnestly to women that they are on the wrong track even in the present movement toward specialization of this sort. She would have women not only face the lessening supply of domestic

---

[5] Charlotte Perkins Gilman, *Woman and Economics.*
[6] Ellen Key, *The Century of the Child.*

servants with composure but dismiss such as they have, and all mothers and intimate women relatives of mothers, live for and with their children and kindred. She would make far more rather than less of maternity and family obligation and by the simple life within a home as complete as possible in itself, make the development of personality, fine, strong, effective, progressive, the only vocation of the average woman. She would, however, make permanent place and opportunity for the exceptional woman, born a specialist, to "burgeon out her powers"; and she would make teachers and nurses "mothers-at-large."

Somewhere between these extremes may lie the golden mean of wise decisions. But, meanwhile, is it true that the lady of to-day, who is cared for by her husband without hard labor either within or without the home, or who has inherited wealth that gives her problems of expenditure rather than of acquisition, is but a parasite? If she is married and bears and cares well for children, and makes a true home, she cannot be idle and must often work hard. If she has not married and has taken on some life-interest, intellectual, artistic, social, she is still employed; but perhaps in neither case in a manner that would make her easily or surely self-supporting. Does that fact alone make her a parasite? Nay, her social usefulness or harmfulness depends upon the *kind of person she is rather than upon the definiteness of her economic status.* "Clear your minds of cant," says Dr. Johnson; and the admonition is useful, whether the cant in question be the religious, the political or the economic. To-day we are deafened by the economic cant, the translation in strident tones of all values into terms of dollars and cents. When a sociologist talks about a "thousand-dollar man" or a "three-thousand-dollar man," he is talking as one who would measure a sunset by a railroad track. Using adequate human standards, a very great man may never be able to earn a thousand dollars a year, and a very small one or very dangerous one may capture his millions. The lady, therefore, should not be overcome with shame by epithets which deal only with commercial budgets. It may even fall to her lot to make the last stand against the over-emphasis of our adolescent social science upon the "pay envelope"! If so, success to her!

The vital element in the modern criticism of the lady, and one which should be heeded with tragic earnestness, is that which calls attention to the wrong side of womanhood; the sinister aspects of a really idle class of women debauched and coarsened by vulgar luxury. When Professor Ferrero [7] shows us historically the "abuses of liberty" of which privileged woman has been guilty, abuses "greater than those of man because she exercises more power over him than he over her," and also "because in the wealthier classes she is freer from the political and economic responsibilities that bind the man," so that she can "easier forget her duty toward the race"—we see the danger that now besets the lady of our civilization, and through her, the race.

There are three dominant tendencies of expression

[7] G. Ferrero, *The Women of the Cæsars.*

which the lady has shown. One, that of the specially gifted, toward individual and creative work. This cannot now be discussed. It belongs to a separate study. Of the other two, the tendency which Professor Ferrero has so searchingly revealed, is that toward the selfish exploitation of man and of all social agencies, even of the friends who love her best, for her own selfish, voluptuous, irresponsible pleasure. The qualities which base or ignorant or pleasure-seeking men have bred in her for their own gratification, grown monstrous in independent social power, at last endanger the very institutions man most highly values. It must never be forgotten that the lady has flowered out of the soil of unselfish service of her kind; that mother-nature which common womanhood expresses. If she rashly and wickedly strives to draw her life-force through the air of wanton coquetry from the sap of healthier growths (like the orchid, beautiful, fantastic, but uncanny), she withers at the centre of her being, and becomes a parasite indeed. That the suddenly acquired luxury of undisciplined classes, that the brazen domination of wealth in our American life, tend to produce among us women of the lady rank, and their pitiful imitators among the ignorant poor, who ignore every duty and outrage every womanly ideal, is terribly true. They are, so far as they exist, the most tragic force for social friction and national disintegration in American society. It is to prevent the increase of the social dangers inhering in a womanhood thus debauched by selfishness, greed and the pursuit of pleasure as the business of life, that the leaders of thought among women should chiefly address themselves. This is more vital than the immediate settlement of the intricate problems of the economic position of the married woman with children.

And to this end such leaders should refuse to accept financial values, especially such as are reckoned only on the basis of the market-price of labor, as the only classification of the useful or the useless in womanhood. The revolution in woman's work caused by the vast industrial changes of the last century do indeed make necessary radical readjustments in her economic life. Only the childish fear to attempt the full solution of difficult problems. Hence all thanks are due to those women who are bravely thinking their own preferred solutions through to logical ends; whether they are ranged with Mrs. Gilman's piquant audacity of wholesale settlements on a new basis, or with Ellen Key's ponderous and solemn moral appeal for a rebirth of the oldest in the newest womanhood. Nothing is out of place in discussion of the unavoidable puzzles of life and labor that to-day press upon enlightened women, except bigotry and cowardice. In this field of vast social changes and their reaction upon womanhood, however, as in all environmental pressure upon the individual, we all live before we can learn a rule of living; and we are taught what that rule must be by necessary experimentation. Some

> "Motion, toiling in the gloom,
> Yearning to mix itself with life,"

ordains our course. In the sphere of character, how-

ever, the light of purpose illumines the path we may
choose to follow. And here the standards are of
moral values and we have as guide

> "The perfect woman, nobly planned,
> To warn, to comfort, to command."

The third tendency of the lady in self-expression,
and happily the one that influences by far the larger
company of the privileged women of our civilization,
is that toward a broadening and deepening and spir-
itualizing of the maternal function to ends of vital
nourishment of the mind and heart of the race. The
briefest recital of the social service of the lady in
modern times would show beyond peradventure how
much of the sharing of the commonwealth of the race
is due to her activity. This service tests the value of
the lady; her right to live and to be cherished as an
asset rather than a parasite, whatever her economic
position. She who feeds the best in the larger life
(as humble mothers nurse their babes out of their
own abundant health) needs no excuse for being.
Said the dying Bunsen to his wife: "In thy face have
I seen the Eternal."

Said Dante, musing on his Beatrice:

> "A new intelligence doth love impart
> Which guides the upward path;
> When I behold in honor dight"

the lady—

> "Who doth shine in splendid light."

Deep in the aspiration of humanity is implanted the majestic and lovely figure of her who is the embodiment of the true, the beautiful and the good. No abuse of women, no tyranny of law or custom that degraded mothers and sold maidens in the marketplace, could ever destroy that ideal of perfect womanhood. Literature and art have brought it forth to sight and named it Wisdom and Justice and Purity and Hope and Joy and Love. In such prophecy it is approved as true. The supreme social need, now as ever, is that living women shall not violate that ideal but help its realization. It is the supreme gift of the lady to social culture that at her best she has drawn man to her as to a "fair, divided excellence" in such fashion that he has been compelled to look above to face her, and thus has linked the marriage of hearts to the up-climbing of the race.

III

THE DRAMA OF THE WOMAN OF GENIUS

"THERE'S no such a person as Mrs. Harris!" exclaimed the quarrelsome friend of Dickens' Sairy Gamp, in her climax of jealousy of the much-vaunted but never-seen benefactress. "There is no woman of genius," says de Goncourt; "women of genius are all men." [1] "There can never be a woman of genius," says the author of *Sex and Character,* in whose view women are hardly human, although it is the duty of men to treat them as if they were.

This book, recently translated from the German into English and already in its third edition, is a curious testimony to the effect of prejudice upon the ability to see facts. The author, strangely precocious in his maturity of thought and style and in his wide reach of learning, yet betrays such an exaggerated and even diseased adolescence in his sex-antagonism that we do not wonder that he committed suicide before he was twenty-four years of age. What de Goncourt puts into an epigram has been laboriously wrought out in many heavy books. What Otto Weininger declares, with that intense hatred of women which the morbid ascetic has always shown, is asserted in more or less

[1] Otto Weininger, *Sex and Character.*

45

good-natured argument by many writers.   In an *Es-say on the Character, the Manners and the Under-standing of Women in Different Ages,* published in 1781, the author, Mons. Thomas, gives it as his belief that women have never reached and never can reach that "very height of human nature from which great men have looked down and examined nature's laws, have showed to the soul the source of its ideas, as-signed to reason its bounds, to motion its laws, to the universe its course; who have created sciences and aggrandized the human mind by cultivating their own."   Thus early, however, and most reasonably, Mons. Thomas raises the question, fundamental in the problem of woman's intellectual life, "If not one woman has ever raised herself to a level with the greatest men, is it the fault of education or of her nature?"   Certainly the absence of women from the highest-placed company of the Immortals in philos-ophy, science and art is too obvious to be discussed.

Plutarch in his account of "The Virtuous Actions of Women" gives recognition of their intellectual abil-ity, but, moralist that he is, dwells most on the high degree of courage and honor in his chosen examples. He, however, has the insight to declare that "the tal-ents and virtues are modified by circumstances and persons, but the source is the same"; thus linking men and women together in his company of the great and the good.   He and later writers willingly grant women place among the lesser, if not among the supreme, geniuses.

At the outstart of discussion of women's intellectual

attainments, it is well to remember how few are the men of first rank. Dr. Clouston,[2] in his illuminating analysis of the "eleven orders of brain," gives the average man "four-fifths of the whole of humanity," while to the great genius he allows "only a few in each generation." To the class of "marked, all-round talent," however, he assigns one-eleventh part of the mass of mankind, and to "genius of the lesser rank" a chance to appear at any time in one to every four or five hundred of the population. It is in these two classes, that of the all-round talented, and that of the specialized genius of the secondary rank, that we count up most of the great women. For example, of the hundreds of religious sects which may be listed only a few can be placed to the credit of women as founders, and none of those is one of the great religions; but women have assisted men in establishing faiths of which they were the first and most important disciples—as in the second century of our era Apelles had his prophetess-friend, Philumene, to help him; and later, Montanus his two women assistants, Priscilla and Maximilla, who seem to have impressed even Tertullian himself with their zeal and ability. In philosophy many women appear of the second and third class, but no one great enough to found a school of thought. [3] In poetry, Sappho, Sulpicia and Erinna lighten with their suggestion of youth and beauty the massive chorus of masculine poets of the ancient world; and

[2] Dr. T. S. Clouston, *Unsoundness of Mind,* chapter *Orders of Brain.*

[3] Compare Havelock Ellis, *Man and Woman,* chapter on *The Intellectual Impulse.*

in our own time Christina Rossetti and Mrs. Browning and many others wear their singing robes by right; but, as is often said, Dante and Shakespeare have no feminine counterparts. In science, mathematics has so far proved the field of women's greatest achievements, counting many eminent women, from Laura Bassi, who graced so well her professor's chair in the University of Bologna, to Miss Herschel, whose work was so interwoven with that of her brother, that no one can know its exact scope and value. The fame of Mrs. Somerville in this branch of knowledge is secure, as is that of Constance Naden, so highly praised by Herbert Spencer as showing that "rare union of high philosophic capacity with intense acquisition," and whose untimely death probably deprived the world of one of its great expressions of feminine power. Sophie Kowalevsky, also, is accepted as a master and found her rightful place in the professor's chair in Stockholm. In music women have made a very poor showing in the field of composition, but a rich display in interpretation of song and in appreciative criticism. In literature, to which some deny the distinction of art, but which it is hard to describe adequately by any other word, women show better results; in the branch of letters, memoirs and journals excelling men, and in fiction now clearly leading the van, with Marian Evans at the head of the line. In acting, a subsidiary but important art of interpretation, women stand at the very top; and in oratory, wherever and whenever allowed by custom to practise it, they easily win first place, in point of numbers of gifted public speakers now clearly excelling the masculine side of the house. In politics and the art of government of States women have chief seats in the Pantheon. Surprise has repeatedly been expressed by students on discovering this fact, which shows how little the true genius of common womanhood itself has as yet been understood. In spite of their legal subjection to men, women have ruled and administered affairs in the family and in the smaller social groups since time began; they excel and have always excelled in power to read human nature, in detail-observation of facts and conditions and in skill in making needed social adjustments. This power, "writ large," is the power of the statesman. Hence there is the best of reasons in the practical, social capacity of women, why the great queens of history have compelled even the most reluctant historians to give them place among the leading political rulers and organizers of the race. Democracy has not yet learned to use these innate powers of women to such advantage as aristocracy succeeded in doing. When it does, the rudely broken line of high display of women's political genius may be reunited to good effect. With this exception, and some rare but significant concessions which are beginning to be called for by such a woman as Madame Curie, women are generally required in respect to the supreme manifestation of genius to echo the plaintive humility of Anne Bradstreet, writing in 1640:

"Men can do best, and women know it well.
Preëminence in each and all is yours,
Yet grant some small acknowledgment of ours."

The failure of women to produce genius of the first rank in most of the supreme forms of human effort has been used to block the way of all women of talent and ambition for intellectual achievement in a manner that would be amusingly absurd were it not so monstrously unjust and socially harmful. A few ambitious girls in the middle of the nineteenth century in Boston, the Athens of America, want to go to High School. The Board of Education answers them, in effect: Produce a Michael Angelo or a Plato and you shall have a chance to learn a bit of mathematics, history and literature. A few women of marked inclination toward the healing art want a chance to study in a medical school and learn facts and methods in a hospital. Go to! the managing officials in substance reply: Where is your great surgeon; what supreme contribution has any woman ever made to our science? A group of earnest students beg admission to college and show good preparation gained by hard struggle with adverse conditions. You can't come in, the trustees respond, until you produce a Shakespeare or a Milton. The demand that women shall show the highest fruit of specialized talent and widest range of learning before they have had the general opportunity for a common-school education is hardly worthy of the sex that prides itself upon its logic. In point of fact no one, neither the man who denies woman a proper human soul nor the woman who claims "superiority" for her sex, can have any actual basis for accurate answer to the question, Can a woman become a genius of the first class? Nobody can know unless

women in general shall have equal opportunity with
men in education, in vocational choice, and in social
welcome of their best intellectual work for a number
of generations. So far women have suffered so many
disabilities in the circumstances of their lives, in their
lack of training in what Buckle calls "that preposterous
system called their education," in their segregation
from all the higher intellectual comradeship, in the
personal and family and social hindrances to their mental growth and expression, that not even women themselves, still less men, can have an adequate idea of
their possibilities of achievement. Nothing therefore
is more foolish than to try to decide *a priori* the limits
of a woman's capacity. What we do know is this, that
there have been women of talent, and even of genius
reaching near to the upper circles of the elect; and
we know also that these women of marked talent have
appeared whenever and wherever women have had
opportunities of higher education and have been held
in esteem by men as intellectual companions as well as
wives and manual workers. The connection between
these two facts is obvious.

Moreover we are to remember in this era of wider
study and more inclusive generalization than the past
has shown, that new scales of value in genius are being
slowly evolved. Each critic and tabulator in the past
has made his own grading of human powers and usually in accordance with his own taste or talent. The
philosopher has put at the head those who have
wrought out systems of thought and built a new universe out of the interior vision; the artist has given

chief crown to those whose creative power has produced triumphs of the imagination; the scientist has placed first those who have discovered most of nature's secrets and put her forces at the service of man; the statesman has honored most highly those who have builded kingdoms and organized society. It so happens now that we are in need of more detailed and flexible administrative genius than has been consciously desired before, and it is not unlikely that in the revision of the lists of the Immortals which Time is always making, certain contributions of womanhood to social culture and social readjustment may loom larger than in the past. We are, however, still under the domination of the philosophic thinker, the pure scientist and the artist in making the record of genius, and women have to accept the conventional challenges of greatness as men have made them.

At this point it is well to remind ourselves not only how few are the men of supreme genius, but also how few have been fortunate enough in their biographies to get their names on the chief lists of the second rank. Not all "inglorious Miltons" were "mute." Many sang sweetly to their contemporaries, but lacked voice to echo down the ages. Doubtless many quite equal to Dr. Johnson, yet lacking his Boswell, received only a fine print recognition in a biographical dictionary. Women, far more than men, it is reasonable to suppose, have suffered hasty eclipse for want of adequate mention in the permanent records.[4] Sappho has been

---

[4] The change of name at marriage has tended toward confusion and loss in the record of women's work.

sadly overworked as an instance of feminine genius; yet to be called "the poetess" as Homer was "the poet" in Greece, nearly five hundred years before our era, was not only proof of her own greatness, but also that there must have been many smaller poetesses to win her that distinction. The ancient world must also have produced numbers of women-philosophers of ability to have made a place for Hypatia at the head of a School; and her powers, which won her a martyrdom for truth equal in dignity to that of Socrates, must have had their rooting in the rich soil of the higher education of women. Indeed, we hear of over thirty "lady philosophers" and students of the most advanced learning in the School of Pythagoras. Again that Pulcheria, of whom Gibbon says, "She alone of all the descendants of the great Theodosius appears to have inherited any share of his manly spirit and abilities," could not have been the only woman of her time and her court to show intellectual achievements as well as noble statesmanship. And that Paula, friend of Jerome, descendant of the Gracchi, and one of the richest women of antiquity, who chose simplicity and frugality for herself, using her wealth for education and charity, could not have carried into effect such noble forms of self-sacrifice had she not lived in a time and place in which women had control over their purses and their lives. [5] Superlative genius, although usually quite unexpected in appearance, always arises out of a group of secondary great ones, and these in turn out of a crowd of the merely talented. Follow-

[5] See J. W. Cole, *Woman.*

ing this general law, when the Lady reached her hey-day of supremacy in the thirteenth to the sixteenth century, her class gave to the world many women of marked intellectual power and of special gifts in many lines.   In these days of girls' colleges and co-educa-tional universities and of increasingly free opportuni-ties for professional work, we remember and call over with a fresh sense of their natural place in the social economy, these learned and gifted women.   But in the eighteenth century and the first half of the nineteenth, they seemed like fairy-tale heroines to the reader who chanced upon their biographies.

Budding genius in the Lady-class naturally devel-oped along the lines of least resistance to the habits and conventions of the age and station of the excep-tional woman.   Writing, scholarship in all the learn-ing of the period, teaching, public lecturing, preach-ing (then thought entirely suitable for the great lady who could do it well), leadership in church affairs and contribution to the higher statesmanship of royal houses and princely courts—these were her achieve-ments.   The "funeral oration" seems at that time to have been a favorite method of public instruction.   It was used by that young girl of the thirteenth century, daughter of a gentleman of Boulogne, who at the age of twenty-three pronounced one in Latin in the great church of her city, of which it is recorded, "the orator to be admired had no need of her youth or the charms of her sex."   At twenty-six this young woman took her doctor's degree and began to read publicly the Insti-tutes of Justinian in her own house, and at thirty was

raised by her learning and gifts of speech to a professor's chair, "teaching the laws to a prodigious con-
course of people of all nations." It was said she
"joined the elegance of the woman to the learning of
the man," and "when she spoke had the merit to make
her hearers forget her beauty." Again, we remember
Casandre Fidèle who wrote equally well in the languages of Homer, Virgil and Dante and who, it is
said, "by her graces embellished even theology." She
gave public lessons at Padua, sustained these in public
debate, and had also "many agreeable talents such as
music." She could not have stood alone, although
probably none of the learned ladies of her town were
her equals; and surely to but few women of any age
has it been given, as it was to her, to prove that higher
education is not inimical to woman's health, by living
more than one hundred years! As to the women
preachers of that time, we may be sure that the Spanish Isabella who often spoke in the great church of
Barcelona, "converting even the Jews by her eloquence," must have had humble followers who were
the pride of their smaller congregations.

This was the period of extravagant praise for
gifted women, as in Venice, where in 1555, Signora
Jeanne d'Aragon had constructed for her a "Temple
of Praise" for her wit, her learning and her eloquence,
to which the greatest writers of her time contributed
in all the principal languages of the world. And
her sister was so nearly her equal in gifts and graces
that it was thought necessary to give her a separate
"decree of praise" made in much the same way. This

genius passed down the family line with the son of Jeanne, a Prince of Colonne, to show that nature never balks at feminine transmission of power.

It was in this period also that books and treatises first appeared discussing the "woman question" and introducing the vexed problem of the relative powers of the sexes. One Cornelius Agrippa labored to prove by a book of thirty chapters *The Superior Excellence of Women Over Men,* calling upon "theology, physical science, history, cabalistic knowledge and morals" to establish his thesis. This man was a soldier of distinction and an all-round scholar, who gave lectures on St. Paul in England, on the Philosopher's Stone in Turin, on theology at Pavia, and practised medicine in Switzerland. Several other men wrote books to prove the ability of women, if not their superiority to men. One of these, Peter Paul Ribera, published a volume entitled *The Immortal Triumphs and Heroic Enterprises of Eight Hundred and Forty-Five Women.* Women also took a hand in proclaiming their own powers. A celebrated Venetian lady, Modesta di Pozzo di Forzi, in 1593 maintained the superiority of her sex in no uncertain words. Her biographer in giving an account of the "great success of her book" shrewdly remarks that "unfortunately for her that whch perhaps assisted in that success was that men could praise her without fear, since she died just as the work appeared." He also confesses that "men always see with pleasure these sorts of works by women; for pride, which calculates everything, makes men regard as a proof of their advantage the efforts which are made to combat them." In the seventeenth century another Venetian lady went so far as to entitle her book, *The Nobleness and Excellence of Women and the Defects and Imperfections of Men.* It is said that she too had "the success that beauty gives to wit." Marguerite, Queen of Navarre, undertook in a letter to prove the superiority of her sex; while Mlle. de Gourney contented herself with simply claiming equality. Then, as now, however, some of the most learned and able women found such comparisons odious, and would none of the merry war for supremacy. One man wrote two books, one on each side of the debate; the first in 1673, entitled *The Equality of the Sexes; a philosophic and moral discourse in which one sees the importance of getting rid of one's prejudices;* and the second in 1675, entitled *The Excellency of Men against the Equality of the Sexes;* but we are told that in the second book "he refuted himself gently, fearing to have reason against himself." [6]

The whole discussion seems to have been a sort of play-battle, doubtless taken seriously by few, if any. It was the prelude to a more serious struggle for democratic rights in government, in education, and in industry which wrought itself out first by and for men, and in which for a long season all claims of women to justice and consideration were forgotten.

Carlyle [7] reminds us that while the French Revolution was smouldering toward conflagration the "paper

[6] See Mons. Thomas, *Essay on Women.*
[7] Thomas Carlyle, *The French Revolution.*

people" (those at ease in their own circumstances from having already profited by class privilege) were playing with radical ideas that were later to make rallying cries in the bloody struggle. It was a time, he says, when "Philosophism sat joyful in her glittering saloons, the dinner guest of Opulence grown ingenuous, the very nobles proud to sit by her, and Preaching, lifted up over all Bastiles, a coming millennium." So in the times when womanhood in general suffered all unspeakable outrage and misery, this little comedy of mock homage, which yet had in it some notes of true reverence, was played out on the stage of polite society.

There were hard days coming, days when the rights of man as man were to embroil the world in conflict; days when the common life was to surge up to the drawing room and rudely break up the dinners of Opulence; days when the Lady was lost sight of and the stern times called even for the woman of genius to bury herself in the primal labors of her sex, that so the home might be kept and the children saved alive and the grain harvested while the men held their hands at the throat of Despotism, until all the common folk were counted as people. When the time came for a genuine movement for equality of education and opportunity for women, it was the great middle class, not the nobility, that led in the sober struggle; and it was martyrdom, not "success," that came first.

Victor Hugo says: "The eighteenth century was man's century; the nineteenth is woman's." In that man's century of revolution against class privilege, the lowest level of "female education" seems to have been reached in our Anglo-Saxon civilization. In our own country, in the early days, the vigor of mind as well as of body of both men and women went of necessity into the pioneer building of our mighty States. So much was this the fact that the oft-repeated sneer, "Who reads an American book?" might well have been answered by a showing of Constitutions, Highways, Schools, ordered Settlements, as the front-row volumes in the library of American genius. This practical devotion to doing things that later historians would write about, made the women of colonial and revolutionary and western-pioneering days great persons, but small students. And the opportunity for learning in schools was even less than the incitement toward "the still air of delightful studies." [8] Although in Massachusetts as early as 1636 the General Court established Harvard College, and in 1644 ordered the several towns to make sure that "Evry family alow one peck of corne or 12d. in money or other commodity to be sent in to ye Treasurer for the colledge at Cambridge," and in 1683 voted that "Every towne consisting of more than five hundred families shall set up and maintain scholes to instruct youth as the law directs," no girls were thought of in this connection. The provision of "free schools," "schools for the people," etc., left the girls entirely out of the count. Hartford, Connecticut, indeed, in 1771, began to allow girls to learn "reading, spelling, writing" and sometimes "to add"; but not until the close

[8] See early records of Massachusetts Bay Colony.

of the eighteenth century did the majority of towns
of New England make provision, even in a meagre
manner, for the education of girls.

At first all the Common Schools for girls were held
between April and October, when the boys were at
work on the farms; and as late as 1792 Newburyport
most reluctantly allowed girls over nine years of age
"instruction in grammar and reading during the summer months for an hour and a half after the dismis-
sion of the boys." This opportunity was extended in
1804 to a provision for "girls' schools," "to be kept
for six months in the year from six to eight o'clock in
the morning and on Thursday afternoons," when the
boys, presumably, were not using the school rooms!
As late as 1788 the town of Northampton, Massachusetts, voted "not to be at any expense for schooling
girls," and only yielded, after an appeal to the courts
by the tax-paying fathers of the girls, a small chance
to learn in the summer months. Up to 1828 girls did
not go to public schools in Rhode Island; and not
until 1852 was the "Girls' High School" securely
established in Boston itself, and not until 1878 the
"Girls' Latin School" of that city to prepare for college.

As Abigail Adams wrote in 1817, when over sev-
enty years of age, speaking of the opportunities of
women in her day: "The only chance for much intellectual improvement in the female sex, was to be found
in the families of the educated class and in occasional
intercourse with the learned." To this should be
added the partiality of men teachers to some bright

girls, which gave an exceptional training to a favored few. ⁹ Thus we read that in 1783 Ezra Stiles, President of Yale, gave a certificate declaring that he had "examined Miss Lucinda Foote, twelve years old," and had found her "fully qualified, except in regard to sex, to be received as a pupil in the Freshman Class of Yale University." We are glad to learn that Lucinda received the full college course, including Hebrew, under President Stiles' private instruction, and that she then proved that learning does not undermine the family, by marrying and having ten children. To similar happy accidents of personal favoritism toward exceptional girls must be added the earliest contributions to co-education made by the religious sects, the Moravians who founded in Bethlehem, Pennsylvania, in 1749, the first private institution in America which admitted girls to higher educational opportunities than the elementary school; and the Friends, who established in 1697 the Penn Charter School in Philadelphia which made provision for the education of "all Children and Servants, Male and Female, the rich to be instructed at reasonable rates and the poor to be maintained and schooled for nothing"; although in this provision the boys were provided with a more extended course of study than the girls.

These reminders of the period before the days of the Ladies' Academies for the well-to-do, of which Mrs. Willard's was the most ambitious, and of Mary Lyon's school in which the poorer girls could earn a

⁹ Mary Eastman, *History of Women's Education in the Eastern States* in *Woman's Work in America.*

part of their living by housework, cannot be omitted from consideration of the intellectual output of women in the United States. Oberlin, with its "Female Department" and its offers of education to black as well as white, the Cincinnati Wesleyan Woman's College and Ripon and Antioch Colleges, were object-lessons long more observed than followed. The establishment of Normal Schools gave the first great democratic opportunity in education to women in America; and, characteristically in the history of women's higher education, this opportunity was given women not for themselves as human beings entitled to intellectual development, but as women who could give the State a larger and cheaper supply of teachers for the free public schools. Even as such it was an innovation bitterly opposed as too radical. [10] We recall the procession of hoodlums of "property and standing" that made an effigy of the gentle and learned Mr. Brooks and carried it through the streets, putting a fool's cap on the head on which was the legend "A Normal School in the Clouds." The valiant Horace Mann had to work hard and long to bring that vision down from the clouds into the actual public school system; and women teachers, trained in co-educational normal schools, shared his labor at every step. In spite of their poverty in education, however, the women of the eighteenth and first half of the nineteenth centuries made some good showing in letters; and their struggles for professional training and opportunity, especially in the field of medicine, show an heroic tem-

[10] Henry B. Barnard, *History of Public Education.*

per as well as a persistent purpose second to no class
of men in a similar effort to obtain rights and chances
in the larger life.

There have been so many definitions of the lesser
genius that one is at liberty to vary the intellectual
challenge to women in order to cover justly the demand upon them. If, for example, as some say, "genius is the power of prodigious industry in some one
direction," then women might certainly win some
prizes in literature—or in what is called that when it
is fresh from the press and becomes "the best seller."
[11] Not only Mrs. Southworth with her near a hundred
books translated into several languages and sold in
six capitals of the world, but also Mrs. Willis Parton
with her article each week for sixteen successive years
in *The New York Ledger*, may challenge attention!
Then we have Lydia H. Sigourney whose day-school
education ceased at thirteen years and who was obliged
to do all the rest of her studying by herself, varied
only by a short term at a boarding school where she
was taught "embroidery of historical scenes, filigree
and other finger-works." She produced over fifty
books and more than two thousand articles in prose
and verse contributed to over three hundred periodi-
cals. No wonder her Muse was anæmic from such
exertion on such small sustenance! Mrs. Hall, col-
laborating with her husband through the forty years
of his editorship in *The Art Journal*, and Mrs. Bar-
bauld, adding to her large original work the editing

[11] Helen Gray Cone, *Women in Literature* in *Woman's Work in
America.*

of fifty volumes of the best English novels, show a like industry with better results.

If, again, as others say, genius is shown by the pioneer entrance into new fields of thought and action, then such a woman as Lydia Maria Child must surely have a place among those distinguished for translating the inventive faculty into literature. Pioneer she was in so many ways—writing the first anti-slavery book; initiating the first series of travel and art letters from a great city; among the first to write novels using home material; starting the first children's magazine in the United States; becoming one of the first woman editors of other than a "Ladies'" magazine in her work for *The Anti-Slavery Standard;* and most original of all, writing the first comparative study of religions published in this country, and one of the first published in the world from the standpoint of rational thought; and this from a stock of learning so small as to make the venture as audacious as it was provocative of thought in the better equipped students of her time. Nor must it be forgotten that in the very beginning of what may be called American literature Margaret Fuller founded the first quarterly published in this country in the interest of philosophy; and added other pioneer contributions as literary editor of *The Tribune* under Horace Greeley to what was the spring-time growth of intellectual life in the United States; besides proving herself the great improvvisatrice of her day in conversation as an art.[12] In fiction, the success of women in introducing new subject-matter is proof

[12] Horace Greeley in *Memorials of Margaret Fuller Ossoli.*

of their preëminence in at least one form of originality. Aphra Behn herself, the first woman in England
to earn her living by her pen and made worthy of her
burial in the Poets' Corner of Westminster Abbey
more by that fact than by the lasting value of her
words, held the stage by her dramas so long chiefly
because they in some degree initiated that realistic
school which Jane Austen first made commanding and
respected as a new type of story-telling. Many women
writers of all the leading nations have carried on this
adventurous spirit and shown high gifts in the imagi-
native treatment of the actual and the commonplace.
This was the master quality in Mrs. Beecher Stowe's
novels, the most popular of which, *Uncle Tom's
Cabin,* attested also woman's tendency toward the dramatic presentation of great moral ideals. The practical nature of women and their deep religious earnestness have often made them servants of their time, as
was Mrs. Stowe, in ways that of themselves sometimes
dwarf permanent results in literature and art. For
example, Jane Grey Swisshelm, with intellectual power
and business ability to found and maintain an influential newspaper in the days when many women could
not read or write, used much of her strength in defending her anti-slavery propaganda against the mobs
that opposed her, and later in nursing soldiers of the
Civil War, and thus in all her life became a type of
the numberless professional women who waver per-
petually between social reform and intellectual achievement.[13] Such devotion to duty, if not inimical to ge-

[13] See *Woman's Work in America.*

nius, harnesses it too early to hard labor for full development of "frolic fancy" or of calm contemplation.

"Talent," says Lowell, "is that which is in a man's
power; genius is that in whose power a man is." If
genius, even in its lesser ranges, be this irresistible
pressure toward some unique self-expression, then
women cannot be left out of the charmed circle; especially when we remember Helen Hunt with her solitary
but wide approach to love and life, and Emily Dick-
inson, that hermit thrush among poets. Nor can those
unique interpreters of art and literature among women
whose vital expression has so enhanced the works of
genius as to make them seem new creations, be left
out of the count. In modern times, the growing company of musicians, some of them composers, and the
artists of pen and brush, and the sculptors among
women who swell the secondary ranks of genius in
numbers and in power, must have increasing recognition.

All this, however, does not reach the deepest considerations involved in taking account of the intellectual contribution of women to art, science, philosophy and affairs. Whatever may be the reasons in
nature for the lower level of women along these lines
of man's greatest achievement, there are the gravest
reasons in circumstance for the comparatively meagre
showing. In addition to the handicap of lack of education, a handicap which no exceptional success of the
self-made man or woman can offset for the majority
of the talented, there is a no less important deprivation which all women have suffered in the past and

most women now suffer. This deprivation is that of the informal but highly stimulating training which the good fellowship of their chosen guild of study and of service gives to men, but which is denied for the most part even to professional women. For example, women have been in the medical profession for a considerable time, and have obtained high distinction in it. They have won just recognition from many influential doctors of the other sex. Yet they can hardly be said to have entered the inner circle of their clan. They may stop to dinner at medical conventions, it is true, provided they make no fuss about smoking and do not mind being in the minority; but there are few men, even in that enlightened group, who can so sink sex-consciousness in professional comradeship as either to give or get the full social value that might be gained from a mixed company of like vocation. The women lawyers and members of the clergy are in even smaller minority, and hence suffer still more from that embarrassment of "the exception" which prevents easy and familiar association. In the teaching profession, where the relative numbers of the sexes are reversed, there is often more adequate professional intercourse; but the woman college professor, or college president, is still that one among many whose reception into her special class, even if courteous and friendly, is too formal and occasional for real guild fellowship.[14]

To this negative deprivation must be added the positive opposition of men to the entrance of women into that professional life and work from which the genius

[14] See M. Jacques Lourbet, *Problème des Sexes.*

arises as the rare flower from a vast field. The whole course of evolution in industry, and in the achievements of higher education and exceptional talent, has shown man's invariable tendency to shut women out when their activities have reached a highly specialized period of growth. The primitive woman-worker, as Jack-at-all-trades, does not develop any one employment to its height of perfection. Gradually initiating old men and boys, not fitted for war and the chase, into these varied forms of effort, women start the other sex toward that concentration of effort upon one process-activity which finally develops separate arts, sciences and professions. When this point is reached, the "woman's work" usually becomes "man's work"; and when that time comes, men turn round and shut out women from the labor which women themselves have initiated. This monopolistic tendency of men is shown most clearly in the history of the learned professions. Women were seldom, if ever, priests but they participated in religious services when religion was a family affair. When a priestly caste arose and became the symbol of peculiar authority, only men entered its ranks. Woman can reënter her natural place as religious leader only through the Theological Schools and Ordination, and these have been forbidden her until very recently and are now seldom open to her in full measure.

A striking illustration of this process of sex-exclusion following the perfecting of standards in training is shown in recent years in the United States in the action of the Methodist Episcopal Church. This religious body, of which Susanna Wesley has been called "the real founder" and Barbara Heck the first and most effective teacher in the United States, had for all its earlier propaganda the services of lay-preachers, later called "licensed exhorters," among whom were many gifted women whose "call" was well attested by the crowds that thronged to hear them. When, however, through an effort to raise all the standards of leadership in the Methodist Church to the plane of an "educated ministry," this lay service was crippled and finally abolished, women were shut out of the Methodist ministry altogether; thus losing to this Church many brilliant and devout preachers.

Again, women developed law and its application to life in the germs of family rule and tribal custom quite as much as did men; but when statutes took the place of tradition, and courts superseded personal judge-ship, and when a special class of lawyers was needed to define and administer laws, which grew more difficult to understand with growing complexity of social relationship, men alone entered that profession. Women can now become members of that class only by graduating from law-schools and being "admitted to the bar," and only very recently have they been allowed these privileges. The prophetess Deborah, who was a "judge in Israel," was not the only woman to embody the ancient authority of woman in formal fashion; and Aspasia pleading causes in the Athenian forum and Hortensia appearing before the Roman Senate against unjust taxes do not stand alone in history as familiar with and influencing legislation. The ru-

dimentary law of the ancient Germans, especially, **took**
care to "represent every woman at the court of the
suzerain, in judicial acts and debates." [15]   The Court
of Maryland in January, 1648, ordered that Mistress
Brent be received as Lord Baltimore's attorney; although when she asked, on that account, for "Voyce
and vote in the General Assembly," she was refused.[16]
These exceptions do not disprove but give point to
that general rule of development of law that in the
ratio of its perfecting as a separate profession women
were excluded from its training and its practice. When
Arabella Mansfield of Iowa was admitted to the bar in
1869 she was a pioneer in the road all women must
now travel to reënter any stronghold of the law.

This process of differentiating and perfecting intellectual labor, the process in which at most acute periods of specialization and advance, women were
wholly shut out of their own ancient work, finds its
most complete and its most dramatic illustration in
the history of the medical profession.   Some phases of
the healing art have always been connected in primitive society with the priestly office and, hence, in the
hands of men.   Three great branches, however, were
always, in all forms of social organization of which
we have knowledge, in the hands exclusively of women,
namely, midwifery, the treatment of diseases of
women so far as those were cared for at all, and the
diseases of children.   The growth of Christian mis-
sions to foreign countries has been due in large part

---

[15] Louis Frank, *La Femme Avocat*
[16] *Archives of Maryland.*

to the employment of women medical missionaries to
enter the secluded homes of women in so-called heathen
countries where the primitive taboo still forbids the
entrance of a man not her husband into the sickroom
of a woman, or into the nursery of her child. That
men should attend women in childbirth, or should become to women that most intimate of friends, a "family physician," is still unthinkable to the modesty of
the Oriental woman. The result of this sex-segrega-
tion in the care of the sick in these important branches
has been that women doctors, unschooled but often
not unskilled, have served all the past of human experience in childbirth, in child-care, and in the special
illnesses of women. This has been true in our own,
as well as in older civilizations up to the 18th century. In our own country, in colonial times, only
women ushered into a bleak New England the potential citizens of the new world. We read of Mrs. Wiat,
who died in 1705 at the age of 94 years, having assisted as midwife at the birth of more than 1,100 children.[17] And in Rehoboth, one of the oldest communities in Massachusetts, the Town Meeting itself
"called" from England "Dr. Sam Fuller and his
mother," he to practise medicine and she "as midwife
to answer to the town's necessity, which was great." [18]
Busied with other matters, the Colonies paid little
attention to medical science until the war of the American Revolution betrayed the awful results of ignorance
in the slaughter of soldiers by preventable disease.

[17] Mary Putnam Jacobi, M.D., in *Women in Medicine.*
[18] Town Records of Rehoboth, Mass.

When the healing art began to become a true science
and took great strides toward better training and fa-
cilities of practice for the student, attention was at
once drawn to the need for better service in the fields
wholly occupied by women. The opening and improvement of the medical schools, however, was a
new opportunity for men alone and the new demand
for more scientific care of women in childbirth and
for higher medical service to childhood and for the
women suffering from special diseases, resulted in the
greatest of innovations, namely, the assumption by
men of the office of midwife and their entrance into
the most intimate relationships with women patients.
Dr. James Lloyd, after two years' study in England,
began to practise "obstetrics" (the new name that dis-
guised in some degree the daring change in medical
practice) in Boston, in 1762. Dr. Shippen, similarly
trained abroad, took up the same practice in Philadelphia and added lectures upon the subject.   [19] Thus
began in our own country the elevation of this important branch of the healing art to a professional
standard and the consequent exclusion of women from
their immortal rights in the sickroom. It was a poor
recognition of the debt the race owed to the mother-
sex, both as suffering the pangs of childbirth and as
helping to assuage them and in caring for the infants
and children of all time! After men entered upon the
task of perfecting the medical profession, and incidentally shutting women out of it, it did not take long,
however, for the thoughtful to see the propriety of

[19] Augustus Gardner, M.D., *History of Art of Midwifery*, 1851.

allowing women those advantages of training which
would put them back again into their rightful place
on the higher plane of science now demanded. What
gave sharp point to this feeling was the common opposition to men engaging in these ancient prerogatives of
women. This was at first as intense and as bitter as
the later opposition to the entrance of women into the
co-educational medical schools. Dr. Samuel Gregory,
who founded, in Boston, Mass., in 1848, the first medical training school for women,—a poor affair but a
prophecy of better things,—wrote a pamphlet which
was widely circulated, entitled "Man-midwifery Exposed and Corrected; or the Employment of men to
attend women in child-birth shown to be a modern Innovation, Unnecessary, Unnatural and Injurious to the
physical Welfare of the Community, and Pernicious in
its influence on Professional and Public Morality."
Dr. Gregory brought forward in support of the claims
of his new School of Medicine with its meagre opportunities for study, that it would enable the "surplus
female population," numbering already in 1849 at
least "20,000 in New England," to prepare for a "useful, honorable and remunerative occupation as mid-
wives"; and as they "could afford to give their services
at a much cheaper rate than men, five dollars instead
of fifteen dollars" would be all the poor would have
to pay in confinement cases. It may well be imagined
that this prospect of being undersold by women, in a
field of medical practice which men were suddenly
finding very remunerative, added fuel to the flame of
opposition by men doctors to any form of medical

education for women which would enable them to receive certificates legally entitling them to any part in the medical profession.   Yet some prophetic and just minds early recognized the justice of the claims of women to such education.   The Right Rev. Bishop Potter of New York declared in 1850, "The especial propriety of qualifying women to practise among children and their own sex will be admitted, I hope, by all."   And the New York *Tribune* in an editorial printed in 1853 said, "Fifty years hence it will be difficult to gain credit for the assertion that American women acquiesced through the former half of the 19th century in the complete monopoly of the medical profession by men, even including midwifery and diseases of women."   This acquiescence of women, however, was inevitable when these branches of the healing art were incorporated in a profession into which women could not legally enter, and trained for in schools from which women were excluded.   The first women who tried to secure training in medical schools in order to re-enter those branches of the healing art from which they had so recently been driven, and on the higher plane of science now properly demanded, endured such hardships as made them veritable martyrs.   In 1847 Harriot K. Hunt knocked at the door of Harvard Medical School to be persistently refused admission. In 1849 Elizabeth Blackwell graduated from Geneva Medical School, having secured instruction as a special favor, and began her great career; devoted equally to securing the best possible medical training for women, and to elevating to higher standards than had as yet been attained by men the whole area of medical training. Among the heroic figures of these early days are to be found many married women whose husbands, often themselves physicians, helped them to obtain their training. Dr. Hiram Corson, who for a generation waged a chivalrous war against the exclusion of women from his profession, helped many a woman to attain desired opportunities; and his niece, Sarah Adamson, afterwards the wife and fellow-practitioner of Dr. Dolley, was the second woman to take a medical degree in the United States. And Dr. Gleason, who associated his young wife with himself in medical work and persuaded the "eclectics" to open their school to women, declared early in the struggle, "In my opinion, the admission of women is the reform most needed in the medical profession." The attitude of the men of the medical profession generally, however, was one of the utmost hostility, showing every form of monopolistic selfishness and injustice. England, which had led the United States in all medical advance, gave belated attention to the needs of women. Not until 1872 was the Medical department of the London University opened to women, and when they were declared eligible for its medical degree many indignant men-graduates of the institution protested that their "property rights had been invaded by this action"; that for women to be able legally to practise medicine "lowered the value of their own diplomas, and, therefore, the University had violated its contract with men by allowing women to share its privileges." [20]   All this was

[20] Dr. Putnam Jacobi, *History of Women in Medicine.*

without reference to the intellectual standing or practical efficiency of the women graduates. The mere fact of women entering the profession meant, in the minds of these protestants, degradation to the men already in it! Earlier than this, in 1859, the Medical Society of the County of Philadelphia passed "resolutions of excommunication" against every physician who should "teach in a medical school for women" and every one who should "consult with a woman physician or with a man teaching a woman medical student." [21]   In Massachusetts after qualified women physicians were given State certificates to practise, the Massachusetts Medical Society forbade them membership, thus refusing to admit the legality of diplomas already sanctioned by the highest authority.[22]   The facts that women medical students, like those of the other sex, required clinic teaching and hospital training for proper preparation, and that, since hospital opportunities could not be adequately duplicated, women must be taught with men in this field, gave the pioneer women medical students a peculiar discipline of hardship. When the gentle Ann Preston and the highly bred and scientifically trained Emmeline Cleveland led their classes of women into the amphitheatre of the operating room of the first hospital opened to women for this clinic training, the men students howled and called vile names and made the women, on leaving the hospital, pass through a lane of riotous men all shouting indecencies at women so

[21] Records, Philadelphia County Medical Society, 1859-60.
[22] Admitted 1879.

far above them in moral height that they could not touch them where their spirits lived, even by personal violence! This Quaker pioneer, Ann Preston, was so unmoved by all the abuse showered upon the early women doctors that her serene spirit guided her pupils toward a conception of life and duty rarely expressed in any era by any class of women. So far from either bitterness or pretence was her attitude that her words of warning to the women graduating from the Philadelphia Medical School were a fitting sermon for all women of to-day, or of the future, who aim toward excellence in newly opened fields of effort. Speaking to one of the first classes, she said: "Every woman physician will be watched narrowly and criticised severely because she is a woman. If she bear herself not wisely and well, many will suffer for her sake. Gentleness of manner, the adornment of a quiet spirit, are as important to the physician as to the woman. Your business is not to war with words but to make good your position by deeds of healing." When women sought to make good in positions of helpfulness as hospital internes, their first examination was signalized by "the obstetrical and gynecological examiners by vulgar jokes" and by the attempt of the "surgical examiner" to wreck them "with unusual demands." Nevertheless, the women did reënter their ancient profession of healing after a brief exclusion. So far from permanently lowering the standards of training newly established, their chief pioneer leader, Elizabeth Blackwell, was instrumental in inaugurating modern preventive medicine, by the establishment in the New York Medical College for Women, opened in 1865, of the first chair of Hygiene ever set apart in a medical college in the United States. In 1882 this pioneer medical college for women set forth the bravest and truest of philosophies respecting women's work in the following words: "We call upon all those who believe in the higher education of women to help set the highest possible standards for their medical education; and we call upon those who do not believe in such higher education to help in making such requirements as shall turn aside the incompetent;—not by any exercise of arbitrary power, but by a demonstration of incapacity, which is the only logical, manly reason for refusing to allow women to pursue an honorable calling in an honorable way."

  This brief allusion to the heroic struggle of woman to reënter the healing art against the positive opposition of men already entrenched in all the coïgns of vantage in professional training and organized professional guilds, furnishes a flashlight picture of the whole course of woman's entrance into the more modern types of differentiated labor. The short time since women were admitted even to the outskirts of the learned professions, and even to the smallest crumb of training for any great art, science or intellectual achievement, must be more justly estimated before we judge whether or not women have shown incipient genius. Certainly in the medical profession, the lovely Susan Dimock, who, even as a girl, drew the attention of the whole leadership of her profession to her powers as a surgeon, might, had not the angry waters destroyed her life in the sinking of the ill-fated "Schiller" in 1875, have given new proof of the possibilities in woman's development.[23]   And Dr. Mary Putnam Jacobi, first woman to be admitted to the Paris School of Medicine and winner of its second prize at graduation, proved, by her all-round talent, clear title to a high place in Dr. Clouston's "second grade of genius." It is she who has summed up in vivid and truthful manner not only for her own profession but, inferentially, for all the higher intellectual pursuits of women, the just basis of judgment of feminine powers. "When," she says, "a century shall have elapsed after general higher education has become diffused among women; after generations have had increased opportunities for inheritance of trained intellectual aptitudes; after the work of establishing, in the face of resolute opposition, the right to privileged work, in addition to the drudgeries imposed by necessity, shall have ceased to preoccupy the energies of women; after selfish monopolies of privilege and advantage shall have been broken down; after the rights and capacities of women as individuals shall have received thorough, serious and practical recognition; a century after this" [24] we may fitly judge of the natural capacity of women for that intellectual leadership out of which genius must spring.

In addition to these handicaps must be named the well-known but scarcely adequately measured interruptions to both study and self-expression which the women

---

[23] Ednah D. Cheney, *Women in Hospitals.*
[24] Chapter *Women in Medicine* in *Woman's Work in America.*

of talent and specialized power have always experienced. Anyone can see that to write *Uncle Tom's Cabin* on the knee in the kitchen, with constant calls to cooking and other details of housework to punctuate the paragraphs, was a more difficult achievement than to write it at leisure in a quiet room. And when her biographer says of an Italian woman poet, "during some years her Muse was intermitted," we do not wonder at the fact when he casually mentions her ten children. No record, however, can even name the women of talent who were so submerged by child-bearing and its duties, and by "general housework," that they had to leave their poems and stories all unwritten. Moreover, the obstacles to intellectual development and achievement which marriage and maternity interpose (and which are so important that they demand a separate study) are not the only ones that must be noted. It is not alone the fact that women have generally had to spend most of their strength in caring for others that has handicapped them in individual effort; but also that they have almost universally had to care wholly for themselves. Women even now have the burden of the care of their belongings, their dress, their home life of whatever sort it may be, and the social duties of the smaller world, even if doing great things in individual work. A successful woman preacher was once asked "what special obstacles have you met as a woman in the ministry?" "Not one," she answered, "except the lack of a minister's wife." When we read of Charles Darwin's wife not only relieving him from financial cares but seeing that he had his breakfast in his room, with "nothing to disturb the freshness of his morning," we do not find the explanation of Darwin's genius, but we do see how he was helped to express it. Men geniuses, even of second grade, have usually had at least one woman to smooth their way, and often several women to make sure that little things, often even self-support itself, did not interfere with the development and expression of their talent. On the other hand, the obligation of all the earlier women writers to prepare a useful cook-book in order to buy their way into literature, is a fitting symbol of the compulsion laid upon women, however gifted, to do all the things that women in general accomplish before entering upon their special task. That brave woman who wanted to study medicine so much that not even the heaviest family burdens could deter her from entering the medical school first opened to her sex, but who "first sewed steadily until her entire family was fitted with clothes to last six months," is a not unusual type.[25]

Added to all this, the woman of talent and of special gifts has had until very lately, and in most countries has still, to go against the massed social pressure of her time in order to devote herself to any particular intellectual task. The expectation of society has long pushed men toward some special work; the expectation of society has until recently been wholly against women's choosing any vocation beside their functional service in the family. This is a far more intense and

[25] Mrs. Thomas, graduated in first class of Women's Medical College of Philadelphia; served as City Physician at Fort Wayne, Ind., eight years.

all-pervading influence in deterring women from success in intellectual work than is usually understood.
"Palissy the Potter" is honored with a volume in the
series on the *Heroes of Industry*. This is well; for
his marked talent, his indomitable purpose pursued in
poverty, his choice of inventive rather than of paying
work, his final success after intense effort, all mark him
as great in his devotion and in his gift to art. We
note, however, that his family pay a heavy price for
his choices in life; and when his wife objects to his
burning up the baby's cradle and the kitchen table in
that devouring furnace which has already consumed
all their comforts, we are inclined to sympathize with
her. She does not feel sure—as indeed how could
she?—that Palissy will get the glaze he wants; but she
sees clearly that the children are hungry and she cannot feed them. His biographer, however, is clearly
of the opinion that men should be sustained in their
heroic efforts to solve problems and make inventions;
and Palissy himself has that conviction of society concerning the worth and righteousness of man's specialized effort to give tone to his ambition. This it is
which makes him feel himself a hero and not merely
a selfish man who neglects his family. No book has
yet been written in praise of a woman who let her
husband and children starve or suffer while she invented even the most useful things, or wrote books,
or expressed herself in art, or evolved philosophic
systems. On the contrary, the mildest approach on the
part of a wife and mother, or even of a daughter or
sister, to that intense interest in self-expression which

has always characterized genius has been met with social disapproval and until very recent times with ostracism fit only for the criminal. Hence her inner impulsion has needed to be strong indeed to make any woman devote herself to ideas.

In view of these tremendous obstacles, it is fair to assume that when women in the past have achieved even a second or third place in the ranks of genius they have shown far more native ability than men have needed to reach the same eminence. Not excused from the more general duties that constitute the cement of society, most women of talent have had but one hand free with which to work out their ideal conceptions. Denied, at cost of "respectability" itself, any expression of that obstinate egotism which is nature's protection of the genius in his special task, and in the preparation for it, they have had to make secret and painful experiments in self-expression after spending first strength in the commonplace tasks required of all their sex.

The genius is at once the most self-centred and the most universal of human beings. He sees only himself and the world of thought or of affairs he would master for his special work. All that lies between, family, friends, social groups, is but material for his elect service. Delight in his own personality, absorbed attention to the processes of his own mind, have made him generally the master shirker in respect to the ordinary duties of life. He has been often "ill to live with," and greedy in demand upon the support and care of others. He is so rare and precious, however, that "with all his faults we love him still" when he enriches the commonwealth of thought, imagination or action with some new gift. But, alas, the "near" genius has too often the character frailties of the genuine great one without his power of achievement. We see therefore the social advantage of the poverty and hardships and lack of immediate appreciation which have so often weeded out from the lists, in advance, all but the giants in intellectual power. Seeing how many small people mistake their own strongly individualized taste for great talent, and feel justified in declining all disagreeable tasks of "menial" work on the plea of absorption in some form of effort which is mainly self-indulgence, we realize that nature has done well to discipline the would-be genius severely. The "artistic temperament" so often drops the final syllables to become mere vulgar "temper" that family life could not well bear the strain of greatly multiplying the type that for the most part only enjoys but does not produce masterpieces. But to suppress in wholesale fashion, and at the outset, all troublesome "variations" in women, while leaving men free to show what they can become and giving them besides a good chance to prove their quality, is to make that discipline too one-sided. The universal social pressure upon women to be all alike, and do all the same things, and to be content with identical restrictions, has resulted not only in terrible suffering in the lives of exceptional women, but also in the loss of unmeasured feminine values in special gifts. The Drama of the Woman of Genius has been too often a tragedy of misshapen and perverted power. Col. Higginson said that one of the great histories yet to be written is that of the intellectual life of women. When that is accomplished, those truly great women whose initiative was choked by false ideals of feminine excellence, whose natures were turned awry for want of "space to burgeon out their powers," whose very purpose to "aggrandize the human mind by cultivating their own" was made a cross for their crucifixion, will be given just honor.

One woman of the nineteenth century might well hold the first place in such a record of the achievement and martyrdom of the woman of genius. Stepping out into the Western world from the dark shadows of Oriental subjection of her sex, this woman of India, Anandabai Joshee, appeals to the future for her full recognition. And if Being and Doing ever come to rank with Thinking and Imagining and Discovering as marks of greatness, no list of the Immortals will be complete without her. The record of her life epitomizes and makes heroic that historic conflict in women's lives between social duty and personal idealism. A child wife at nine years of age; a child mother at fourteen, her baby's death making her determine to study medicine for the benefit of her countrywomen; at seventeen overcoming tremendous obstacles in order to carry out this purpose, which obliged her to become the first high-caste Hindu woman, still loyal to her inherited religion, to leave her country for a foreign land; at eighteen years entering upon her studies in the United States and showing marvellous powers of scholarly acquisition and still more marvellous breadth of mind and exaltation of moral nature; at twenty-one graduating from the Woman's Medical College of Philadelphia, the first Hindu woman to take a medical degree in any country; and dying at twenty-two, just as she received her appointment as physician in charge of the Female Wards of Albert Edward Hospital in Kolhapur, India—her life reads like an incredible romance.[26]

It has been said that although genius is so often allied to instability of character, we have in Darwin and in Shakespeare two examples of the wholly sane. In Dr. Joshee we have another; one whose mental power was so exceptional that it could bridge the chasm between centuries of intellectual development and continents of racial difference to make itself at home in the Anglo-Saxon civilization, whose finest fruits were so quickly made her own; and yet one whose gentle, unselfish, loving spirit showed no flaw in most intimate association. Writing to friends in America just before her voyage, she said: "When I think over the sufferings of women in India I am impatient to see the Western light dawn as the harbinger of emancipation." In that spirit of world-citizenship, without giving up her ancient faith, she so enlarged and purified it that she was able to say: "I have nothing to despise; the whole Universe is a lesson to me." When, before leaving India, she was urged by all who loved her not to undertake so perilous a venture, she calmly replied: "I am sure nothing will harm me, or if it does it will be for my good." Ad-

[26] Caroline Healey Dall, *The Life of Anandabai Joshee.*

dressing a great multitude of her wondering fellow-country people on the eve of sailing, in answer to the question, "Why should you do what is not done by any of your sex?" she made the answer that might well become the formula to justify all exceptional service —"Because society has a right to our work as individuals." Yet this woman, so rare in heroism and in mental and moral power that there are few to place beside her, declared her intention "to live and die a faithful Hindu wife." Knowing what that meant in personal subserviency and in chilling repression, her biographer declares that Dr. Joshee's untimely death was due most of all to this attempt to do the impossible, to be a servant in the home and a social leader in the community. However this may be, and with all due tribute to her husband's devotion and willingness for her to live the larger life, it must be true that the hurtful conditions of Hindu wifehood had already sapped the strength of Dr. Joshee before she left India; and the unique loyalty that made her seek to return to her caste restrictions while carrying the torch of enlightenment to her sisters in India entailed a double burden too heavy for her frail body. What women of less heroic mould, and in more favored circumstances, have suffered in the effort to do all that their world expected of them and also something of what their own inner natures demanded—and that toll of suffering is long and heavy indeed—Dr. Joshee embodied in the pathos and in the sublimity of her unique experience.

In this country of free opportunity, and in this time,

when to work one's own way to one's own ends is so much easier for women than ever before, it is in the life and work of such a woman as Anandabai Joshee that we perceive the full significance of the Drama of the Woman of Genius.

IV

THE DAY OF THE SPINSTER

THE day of the spinster did not dawn until women, married and single, and of all ages, had generally ceased to use the distaff and the spinning-wheel. The name came, indeed, from the useful service rendered by maidens, young and old, in the days of domestic handicraft, when the economic pressure was so heavy upon the house-mother that she could not fulfil her task without the labor of the unmarried in the home. But "spinster" came early to have a legal significance as descriptive of the unmarried state of an adult woman, just as still earlier the word "distaff" stood for collective womanhood; Dryden saying of woman's rule, "The crown usurped, a distaff on the throne." So closely related were woman's work and woman's existence in ancient law and custom, that the name of her labor became the title for herself. To-day we use the word spinster in colloquial speech as the designation of all sorts of maidens, of "certain" or "uncertain" age. The spinster may be the lady who must never be called anything which suggests hard work; she may be the "bachelor girl" whose professional success assures her an independent habitation and high social standing; she may be the working-woman whose manual or commercial labor ensures her her own latch-key and her own bank-book; she may be, and often is, the staid teacher upon whom is placed the heaviest burden of public service borne by any class in the United States. In any case, the modern spinster has at last her innings in the great game of life.

Celibacy, although said to be a practice of the ants and bees for economic reasons in the division of labor, is, comparatively speaking, a recent experience of the human race. In primitive life no one, man or woman, could shirk the duty of marriage and of participation in the race life through parenthood. The whole system of ancient social order was based upon this universal sharing of the marriage state. The early religion of ancestor-worship, the customs of family ritual which ruled all details of existence, the basis of property rights and of political privileges in specific forms of descent and relationship, these all demanded the active membership of all adults in the family. The ancient Hindu law declared, "The extinction of a family causes the ruin of the religion of that family; the ancestors, deprived of the offerings of sons, fall into the abode of the unhappy."[1] At Athens the law made it the duty of the first magistrate to "see that no family became extinct"; and Cicero said, "There is no one so careless about himself as to wish to leave his family without descendants; for then there would be no one to render him that worship which is due the dead." Because

[1] Laws of Manu.

of this religious basis of the family the sterile wife must be divorced, the sterile husband must raise him up sons from a brother or other relative, or by adoption an heir must be secured; as the Hindu law put it, "He to whom Nature has denied a son may adopt one so that the funeral ceremonies shall not cease." [2] This demand of ancient society that each man should have a son to carry on the worship of the dead has no longer place in our thought; when we deplore celibacy or "race suicide," it is in the interest of the future, not the past; the unborn, not the dead. We need, therefore, to think ourselves back in order to realize in any degree the religious significance of marriage. The hearth-fire that in Greece and Rome was so sacred that it must never be neglected, dates back to earliest Aryan life. "Agni," says the Rig Veda, "must be invoked before all other gods." The sacredness of this fire was attested by the fact that no criminal or wrong-doer could approach it until he had purified himself; and not even in legal marriage could the union of the sexes be brought too near it. When the gods became persons, the Hearth-fire became Vesta, whom Ovid declared to be "naught but a living flame"; Vesta, the virgin goddess, "neither fecundity nor power, but order, moral order"; the "universal soul." Marriage, however, was a religious necessity; and for that reason, in Rome a man who had enough children felt it a duty to lend his wife, either temporarily or for life, to some childless man: while in Sparta, although a man should lend his wife for kindred purposes, he was required to keep

[2] Laws of Manu.

her in his own house, and, if old and decrepit, should invite under his roof some young and strong man to bear him children.   Lycurgus had women marry when "of full age and inclination," while Romans gave their daughters in marriage at twelve years and under; but all women in the ancient world had to marry, and primitive customs of all ages and lands multiply varieties of dealing with this inexorable command.   Not only must the ancient woman be married once, but she must be married all her life, or suffer, as in India, terrible penalties.   If a widow, she must be replaced under a new husband's control as speedily as possible, lest she get into mischief; if deserted, she must find her sole protection and support in marital rearrangement.   In any case, not until our own civilization is reached do we anywhere find celibate women numerous enough to form a class.

Men were first allowed some freedom not to marry, but this was grudgingly given and with many penalties for the idiosyncrasy.   In Sparta, we are told, bachelors were under ban, disfranchised by law, excluded from witnessing the great public processions which were the pride of the State; and in winter time compelled to march naked around the market-place, singing as they went a song testifying to their own disgrace by which they "justly suffered punishment."   And in this land, so insistent in all other respects upon reverence for the aged, there was one exception: a youth might refuse, and without reproof, to rise and give a seat to a venerable bachelor, even to one who had done honorable service for the State, saying, "No son of yours will

ever rise to give me a seat."[3]   This punishment of
the bachelor has been common in many ages and countries, and extended down to the early days of our own
history.[4]   In Connecticut, in 1636, a law was passed
which would not "allow any young unmarried man to
keep house," and Hartford taxed "lone-men twenty
shillings a week" for the "selfish luxury of solitary living."   In 1682 a special town order gave permission
for two bachelors to keep house together, "so they
carry themselves soberly and do not entertain idle persons to the evil expense of time by day or night," while
as late as the eighteenth century, a general statute of
Connecticut forbade any "householder" under penalty
of fine to "give entertainment or habitation to single
persons without special allowance of the selectmen;
and such Bourders, Sojourners and Young persons"
as they were permitted to entertain were required to
"attend the worship of God in the families where
they live and be otherwise subject to the family discipline or pay five shillings for every breach of the law."
In Rhode Island, although not so strict a community
as that of Connecticut, "single persons of three months'
residence must pay a special tax of five shillings," while
the "rate of faculties and personal abilities" was left
to the discretion of the assessors.   One wonders in this
case whether pride in "personal abilities" or thrift in
saving operated most strongly on the taxpayer's mind!
In Plymouth the law declared that "Whereas great In-
convenience hath arisen by single persons in this Col-

[3] *Plutarch's Lives.*
[4] See George E. Howard, *A History of Matrimonial Institutions.*

lonie being for themselves and not betaking themselves
to live in well-gouverned families, no single person shall
be suffered hereafter to live by himself but such as
the selectmen permit"; and in Massachusetts there was
a general statute that placed all "single persons who
take journeys merely for pleasure" under suspicion in
such manner that they could easily be haled to court
and made to pay "forty shillings," or go to jail if they
could not give a satisfactory account of themselves.
"Single men" in Massachusetts for a long time could
be "convicted of living from under family government"
and made to "submit themselves to some family rule,"
and put on probation, as it were, being required to
"bring with them to Court a certificate" that they had
thus mended their independent ways.

There was little trouble with "old maids" in a society in which, as in colonial days, and early post-rev-
olutionary times, women were at such a premium because of economic value as workers, that young girls
married very early, and a widow might expect (as was
the case with one of Judge Sewall's friends) to be
invited to "keep house together" by a widower who
attended her home from her husband's funeral! Yet
there were a few women called "antient maydes" at
the great age of twenty-five years! "An old maid in
Boston is thought such a curse as nothing can exceed
it and looked upon as a dismal spectacle," says John
Dunton in his *Life and Errors;* but nevertheless he
praises one such who by her "good-nature, gravity and
strict virtue convinces all that it is not her necessity
but her choice that keeps her virgin. Now about

thirty," he adds, "the age which they call a Thornback, yet she never disguises herself and talks as little
as she thinks of love." Courtship, also, was under
strict rule when a man in New England might be fined
and even given corporal punishment for making any
"motion of marriage to any man's daughter or mayde-
servant without first having obtained leave of the
parents or master." So that marriage itself was not
easy, it would seem, in those days, unless one always
chose with the parents; but to refrain from marriage,
with such a sentiment against old maids (even in Boston!), must have been almost impossible, even for the
most hardened or good-natured "Thornback."

Although, however, primitive life allowed few
women, if any, to escape mating in some fashion, and
although all sorts of difficulties later encompassed the
path of the woman who chose not to marry, or who
wished to marry against the parents' wish, there were
some women, as we know, in classic civilization, who
stayed outside the marriage bond and yet attained a
place of peculiar social power. The unique phenomenon of the hetaira in Greece testifies, among other
things, to the fact that no class in society can be permanently shut entirely out of the leading influences
of their time and country. [5] While the Greek wife
had no part in the intellectual development which was
her husband's privilege, by the sure law of nature,
fathers in Greece, as elsewhere, gave daughters mental gifts; and some of those daughters broke the bars

[5] See W. E. H. Lecky, *History of Morals,* chapter *The Position
of Women.*

of the home cage to become the only free and educated class of women in Athens by the only manner of life open to them. Only courtesans among women shared the glories of the Age of Pericles, and they thus formed the one *élite* class of "irregular women" the world has known or probably will ever know. Given a land where beauty was worshipped as the highest good, a land in which not abstinence but temperance in all physical indulgence was the law of virtue, a land that by a strange inconsistency in evolution left the mothers wholly behind in mental training and stimulus, it is not quite strange that the rare combination of beauty, devotion to study, interest in public affairs and intellectual gifts should have made a few women outside of marriage chief representatives of the higher companionships of the sexes. Only for such reasons could Socrates, chief moralist of his day and country, see it right to record his indebtedness to one such courtesan for her aid in his teachings and in his public service, and visit others of her class as equals and honored friends. This shows their high standing among the great and good; but perhaps excuses, even then, the acrimony of poor Xantippe! That many men took their wives and even their daughters into the houses where these brilliant women held court is proof that they were not denied "good society," and hence were not outside the pale, and hence again could never have suffered deep disgrace. For the sake of their learning and their wisdom in public affairs and their constant devotion to their lovers' work, a few such women have come down to us in the grateful memoirs of great men, in proof that they broke the bonds of women's duty to the family for the sake of freedom and at the behest of unquenchable impulse toward the mental and even the moral development of their age. The Vestal Virgins of Rome trod another path toward independence and self-development. These and the Flamens, as is well known, constituted the most sacred religious orders of the Imperial City; and while the Flamens were the symbolical priests of domestic life (even the death of a wife making them ineligible for service in the temple), the Vestals, in their guarding of the sacred fire of the city, symbolized that spiritual essence of devotion for which the celibate only was deemed sufficiently pure.

The history of the courtesan class of Athens and that of the Vestals of Rome outlines the only two ways in which the women of the past could attain a life of their own detached from the family. This first class had its parallel in a group of Grecian men. When Roman citizenship was the most desired of political conditions, we read that many freemen of Greek cities sold themselves as slaves to Roman citizens in order that manumission might carry with it induction into Roman citizenship. [6] So some women of Athens sold themselves to rich men of intellectual and social power, in order that they might gain entrance into the true life of their country; or foreign women thus escaped the manual labor of ordinary slavery, with its accompanying degradation. But because the courtesan could never have the State behind her in support of

[6] E. M. Smith, *Law of Nationality.*

her claims upon the community (as even the enslaved wife of the Greek citizen could do for her narrow range of rights in marriage), she could never be manumitted into true freedom; and like all women supported by the personal favor of men outside the family life, her last estate was often worse than the first, and left her friendless in the city she loved.

The Vestals, on the other hand, were a picturesque embodiment of the city's reverence and the city's pride. The altar flame they guarded was the symbol of the collective worship of the many families that had united to build the city. For that reason the high honors which were paid them had a civic dignity which made magistrates step aside for them in the streets, which made criminals flee to their all-powerful protection for succor, which made their persons sacred even from careless touch, and gave them rights over their estates only equalled by the mothers of three children when the right of other women to personal property was finally recognized. The Vestals had also their parallel in Roman history, in the Stoics, who, in the time of Rome's decadence, lived in their world but not of it, and guarded in sublime isolation, amidst the bestiality and greed of their time, the sacred flame of a pure patriotism and a noble humanity.[7]

It must always be remembered in considering the paths by which freedom and opportunity have been opened to women, that so long as religion was of the family, or the city, of the nation or the race alone, woman had in it no place of her own. The head of

[7] See F. M. Holland, *The Reign of the Stoics.*

the Jewish household determined the faith of the family and the wife and mother would have been the last of the flock to differ from the patriarch. In all ethnic religions, which are but family faiths writ large in racial types, the sons of the family alone bear the torch of devotion from generation to generation. There are exceptions in the position of priestesses and sibyls; and in the old Teutonic strain are many traces of freedom and power among the women: but the civilizations that have stamped our laws are those in which all descent, spiritual, political and monetary, has been "through males and the descendants of males." The simple liberty of personal choice as human beings, which is now granted to women as to men, was unthought of in any past we know. To make it possible for the respectable woman, and for the secular woman and for the average woman, to refuse marriage or to live a normal life without a husband, it was necessary that at least two world-events of supreme importance should occur. One was the proclamation of Christianity, that every individual, "Jew and Gentile, male and female, bond and free," had a right to his or her own soul, and must bear individual responsibility for its salvation. Buddha before had announced, "My law is a law for all," and had thereby broken the outer wall of caste in India. For our civilization, however, the first Bill of Rights for women was the spiritual Magna Charta that sent every human being to the altar solitary and by inner compulsion. Priests might afterward assume powers of exclusive representation of the divine, but even then each soul must receive this ministration on its own account and for its own behoof. Under Paganism in Asia Minor women had held high priesthoods and official rank and office; and in the last days of the Roman Empire highly placed women had received personal property rights and power to plead in courts and to order their lives freely as never before. Latin Christianity lost to woman much of this freedom, it is true; and after a time degraded its conception of womanhood by teaching ascetic disdain of marriage. One thing, however, Christianity gave women in the mass—a dignity they lacked before, this direct approach as individuals to the Infinite Ideal. Symbolized as that ideal was, in the feminine virtues of Jesus, the imagination of women was appealed to in a new and intense fashion, and women in crowds took advantage of their new spiritual franchise. The chaos of the time when the old order was breaking up and the new not yet formed, the separation of families, the woeful plight of young maidens bereft of protectors, the poverty of the old nobility, all did much to cast a large class of gentlewomen helpless upon the world. This made the establishment of religious houses a natural and necessary thing. But nothing did so much to give women a high position in the early Church, or to establish for them unique careers in those religious houses, as the doctrine that the woman and the slave, as truly as the man and the master, whether inside or outside the family bond, must worship as equals and each manage his or her own spiritual concerns in individual responsibility. This it was which made it honorable for women as for men to follow the Inner Light.

The Christian Church thus early offered women such a place of power as they had not held before.[8] Education, art, affairs, companionship with learned men and rulers of States, these all belonged to the realm of influence and activity presided over by the Lady Abbess. Great property holdings were hers, in her own name and the name of her order. Like St. Hilda, under whom several bishops were trained, she sometimes presided over mixed religious houses. In many cases she must be summoned to Parliament, like great lords, but might send a proxy; and often she furnished military forces second only to those of kings. That Spanish abbess who ruled sixty towns and villages; those two women rulers of the Holy Empire, who in Germany issued coins on their own account and were represented in the Imperial Diet, were but a few of the great ladies who gained their highest powers of achievement through the Church. If women of this class lost, later on, their rule if not their influence in the conventual orders, some of the most noble and able live now as canonized saints.

The Lady Abbess was not always a maiden; she was often a widow, and sometimes a wife whose desertion of her husband and her family was counted to her for righteousness, if she embraced the true faith and he and they did not. But she must be celibate at least in profession while she held her stately

[8] See Louisa I. Lumsden, *Woman in History* in *The Position of Woman*, London, Nisbet & Co.

offices. She thus introduced to the ideal conceptions of humanity a new sort of woman; one who could be reverenced, and powerful, lovely and happy, and yet be independent of the family relationship. She thus made the modern spinster possible.

A second great world-event, without which the day of the spinster could not have dawned, was the abolition of slavery, the establishment of the legal right of the manual laborer to his own liberty and to his own possession of the fruit of his toil. Slavery is yet so near to us that we can smell its torment. It has been for man the debauchery and the exploitation of his work-power, that which is the commodity by which he must buy his right to "life, liberty and the pursuit of happiness." Slavery was for woman, besides this, the debauchery and the exploitation of her sex-relationship. Looking over the world to-day, how few are the women who have emerged from this double despotism! The savage woman still is held by customs that treat her person as a communal property; the women of oriental civilizations still are segregated as members of the sex that must be watched and guarded; the very princesses of royal houses (which preserve in unreal pageant the outgrown customs of the past) are still given in marriage for purposes of State; unenlightened parenthood still barters its daughters in the marriage market for place and money; the day of woman's self-ownership and self-direction as a responsible human being has hardly yet dawned for the mass of the world's women. But for these few who have arrived as persons there are a new freedom

and a new enticement to activity and a new embarrassment of riches in personal choice which are almost
an intoxication of liberty.

Of this new draught, the unmarried woman of to-
day drinks the deepest and with the easiest abandon.
Liberty brings its dangers as well as its delights, and
the pathology of woman's independent work and the
consequences to her, as to others newly emancipated,
of having liberty before receiving preparation, are
sometimes in sad evidence. But the spinster, as we
now consider her, is that woman who is at the top
of the new opportunity, not beneath it. As such, she
is opening, in this, her day, new avenues of work for
woman, and applying the general rules of labor to
her own case with success. She is thronging the courts
of higher learning and making significant her entrance
therein. She is winning distinction in all the higher
professions. She is becoming at ease in commercial
spheres in the business offices of the world. She is
acting as close second to many of the greatest and
most useful men of the time as secretary and helper.
She is proving, over and over again, with that cumulative guarantee of success which is the only way of
impressing the mass intelligence, that women's bodies,
brains, powers of constant and effective activity and
moral characters can stand the strain of manual, clerical, professional and artistic service on a high level
of competition with men. Scientific research, the gath-
ering and applying of statistics, the administering of
great concerns, of civic and State affairs—in each and
all of the great divisions of specialized labor the spin-

ster is making good in a quite new fashion for women. No equal number of married women of equal ability or of occasional opportunity to demonstrate greater ability than the majority of able spinsters show, could make this cumulative proof of women's independent powers. The demands of marriage and maternity which for many years require a daily choice as to which of several duties shall rank first in honor and requirement, hinder a straight course to a single aim. The obvious proof of woman's ability as individual worker must therefore first be made by those of persistent and uninterrupted vocational work, those who can enter without personal doubts or social opposition the man-made channels of modern labor, and enter to stay. Whatever may later be done to enhance the value and effectiveness of women's lives when divided between family claims, the lighter and more intimate social services, and personal achievements, the first common appreciation of feminine power in socalled masculine fields of effort must be the result largely of the work of the spinster and the young widow. Women unencumbered by the claims of children to immediate and personal ministration, unfettered by the need to balance at every step their husbands' economic and professional success against their own, can alone walk this new road of free competition in sufficient numbers to make a broad pathway of commonly accepted opportunity for their sex. The day of the spinster has, therefore, great social value in this respect. No one can doubt this who believes that we ought to have a democratic State, and that a democratic State must rest at last upon a democratic home, and that a democratic home is only possible when there are "two heads in council" as well as "two hearts that beat as one," and who sees clearly that there can never be two heads equal in wise counsel until both have access to the high disciplines of rational responsibility and full development of personality.

That the spinster, as we know her, is to last forever as a large class, or that her day is the beginning of a social millennium which is to make over all women into her economic similitude, we cannot think yet proved. [9] The complacent assurance which Dr. Sheavyn expresses that there will be always "need for a large class of disengaged or detached women," as she calls the spinsters, to do the larger social work of womanhood, the teaching and caretaking and the safeguarding of young and ignorant women in inspectorships and the like, cannot be shared by all of us. It is the normal and the average that in the long run must serve the purposes of social uplift. The unusual and the "variant" may serve peculiarly some preparatory process for a higher plane of common life. The Japanese, for example, had to enter the family of nations through the gateway of military achievement, a backward reach for a forward step. We all hope, however, that the union of Orient and Occident will bring the races together in sympathetic understanding in a way to give a new assurance of the needlessness of war. So must women enter all the higher paths of

[*] Phœbe Sheavyn, D.Litt, *Professional Women* in *The Position of Woman.*

intellectual life and achievement through the hard and fast lines of specialization which men have laid down for their own guidance; and often to the narrowing and mechanizing of the feminine nature. This means that the women who "survive" and succeed in the competitive struggle with men for positions of place and financial power must be, for the most part, those to whom the purely intellectual or the personally ambitious makes strongest appeal. This means again that in those women who can most easily maintain a lifelong and successful equality of effort with men (at least in the present commercialized organization of even the higher life of thought and imagination), the individuating sense must be keen, and the power of grasping all those opportunities that make for self-advantage strong. This means again that in the long reaches of selective influences, should the day of the spinster continue unchanged by any new social impulse, we might breed a "detached class of women," who should form the intellectual and economic *élite* of the sex, and leave marriage and maternity for the less developed women. [10] A writer already speaks easily of "marriage as the frequent refuge for the incompetent woman"; and long ago we read of a woman poet of the very "minor" variety, that she "was obliged reluctantly to resort to marriage as a recourse from destitution." The biting acid of Cicely Hamilton's *Marriage as a Trade* eats away all flesh of sentiment and blood of affection and even sinew of moral appeal, to leave of marriage a skeleton of economic bargain in

[10] Ida Husted Harper.

in which man intentionally cheapens the ware he would purchase to lower its price, and woman is the poverty-bound seller who must take what can be got. The satisfaction this author reveals at the growing company of independent women who refuse to enter the matrimonial market and who become comfortable and happy in their own way, indicates that so far as her influence goes, she would have all girls of high quality become too prudent to "fall in love," and would not be made uneasy at a great army of the "best women" encamped for all time outside the home life. The sober sense of others, however, already affirms that "we cannot countenance a theory which deliberately leaves maternity for the less intellectual." It is surely imperative that maternity be not left chiefly to those who cannot make the highest success in any other craft. If marriage should become, even for a generation or two, chiefly a refuge from destitution or a harbor from the world of individual effort for those who have failed, the disastrous results would be a heavy burden for later times. Unless, indeed, as one has passionately declared, "it is best to force God to a finish with humanity," we cannot contemplate with equanimity any ranking of womanhood that gives to motherhood the least developed persons. Hence we may well look upon the day of the spinster as but a bridge of feminine achievement—which shall connect the merely good mother with the mother that shall be both wise and good; just as the women's clubs and segregated enterprises of women, important and useful as many of them are, constitute at best the training schools in which women are preparing for full and equal participation in social control of the higher interests of life.

One figure rises before us to-day as the embodiment in peculiar fashion and largest measure of the social value of the spinster in this, her day. This figure is the woman head of the Social Settlement. The Settlement is the modern retranslation of the early Christian brotherhoods and sisterhoods. As the monastery and the abbey and the humble convent for women, in a time of social change, preserved the learning of the past and found place and useful work for men, women and children left without family support and protection in the wreck of the patriarchal order, as they formed centres of order and industry, charity and teaching, and gave high companionship to the leaders of thought and of social power, so the Settlement has arisen in our day of profound social reorganization as a fresh instrument of interpretation and progress. It is set to aid by conscious purpose the movement which stirs in all modern life, the movement to spiritualize democracy and to make religion social as well as personal, in function and in aim. In this new venture in fraternity life men have indeed been prominent, and there are not wanting instances of successful use of this instrument of social leadership by husbands and wives with young children, who manage to harmonize a fine domesticity with public household arrangements, and to preserve for their children a right atmosphere in a wrong environment. There are also a few happily suggestive cases of older couples, upon whom the demands of parenthood do not press, undertaking the conduct of a neighborhood house. Yet for all this, the Settlement is essentially, distinctly and logically a celibate movement. It is also, to a great extent, a movement of celibate womanhood, the bachelors among the Settlement workers being a less numerous and less stationary class than the maidens. No one can study this movement without appreciating its social value. This is a time of such profound political, economic and domestic reorganization that apparently only some agency outside the Family, the School and the Church, distinct from State and free from the domination of the Industrial Order, can make clear to the common perception what these basic institutions of society were meant to become in a spiritualized democracy. [11] This agency must seemingly be one capable of arousing popular interest and stimulating the idealism of youth by picturesque and unusual features. In answer to this demand, the Settlement has arisen to carry—often with unsteady hand and confused step, it must be confessed—the torch of illumination from the past to the future. In the course of time it seems clear that the Settlement movement will be absorbed by the basic and permanent institutions of society, perhaps by the Church on the ideal, and by the School on the practical side. Such a process, however, would but enhance, not diminish, the present value of this new Order of Social Service. In this Order women are taking first rank. Those women

[11] Jane Addams, *The Subjective Necessity and the Objective Value of a Social Settlement,* in *Philanthropy and Social Progress.*

who are at the head of some of the most important
Settlements of our largest cities not infrequently hold
chief places of light and leading in their communities.
The Lady Abbess reappears to-day as the administrative head of such neighborhood houses. Like the Lady
Abbess of the early centuries of the Christian Church,
her modern counterpart leaves her family, not to "re-
tire from the world," but to enter its larger life. She
obtains thereby, like her prototype, the special companionship of men of affairs, carrying into mixed
counsels of high debate, in which she is often the first
or chief of women to enter, not only the distinction
of her personality, but the great weight of her institution. Like the Lady Abbess also, the head of the
modern Settlement has an immense social advantage
in being able to live simply and even frugally while
retaining the dignity that now attaches to choice of
such a way of life rather than of compulsion toward
it by reason of slender means. Most ministers of religion, teachers and other social workers have to be
prudent and to live amid surroundings not to be chosen
for their beauty. The Settlement worker, rich or poor,
is invested by the popular imagination with the power
to live anywhere, but with a noble choice of the locality that seems to need her most. Moreover, her
community life enables her to entertain in the easiest
fashion not only men and women of great importance
in the world of art, education, of statecraft, and of
social leadership, but even "Opulence" itself covets
invitation to her "dinners" in which free rein is given
the social imagination and the flow of soul makes up

up for the slender menu even to the confirmed syba-
rite! The woman head of the modern Settlement has
thus established a new type of salon. So much is this
the fact, that the larger and better known Settlements,
so far from being places of self-sacrifice, are the most
coveted of social opportunities by young people of
keen perception, high ambitions and wide outlook,
who yet lack the wealth or family position for independent leadership. In this respect the Settlements
presided over by women peculiarly resemble the ab-
beys and mixed religious houses of the first centuries
of the Christian Church. The Lady Abbess of modern times is thus doing a finer and more vital work
for social culture than even that of the more external
philanthropy which she shares with men of her class—
she is preserving the best of the old feminine ideal
in the new conditions, to dower with it, let us hope,
the collective womanhood of the future.

The spinster who is succeeding in efficient and well-
paid work in any intellectual or business line, in free
and open competition with men and through a long
course of uninterrupted personal achievement, is doing
an inestimable service to her sex and to society by proving beyond peradventure that the higher education
of women and the vocational independency and the
economic security of women are socially worth while.
Such successful work of the unmarried woman is
showing clearly that women in general only lack opportunity and preparation to do a fair share of the
world's most esteemed work. This must in time react
upon the home life to raise domestic standards and

make mothers more efficient. The spinster of to-day, therefore, is contributing largely to social culture when she is simply earning her own living, on as high a plane as she can attain, and with fidelity and some sense of social relationship. She need not affect the sentimental intensity of Olive Schreiner's approach to woman's work to prove her usefulness. The less conscious she is of any "heroic mission," and the more definite and practical she is in her work, probably the more she is wanted and the better she fulfils her function in the modern world.

The woman head of a great Settlement, however, one which has a recognized place in the social control, reform and uplift of a vast city, adds to these services to womanhood and the race another and a priceless one. She carries into the new freedom and power of womanhood the old ideal of woman's consecrated service to her kind, translated in modern terms. She might be painted as the new Portia pleading at the bar of Justice, her cap and gown not assumed for the occasion, but worn by right as certificate of her assured place in the world of letters and of thought, not used as a disguise, but as token of her official standing. She should be painted, not as playing a part for the sake of a lover, but in serious earnest responding to the call of the Time Spirit with a passionate affection for Good. She should be represented facing the Judges of the earth, and the powers of the underworld of greed and oppression, with her womanhood in frank bravery confessed, not concealed, and making majestic and moving appeal for her clients. Her clients—the neglected children, the wayward girls for whose mishaps society itself should be scourged, the rebellious boys whose unsteady feet have never known true guidance, the men and women incompetent to life's demands because a grudging fate has given them so small a portion of life itself, the prisoners whose poverty and ignorance demand a special plea, the "stranger within the gates" who rightly claims a friendly interpreter, the despised and misjudged whom race prejudice alone makes alien, the heroic but defeated on the field of labor who go down as those who face too heavy odds at cannon-mouth—these are her clients!

Our modern Portias, Attorneys of Compassion, to whom all juries must at last give heed, these are they who make radiant with prophecy this day of the spinster.

V

PATHOLOGY OF WOMAN'S WORK

An immigrant, living in the slums of New York City, once said of himself and others of the sweat-shop community to which he belonged, "We live *under* America, not *in* America." To-day, the able, well-trained, socially-advantaged women in "gainful occupations" are in the world of man's organized labor; the ignorant, unskilled and poverty-bound women are *under* that world of machine-dominated, capitalized and specialized industry. While the capable "spinster" has demonstrated the social usefulness of training and opportunity for the woman who, in professional or business life, is making her lifework respected in equal balance with that of men in the same field, the women wage-earners in manual labor, the "factory girls" and the "shop girls," are seeing chiefly the wrong side of industrial competition. The majority of girls have always worked at some kind of labor, of definite economic value, between the period of leaving school and of marriage; but they have for the most part worked at home. To-day, hundreds of thousands of girls, between the ages of fourteen and sixteen years, leave school and enter the ranks of wage-earners outside the home. The industrial condition of this large class of girls is intimately connected with five specific social evils which demand constant attention from all who work in "needy families" and from all who try to aid human failures toward a better condition.

These five social evils are related to charity and correction on one side and, on the other side, to the industrial training and vocational guidance of girls. They are:

I. Prostitution.

II. Poverty; as caused by physical weakness and disease.

III. Poverty; as caused by character-weakness and by mental incapacity not due to actual defectiveness.

IV. Poverty; as caused or increased by the lack of thrift, of judgment and of household capacity on the part of the house-mother.

V. Poverty; as caused or increased by the general economic incapacity and weakness of the deserted wife or widowed mother upon whom the children depend.

This many-sided evil, so patent to all social workers, obliges the candid and earnest student of the problems involved in the condition of women in modern industry to consider the pathological as well as the normal side; the philanthropic as well as the educational significance of that problem.

What is the problem of women's industrial position?

Not that women are newly in industry—they have always been there. Marriage customs and laws fixing the economic value of the service of women to the family reach back to the beginnings of social organization. Women have but recently acquired the "pay envelope," it is true, their compensation through unnumbered centuries being given them in "truck" or in "kind"; but that fact did not prevent their constant labor.

It is the movement from domestic handicraft, and personal tool, and individual process, to the present power-driven machinery with its capitalized plant, that makes the worker go to it for his labor instead of taking his labor to the home, which creates the new element in women's work. The change which created the shop and the factory, makes the new problem of women's labor. Women, as cannot be too often insisted upon, are doing the old things—spinning, weaving, making garments of all kinds, manufacturing, preserving, preparing the food products, and continuing a thousand processes that give comfort to personal and domestic life; but they are doing these old tasks in a new place and by a new method.

The majority of women, however, have not changed the method and place of work wholly or for the whole of their lives. They have only as a large and increasing minority, which promises to become a majority, of the sex, adopted the new methods in the new place of work for a portion of their lives. Herein lies the reason for much that is confusing in the problem of women's labor to-day.

Let us examine these conditions:

[1] From 20 to 30 per cent. of women and girls between the ages of 10 and 60 years are listed by the census and other official reports as in "gainful occupations," that is, in receipt of wages or salary; as contrasted with between 80 and 85 per cent. of men and boys of the same ages thus engaged in "gainful occupations." But this is not an accurate indication of the relative numbers of men and women employed for some portion of their lives for wages or salary. The facts show that fully one-half of the women over 16 years of age spend from 3 to 10 years of their lives in some forms of compensated labor outside their own homes, one-third of the young women between 15 and 24 years being so employed. The average working term for the wage-earning women is from 4 to 5 years; so that in a period of 20 years, in which the personnel of the wage-earning class of men would be fairly stable, the personnel of the wage-earning class of women would be four to five times changed. That means, that the number of women and girls at work at any given moment is not a fair showing of the number of women and girls working during some portion of their lives. It must be particularly noted that this wage-earning period is in early youth. The overwhelming majority of women engaged in gainful occupations are under 25 years of age; and most of them, the larger number, under 21. The youth of these workers and their short term of service in or-

See Florence M. Marshall, *Industrial Training for Women*, Publications of "National Society for Promotion of Industrial Education."

ganized industry outside the home are two facts bearing directly upon the pathological elements in women's work.

These twin facts make natural another fact, namely, that about 75 per cent. of girls who enter trades and occupations between the ages of 14 and 17 years (and this class in the United States constitutes a large part of that wage-earning army of 7,000,000 or more women), enter occupations which offer no future of either financial or educational advance. The work is taken up without serious choice or preparation and without personal ambition or special training. Such work demands only the lowest faculties and, hence, can rarely, if ever, furnish a living wage on the basis of a really human standard of living.

Moreover, added to the facts respecting the proportions, the age, the low grade and, therefore, poorly paid labor in which working-girls engage, is another of great importance, namely, that although 205 out of the more than 300 industries listed in the census employ women in considerable numbers, these women are, for the most part, doing the unskilled parts of this varied industry, even when that industry offers a chance for rising in skill and compensation, and even when they continue many years in it. This shows that the minority of women of unbroken employment, who do continue for a long period in a trade or occupation, suffer permanently from constant competition with an ever-changing army of young girls who enter and leave without really feeling themselves a part of organized industry.

This again leads to the slowness of perception on the part of employers of women and girls that they must or should be dealt with as men are dealt with on the basis of an independent, self-supporting class.

The "working-girl" (and the youth of the average woman worker makes the name most appropriate) is still looked upon as one engaged in a transient effort to help in the family support, and her employment for wages outside the house is still looked upon as either a temporary, if necessary, evil, or a negligible incident quite outside her true and permanent way of life. Most people have yet to learn that this new way of doing the old duties of "woman's sphere" is simply a new form of the economic contribution of women to the world of work, and, hence, must be adjusted to the new industrial conditions as a permanent part of labor, and in such fashion as will best conserve the well-being of men, and women, and of the family. Among the adjustments imperatively demanded is that which has to do with the present divorce, both in interest and process, of the wage-earning period of the young working-girl from the home life she usually re-enters after this wage-earning period has passed. As Miss Summer so well puts it in her history of *Women in Industry,* the work of most girls "no longer fits in with their ideals" and has, therefore, "lost its charm."[2] It constitutes not a preparation for their permanent activity, but an interlude or interruption in the main business of their life as they naturally conceive it.

The old forms of domestic work were not only

[2] Helen M. Sumner, joint author, *Labor Problems.*

trained for in the home, and directly and obviously aided the comfort of the home, but they were, also, admirably calculated to prevent the woman from too early specializing in her work. They were particularly helpful, therefore, in the development of an all-round "faculty" and adaptability in the mastery of things for human use and comfort,—the qualities most needed in the average house-mother. The girl learned all the manifold processes of the old-fashioned household industries from the mother at home. She specialized, indeed, to some extent as natural talent indicated, becoming noted as a "good cook," or a "skilled weaver" on the hand loom, or a gifted dyer of home-made cloth, or an expert cutter or maker of clothing, or what not; but it was a purely natural specialization and never could become a narrow and monotonous doing of but one thing. This was hard upon the genius, and almost equally so upon the woman of marked talent, intellectual or artistic, who, undoubtedly, should have been released from the universal bondage to "general housework" and allowed to specialize in her chosen way. This general training formed, however, a fine technical and moral discipline for the average girl; and it resulted in saving for Nature's uses in the family one-half the race at least from that tyranny of over-specialization which has hampered the average man in his personal development. In modern industrial organization the girl who, at 14 to 16 years of age, goes to work in a shop or factory is specialized at once, and usually on the least educational parts of the industry she is employed in, and along some line she cannot pursue at home as a house-mother. There-fore, her brief incursion into this outside world of organized labor is not only short, not only made at a time of life when she is least able to take educa-tional advantage of it without educational guidance, but it is so unrelated in obvious detail to the marriage she wants, and the re-absorption in home life she seeks, that all concerned fail to see its relation to her char-acter development.

The experience of the race shows that we get our most important education not through books but through our work. We are developed by our daily task, or else demoralized by it, as by nothing else. The training of books is recent and superficial for most of the race and only touches the outer and upper edges of the social consciousness. The training by one's necessary work reaches back to the beginnings of social discipline for social ends. It still forms the most vital part of physical, mental and moral train-ing. Hence, the fact that one-third of one-half the race, and that the mother-half that perforce stamps its quality most irrevocably upon offspring, spends from 3 to 10 years in work entered upon without plan, pursued as a mere and often disliked incident on the way from the father's to the husband's home, and therefore accepted with all its evil concomitants of poor wages and bad conditions as *something not to be bettered but to be escaped from as soon as possible,* constitutes a social evil of the first magnitude. Any work not made an education and a discipline becomes inevitably a source of mental or moral injury; and the greatest evils connected with the modern forms of women's labor grow out of the failure to treat the wage-earning of women as a serious and permanent educational opportunity. The low wages, the philanthropy which makes a hard-working girl a subject of charity in the provisions of "boarding homes" to piece out the too low wage, the long hours, the unpaid overtime, the tyranny of inhumane or vicious overseers—these evils would not be tolerated for a decade if it were clearly understood that the working-girl in "gainful occupations" is a fixture. Were it clearly understood, also, that the married woman earning salary or wages is in the field by right if she can guarantee society that her motherhood is not injured thereby; that the deserted wife or widow, held responsible for her own support and for as much of her children's as she can justly meet, is but fulfilling woman's old economic debt to society under new industrial conditions, in a new place and by a new method; were these things once clearly understood all would see that women must be aided to fit the new processes of self-support into harmonious relation with the full social demand upon women. The poorer the class of women, the greater the demand for this readjustment, and the greater the need for social aid in the process.

With all this in view, let us consider more definitely the social evils bound up with the pathological industrial conditions of women's work.

I. *Prostitution.* It is not true, as a celebrated minister of religion has stated, that "prostitution is solely an economic question." The ancient enemies of human progress, greed and lust, and the ancient drawbacks to human progress, ignorance, laziness, self-indulgence, vanity and lack of moral responsibility, are now, as ever, causes of the social evil. But prostitution is and always has been in part, and often in large part, an economic question.

Women in older stages of social and domestic organization were mostly cared for within the household, but not all in a form of marriage we should now consider honorable. With the increase of individual economic responsibility among women, there has been a corresponding increase in *the ease of access to young girls by the exploiting forces of evil*. There has also been a clearer conception on the part of young girls of what economic conditions actually are, and of that "easiest way" of earning the more luxurious life, which so soon becomes the hardest and most suffering way. We have often had pictured to us the effect upon the hard-working man who comes home at night with a dollar and a half of earnings, of his neighbor's condition in the same tenement whose begging has resulted in a total of three, five or even ten dollars. This produces paupers, we rightly say; and we, therefore, beg people not to give to beggars. Who can rightly picture the effect upon a young girl of 14 to 18 years of age, living in a tenement house where everyone knows everyone else, returning from a week's hard work, with her pitiful wage of two, three, four or five dollars, when she meets a friend who has earned in nameless ways enough to buy finery to wear on "rides" and to "shows" for which the youthful soul longs? The low wages of women are a direct incitement to vice; they constitute the great disadvantage of virtue; they make it easier for all the evil elements that prey upon ignorance and innocence and weakness to secure their horrible maiden tribute each year. The only lasting protection of womanhood is in its own power of self-support and self-direction. We shall be fatally handicapped in endeavors to check the social evil until girls enter the industrial field better safeguarded by intelligence; better trained for special work which is needed and, hence, well paid for; stronger industrially to demand and secure decent treatment; and, above all, with greater desire to do good work and rise in their positions by merit and not by favor, because made conscious by preliminary education of the real significance of their partnership in organized labor, however brief that partnership may be.

Reading from a social worker's diary, we note the features of a common type found in the class of wayward girls; "Mary J., 17 years old, went to work in a candy manufactory at 12 years of age; told the Boss she was 14; mother told him so too; stayed there six months; Boss fired her because she stayed out a day when he wanted her to work. Went into another candy place; the foreman was 'fresh,' all the time fooling with the girls; he was good to her though, gave her tickets to dances; she stayed there longer but left to be with a girl she met at the dance; went around with her a lot but did not stay longer than two months in a place; couldn't do the work sometimes, other times didn't want to stay, thought she could do better elsewhere; mother hadn't 'no right to kick'; she was 'looking out for herself'; went to stay with this friend who had a 'gentleman'—nice man with money; then she got a gentleman friend, too, but 'he done me dirt' —'I had to go on the street'; 'Yes, worked off and on in a good many shops,' but it didn't do any good, 'got took up just the same.' 'No, don't want to work in a family—just want to get out of this place and do as I please; no chance for me in anything decent— now!' "

In all discussions of the causes and reform of the "social evil," let it become clearly understood that prostitution requires for its diminution not only laws, well enforced, to abolish the traffic in womanhood; not only better social protection against harpies who seduce young girls seeking an honest livelihood; not only better chaperonage of young girls in exposed occupations; not only better opportunities for natural enjoyment of youthful pleasure under morally safe conditions; not only these—but most of all, greater power on the part of the average young girl to earn her own support under right conditions and for a living wage.

II. That measure of excessive poverty which is due to physical weakness and disease is intimately connected with the conditions of wage-earning women and girls. All know, and social workers keenly realize, that at least one-third of the "cases" demanding charitable relief have thus to make appeal because of sickness or accident. The connection between this fact and the work conditions of girls of the poorer classes is now so obvious as to constitute matter for study alike by physicians, publicists and philanthropists. All the more important movements toward legally safe-guarding the health and morals of manual workers are now aimed most specifically toward bettering the conditions of "women and children."

This linking of "women and children" together in statutes which not only protect against industrial ex-ploitation, but also render more difficult women's com-petition with men in the labor market, rests on the deep social consciousness that society demands of po-tential motherhood such health and strength as future children need. There is grave difference of opinion between those who stand, on the one side, for the right of women workers to a fair field in the competi-tion for self-support, and those on the other side who look upon all women as social wards, because of their social value as "human beings of the mother-sex." Most labor reformers are hazy as to the fundamental principles involved. Some of the most ardent of these labor reformers at one and the same moment declare for woman's right, equal and equally guaranteed in law, to all opportunities for educational work and professional careers, and also declare for society's right to fetter the married woman in her competition with men in labor at every point by legislation that places adult women and little children in the same cate-gory. Such illogical leadership naturally confuses hopelessly the public mind. Those who believe that the chief social need (especially when the evil of prostitution is considered), is that women shall be given industrial freedom and opportunity in order to readjust themselves in a new industrial order to their old economic burdens, must, it seems clear, be chary of ranking adult women and children together in labor laws. Those, on the other hand, who believe that such economic readjustment of all women is less important than the protection of those women who are married or who may marry from diseases injurious to motherhood, must go much further than they now propose to do in the economic support of both girls and women by social provisions. This grave but often unconscious difference in leadership in the "woman movement" may be eased, if not resolved into agreement, if the youth of the average wage-earning girl and the short average term of her wage-earning be considered. We may well be cautious about interfering too partially by law with the work of women of mature age, and with those who have an industrial experience leading them to trade-union organization, through which a more democratic form of protection may reasonably be hoped for. There can be no question, however, that girls under 21 are fit subjects for as much legal protection from industrial exploitation as we can possibly secure and enforce. Further than this, there is no question that to deplete the vitality, to injure the health, to undermine the constitutional vigor of the potential mothers of the race, before they have reached their maturity, is to poison the fountain of life at its very source.

We must make haste to equalize for boys and girls

a legal majority of 21 years; then, whatever may come to be the decision as to what the State shall do, or not do, in respect to women over 21, or in regard to women who have been employed over 5 years in a given trade, there can be no question that the working-girl, flitting about from one bad employment to another, and not stopping in any one long enough either to learn its value or master its conditions, and flitting out of all organized industry back to the home in less than a decade, should be protected against evil conditions she neither understands nor can change. Legal protection, however, is only one side. Better training for more skilled and promising employments, those that pay better at first, and offer more rapid advance, is the other and quite as important side. The proof that ill health and consequent incapacity to give vigor to offspring does result from a long list of evils connected with the working life of young women, even when not continued above three or four years, is ample. That many trades are specially inimical to women's physique, that monotonous and too rapid machine-work injures the delicate nervous organism of young girls and produces a positive poison of fatigue, and that all this is connected with under-vitalization, the indolence of weakness, the general debility that does not kill but hopelessly incapacitates and which so invalidates motherhood—this is clear and sinister in suggestion.

Another quotation from a social worker's diary gives the story of Rosie J., which might be multiplied many thousand times. "Rosie J., aged 18, is found in hospital; she went to a Settlement class and her teacher visits her. She has worked hard ever since she can remember; helped 'make pants before she went to school'; got her working papers at 14; hadn't got through the sixth grade—was out so much 'taking care of the kids when mother was sick.' 'Liked school'? 'Yes, but didn't get on very well; teacher thought she was stupid; used to go to sleep in school sometimes; so tired. Worked in store, cash girl and bundle girl; had a place at counter at last.' 'Yes, the work was good enough; but father was took sick, went to hospital, died; mother, and the children, all younger than me, had to have all my wages; earned $4.75; didn't have much myself with eight of us till the two boys got to work; had bad cold; couldn't stay at home; doctor at dispensary said I must have milk and eggs; didn't tell how we could get 'em; got worse and worse; had to come here; doctor says he's going to send me away for two months, but they can't get along without my wages; must go home.' "

Is it not clear that Rosie and her like should be legally held as minors until 21 and that all power of social control we have achieved should be used to prevent such exploitation of girlhood?

The social demand for this prevention of health-destroying overwork under bad physical conditions of the young girls who are potential mothers and whose vitality and vigor are our dependence for the people's strength, can need no argument for its support.

The third and fourth evils of poverty due to lack of moral and mental power and of work-efficiency are distinctly traceable to defective homes, and defective homes everyone knows are largely the result of incompetence in the house-mother.

[3] Dr. Warner gives us as "subjective causes of poverty," "shiftlessness," "unhealthy diet," "lack of judgment," and other elements of personal character which depend markedly for their eradication or substantial diminution upon an improved home environment in early youth. Those finer elements of relief which involve education and disciplinary measures to increase the personal power of the "charitable patient" are all the outgrowth of a clear perception that, in the case of many people, it is themselves and not their condition, that first needs mending. The inability rightly to use existing opportunities for bettering one's lot is a common complaint; one that no proposed mass-uplift, by change of circumstance, without any active coöperation of the classes or persons to be benefited, will wholly cure. The connection between the capacity to make the best and most of existing possibilities for personal advancement and family health and well-being, and the mental and moral power of the house-mother, needs only mention to be appreciated. But the connection between the untrained, unambitious, shirking, careless attitude of the girls at work for wages, and the lack of character and ability to manage a home afterward, is not often clearly seen. It is not alone the absence of that specific training which the old domestic forms of industry gave the girl in the specific processes she would later need in her own

[3] Amos G. Warner, *American Charities.*

home that makes her brief wage-earning period inef-
fective as preparation for later responsibilities, it is
also, and quite as important a factor, the positive
injury to the *work-sense, the demoralization of the
faculty of true service,* that her shallow and transitory
connection with outside trade or occupation so often
gives.

If a person has been really disciplined by her task
in any form of effort, she can transfer that power of
using means intelligently to ends, that mastery over
obstacles, that capable and effective use of work-
processes, from one to another sort of effort, with an,
ease proportioned to native power and the thorough-
ness of this previous training. But if she has merely
"held down a job" for three to five years without interest, ambition, mental grasp or moral faithfulness,
she has acquired no principal of work-power to invest
in the new occupation. Herein is the worst of all the
effects, because the most subtle and far-reaching in
moral character, of the short wage-earning experience
of the average girl of the poorer classes.

Poverty resulting from character-weakness or mental deficiency depends for its substantial diminution
not only upon radical economic reforms, not only upon
the general disciplinary and educational influences of
enlightened charity, but especially upon a training of
young womanhood which shall raise the standard of
the home environment in early life and produce a
higher grade of mother, more definitely trained for
her work with her children.

V. Poverty as related to the work of women after

marriage and in widowhood, is a vital concern. The
fact that a decent standard of living cannot be maintained in many families without some compensated labor of married women, and the further fact that widows and deserted wives must generally use their full
earning capacity in the care of self and children, definitely relate themselves to women's present industrial
training and opportunity. The further fact that
among the most pitiful of all "charity cases" are those
of women of mature years suddenly confronted with
the necessity for self-support and having only "general
ability," and that of a low grade, to bring to the market, shows that the education of the average girl does
not fit for "real life" because leaving out that great
essential—the fitting for earning a "livelihood." If
these three classes of women (married mothers, widowed and deserted wives, and middle-aged self-supporting women) are forced to take the "labor leav-
ings," as it were, the poorest paid and most sweated
kinds of work,—it is a social evil as well as a personal
wrong.

The amount of work that a mother of young children can safely and properly do is a matter of dispute;
but it is already clear that she is the last person in
the world to leave untrained and unprotected to suffer
the worst evils of industrial exploitation. The finest
social use of the average house-mother needing paid
occupation has not yet been devised, still less applied
in work-opportunity; but it is already clear that any
person who wants compensated labor, especially when
past the bloom of youth, must not only be "good," but

economically good for something the world wants done and will compensate therefor. To leave a woman to find out that fact at the age of 40 or 50 is a grotesque and inhumane mistake.

All labor difficulties centre in their final and most puzzling questions about the home, the adjustment of the work of men and women to each other's task, and of the tasks of both to family and social welfare. To settle upon a more reasonable, and a more self-protecting, and a more economically effective relationship of the average woman to the modern industrial order, would be to aid greatly toward the solution of all problems of a "living wage" and a "better standard of living."

The period between 14 and 16 years of age (our most difficult period both for the favored in circumstances and the poorer class of children) must, we are coming to see, offer right opportunity for trade-teaching in the case of those who must earn their living as soon as possible. This is acknowledged generally in the case of boys. It must become equally apparent, and that soon, in the case of girls. For the reasons already given, it has become socially criminal to leave a young girl without training for some specific form of vocational work which will yield her a fair living wage, and will furnish some opportunity for rising in her work, if she remains in it, to a position of honor and adequate compensation. The few attempts at intelligent vocational education of girls prove its feasibility.

The kind of trade-teaching for girls must be varied

and adapted to the locality; being in line with the need for women workers in or near the girl's home. Trade schools must also be more or less organically related to the public-school system according to the local conditions. All vocational training for girls, however, must be based on certain considerations of the social demands upon women. For the most part, the "three roots" of women's employment on which the curriculum of that pioneer enterprise, the "Manhattan Trade School for Girls" in New York, was based, will probably be our constant guides; these are:

1st.   The needle, leading through plain sewing up to millinery and dressmaking.

2nd.   The hand-machine, leading up through simple to elaborate clothing, gloves and shoe manufacture; and to the power-machine and its relation to wholesale production.

3rd.   The paste brush, leading up through "sample cards" and small fancy articles, to bookbinding or works of art.[4]

These three roots of trade-teaching for girls meet the needs of the majority because most closely related to ancient lines of women's work. The demand for trade-teaching for girls is not one of charity, for aid of a few poorest in circumstances. It is not created by effort for the wayward. It is a demand of social requirement that all girls be trained to make more ef-

[4] See Mary S. Woolman, Reports of *Manhattan Trade School for Girls*.

fectively in the new industrial order the same contribution to the economic commonwealth which they so well made by the old methods under the old régime of labor.

We shall work out the right methods in this industrial training for girls when once we have clearly and definitely perceived the higher social demands for it.

Tax-supported schools should and must supply this imperative need in education. Such schools must offer enough trade-training to enable the average girl to "catch hold higher up" in the mechanism of modern industry. They must offer such a vocational training and vocational guidance to girls, as to boys, as shall insure more rapid advance in kind and in reward of labor.

In many trade-schools for boys, we see the sobering effect upon the boys of 18 to 20 years of age of the new-born consciousness of need to choose a life-work and a "good job for good." The average girl, with her 3 to 10 years' period of wage-earning, rarely gains from her wage-earning itself that salutary sense of economic responsibility. If, however, her briefer relationship to the splendid organization of modern industry could give her some of its character-products, she might take a much-needed social value back into the home life.

That economy of force, that cunning adaptation of means to ends, that use of labor-saving devices and that systematic development and application of brains to labor,—in what dire need of these stands the average household management!

Rightly interpreted to her consciousness and rightly used in educational fashion, the wage-earning experience of the average girl might lead to the improvement of the whole domestic machinery. The personal economic advantage, also, of such a definite, specialized training and labor, to a young girl, would give the older unmarried women, the wife continuing to earn, the deserted or widowed mother, the woman in middle life seeking paid employment,— a better chance all around. It would immeasurably lessen the present exploitation of women in industry.

Nothing short of a training that makes all young men and all young women easier masters of their economic fate can satisfy the modern demand of vocational preparation for life. The silly cry of the "manless land for the landless man" as a measure of relief for the unskilled laborer who has no "sense" or "faculty," is already discredited. Only the man who as a boy coaxed and helped the "green things growing," is likely to free himself from the despotism of greed in labor crises by efficient use of the farm. The equally silly cry of "domestic labor, well paid and useful," as a measure of relief for women who were never trained in any household art in childhood, is to be equally discredited. The true economic value of woman's work inside the home can only be secured and rightly recognized by and through a higher efficiency and security of wage-earning on the part of the average girl outside the home. The placing of a just market value upon the labor of the house-mother waits for a more rational and consistent attitude of mind toward the average wage-earning woman.

The expense of needed industrial training, in the case of girls at least, should not be considered for a moment. Women, as a sex, have paid society in advance for any possible cost for their education in any line needed either by the gifted individual or by the masses of common womanhood. They have worked unceasingly, before and since labor laws regulated "hours"; they have worked for "board and clothes" only, secured no more than the babies in their arms in legal ownership in the family estate; they have labored in every form of drudgery and taken over all the things men did not like to do and added them to their own natural service. Only sages have had insight to cry, "Give her of the fruit of her hands and let her own works praise her in the gates." Women have been for the most part "silent partners" in every great industrial as in every great moral enterprise of humanity. Their own development as individuals has been postponed until the whole foundation of social order has been laid in the very substance of their social service to common needs. If women, as a whole, need a new education to fit for more efficient adjustment their old economic burdens to the new conditions of professional and industrial life, then society owes them that education as a debt. The daughters of the race to the remotest future should receive as an "unearned increment," but yet a rightful inheritance from the mothers of the race to the remotest past, every advantage of training for life that any community

can give. It is no favor of men to the exceptionally
gifted woman which has grudgingly opened college and
laboratory to the brilliant members of the sex which
has waited so long for recognition of its right in education. It is no gift of generosity to girls of average
talent and circumstance which starts belated trade-
schools, and makes the High and Normal Schools
more accessible to them as preparation for wage and
salary earning. The unpaid service of women to the
home and to social order throughout the ages demands as merely decent recompense every chance to
live and to grow, to do and to be, that the world of
to-day can offer. For men to refuse this, now that social science has revealed the race-indebtedness to
women, would be to proclaim themselves bankrupt of
honor in the Court of Justice. For women to fail to
hear the new call to social service which the new time
sounds in their ears would be to throw the assets of
ages of drudgery into the waste-heap. For women of
the privileged few to fail in perception and realization of that sex-solidarity which is not sex-antagonism
but simple fidelity to the Guild of Womanhood, is pitiful proof of the dwarfing effect of past subjection.
[5] The "new conscience," of which Jane Addams speaks
so convincingly in her recent articles on the social evil,
is but one expression of the growing conviction that
the problem of woman's personal freedom and woman's social duty is one and the same problem. It
reaches from the dark chasm of traffic in womanhood
by greed and lust to the heights of honor where the

[5] Jane Addams, *A New Conscience in Regard to an Ancient Evil.*

women of light and leading enrich and beautify the world. [6] To-day this problem is acute, and many of its elements confused and confusing, because all the other special problems of our time, political, economic and social, reach their deepest significance and most vital application in relation to womanhood and the home. Here, as in all other crisis-efforts toward human progress, education, more and more effective education, is the watchword. Here, as elsewhere, it is only "culture that shall yet absorb chaos itself."

[6]Lavinia L. Dock, *Hygiene and Morality.*

VI

THE VOCATIONAL DIVIDE

A LECTURER on educational topics was once riding over a bleak hill in New England to reach an evening appointment and fell into conversation with her young driver, who was secured for the occasion by the proprietor of the livery stable because he "couldn't spare a man to go so fur." Talking with the lad, the lady ascertained that he was regularly employed in the mill which loomed so large in the valley landscape they were leaving behind, and that he had learned to drive so as to get an odd job now and then when, as in the present instance, the "mills shut down" for any reason. The boy was frank and somewhat boastful about his family affairs. His father "worked in the mill," he said, "was a weaver; got nine to ten dollars every week." His sister worked too; she "got as much as five or six dollars most weeks." His brother was beginning and he got sometimes a dollar and a half. His aunt, "she lived with them, and she was awful smart, most the best weaver in the mill," and she got eleven or twelve dollars a week and "didn't have to pay hardly any fines, she was so careful." "And your mother?" asked the lady; "what does she do?" "Oh," answered the boy proudly, "she ain't in the mill; she used to work out, but she don't have to now—we take care of her." "Oh, I see," said the questioner, "she does not work; how nice that is." "Why, yes, she does work, too," said the boy rather resentfully, "she works all the time—she's the best mother in town; she takes care of the house and cooks for us and puts up our dinners and mends the clothes and does everything."

"Ah," said the inquiring economist, "I see, she is most useful—and what wages does she get?" "Why, she don't get wages at all," responded the boy, beginning to be a bit confused, "she does the things in the house. She works, of course she does, but there ain't no money into it." "Oh, I see," again said the lady, and closed the brief interview with the conventional hope that they were all kind to the best mother in town.

A young couple, just nearing the wedding day, were discussing ways and means relative to housekeeping in that delightfully engrossing manner suited to the intimate character of the situation. Not "standards of living" was the subject in hand, but how "he" and "she" were to live together in the new Paradise they were to enter. They had reached the critical stage when the parallel columns of "must haves" and "want to haves," being set down with careful precision, mount up so frightfully in the sum total. Having in mind the small salary of an instructor in college, they soon reached the conclusion that the things one must do without are far more numerous than those one can secure. Suddenly the bride-to-be exclaimed: "But, Henry, we are trying to put all the things we have both had and both want into one income. You are earning $2,000 and I am earning $900 and that is $2,900, and not just your $2,000. Can't I earn something, too, so we won't have to do without so many things?" "No, indeed, my beloved one," said the groom-to-be, "I should despise myself if I could not take care of you, and properly. No, you can never earn outside the home after we are married." "But —but," faltered the beloved one, "you see we have not yet allowed anything for domestic help in either of our lists. We should have to have a scrubwoman and a laundress and that would cost something even with no maid, and it mounts up frightfully without that. Couldn't I do something to earn as well as do all the housework to save?" The answer came with hesitancy: "Of course, you ought to have a maid; but I don't see how we can afford it just at first. Of course, I shall earn more later on, and with you to inspire me very soon. I don't know, how these household things are managed. My father, you know, was a minister with a small salary and mother did everything about the house. Is it very hard?" he asked tenderly. "Perhaps not," she said; "you know I have been at school and college and teaching and I don't really know; but I shall learn to do everything perfectly, of course, and make the little home what it should be. But that does not seem to make me save more than the maid's wages and what her food might cost. We still have to do without a frightful lot of things we both want and are used to." "Well, you can't earn money outside anyway," he settled the question. "People would talk and with justice, as if I were a poor sort of husband if I couldn't take care of you." The young wife acquiesced and began soon to engage in much hard work that had "no money into it" in order to make the home of which they were both so proud. The only times, however, when she was fully convinced that she was "supported" were the occasions when she needed some article of dress and had to mention the fact to her husband, who, thinking she "looked lovely in anything," was often oblivious to the fact that women's wardrobes had sometimes to be replenished. And the larger income the young professor in time earned was more than swallowed up by the demands of the fast-coming children. Hence, her saving by working was still essential.

A married couple with no children, he a doctor, and she a music teacher, continuing professional work after marriage had a combined income allowing more than ordinary freedom of expenditure. One day there came a crisis in their lives which involved both professional and economic questions. The husband received a flattering call from a well-known physician in a large city to become junior partner, with the prospect of becoming his successor later on. The offer did not secure for the first few years a much larger income than the doctor alone was earning and not so large as her additional income made their joint possession. It was reasonably certain, however, that the economic advance would be very considerable after the first years

and that the position would give the young doctor a
most enviable place in his profession. There was no
question in the mind of the husband as to the acceptance of the offer as he joyously read aloud to his wife
the letter from the distinguished physician and his intended reply. To have such recognition of his professional standing while still under forty was indeed a
good fortune which could not fail to cause elation.
His wife was sympathetic and rejoiced with him in this
proof of his powers; but he could not fail to notice,
after a while, that she was not as entirely happy as he
in the prospect of the change. "What is it, wife?"
he asked at last; "don't you like the big city this will
make us live in?" "Oh," she answered, "any place
where we both are, and you are happy and useful,
would be home to me; but my own work—what of
that? I know the conditions in this city you are called
to; it has a big Conservatory of Music and the crowd-
ing of its graduates into the teaching field each year
would make it almost impossible for any stranger to
get a chance for pupils. I might some day break into
the line, but not for a long time and only then if I
could work up some specialty of teaching not now over-
crowded; and that would mean that I must myself
study and that would be too expensive with the income you are offered. You know," she added, with
the gentle deference to men's pride which all wise and
loving women practise, "I have paid for the extra
maid service and my own personal expenses, as I
should do, with my separate income, and I can see
that it may be difficult for me, for us, to manage af-

fairs on the new basis." "Why, wife," he said, with
evident disappointment, "I supposed, of course, you
would feel with me that my professional advance and
the permanent, if not present, increase in income which
it would bring were wholly your gain as well as mine.
If you have more leisure, by reason of not teaching,
I suppose you could easily do some of the things you
hire help for now and, of course, I should do everything I could to have you miss nothing. You must
keep up with your music all you can, for your own
and our friends' enjoyment; but I suppose we couldn't
afford lessons yet awhile. I shall have to brush up
a bit at the hospital and learn the ways of the city-folk
in my profession, and that will cost something, I am
afraid. But surely you appreciate how great an opportunity this is for both of us?" "Yes," of course
she "appreciated," and equally of course she did housework and sewing and mending which she hated, instead of teaching music which she loved, during the
years when such sacrifice was necessary. She did not
enjoy, however, overhearing one of his family say
to her husband: "Well, one thing, Doc, I am glad of,
this move breaks up Fannie's teaching. It queers a
man to have his wife work after marriage and it's
lucky you left that village when you did and had
your home where she couldn't keep on doing what
would make every man wonder what was the matter
with you." It crossed the mind of the woman who was
valiantly trying to acquire belated efficiency in managing a household, and one in which a doctor's irregu-
larity made three meals a day a serious proposition,

that her present occupations bore a strong resemblance
to "work"; but, obviously, they could not be real
labor since she was now being "taken care of" for the
first time in her married life!

Another couple started out on their wedding day
with a clearly defined plan which marked them as
"new" and "different." They were both artists; he
also an instructor in an art school of distinction. All
went well in their mutual regard for each other's
work, "self-reverent each, and reverencing each" their
living formula. All went well until the children came.
Then it became clear that it was not right to have
little ones tumbling around in a studio, however picturesque it might be, and sleeping behind screens that
shut out no sound of hilarious callers in the late evening, and subject to the gastronomic hazards of irregular breakfasts, "bohemian lunches" and "dinners
out." These things were eminently satisfactory to the
parents, both of whom loved to do the unexpected and
take the consequences, sure for them to be far happier or funnier than any planned-for arrangement
could be. But they did not suit the needs of little
people. They must be brought up in a "regular manner," terrible "strait-jacket" as this seemed to be
to the lovers who were responsible for those infants.
There was not the slightest wish on either side to
shirk parental duty; but, on the other hand, neither
could wink out of sight the fact that the proper care
of the babies required an immense sacrifice on the
part of both parents, and a revolution in her way of
life for the mother. It was clear that economic re-

sponsibility for the household must be given over
wholly to the husband, who had a steady salary, as
well as a greater capacity to do the conventional things
that sell readily. Yet he, as well as she, he more than
she (such was his rare grace of humility in view of
another's powers), realized that hers was the finer
insight, hers the rarer touch in expression, hers the
spark of genius most likely to be recognized after she
was dead, if not before. It chafed that she must stop
steady growth just in the morning time of her development, and lose technique for want of use, and
dismiss thronging visions because it was time to feed
the baby. So infatuated were they with their art and
with each other that, had it not been for the children,
blessed encumbrances as they both felt them to be, the
studio life together would have wrought out a companionship rare in its adjustment of each to each and
of both to an ideal. As it was, they planted a home
in the suburbs where it would be "healthy for the
children" and, as the income was small, even with all
the man could do, the wife and mother set ardently
to work to do all the housework and take care of the
children in the best manner possible. And lo, and
behold, she found she liked it! Welling up from her
subconscious self in proud delight at her cooking and
her gardening and her sewing and her teaching of the
little ones, rapidly becoming a charming quartette,
came a deep satisfaction, not only at the well-being of
the family for which the service was undertaken, but
also in the perfection of her service itself. As she
remarked often to her husband when a new house-

wifely talent displayed itself almost unbidden: "I feel all my ancestral mothers patting me on the head and saying, 'Now, Winifred, you are doing something useful in the world—at last you amount to something.'"

The easel stood untouched for days together; and the sunrise dreams of how a picture might look chased themselves away as she blithely ministered to her flock. But, in moments of quiet, when the children slept, or as they picnicked together in the deep woods where the teasing sunbeams called for her brush to hold them in lasting beauty, she had the old craving for self-expression. Her husband never ceased to bewail the sacrifice, and viewed with jealous eye the professional success of women much her inferiors, unable to help feeling that something was wrong, if her rare insight and lovely interpretation were to be wholly lost. "By and by," was her watchword, "by and by when the chicks are grown." He offered her a "Sabbatical year" in which she should have the studio and he the suburban home and its cares; but her merry refusal to subject the children's digestion to his brilliant but erratic cooking, and their health and teaching to his well-meaning but clumsy direction, was clearly wise. "If we were rich and could afford good servants and the best possible caretakers for the children, and I could thus have peace of mind for a good day's work, it would do to keep on painting, to try to be both a constantly growing artist and a serviceable house-mother. But you know that for me to depend upon selling pictures enough to pay for the horribly regular demand for wages for such helpers would be a fatal gamble in futures. Besides," the mother said, with shining eyes, "just here and now the things I do keep me close to the babies, and it is not clear that anything is better worth doing than that." So, to the tune of "By and by when the chicks grow up," she answers the beckoning of breeze and sky and brook and tree and vows to keep tryst with them when she has leisure to "tell again the tale" they tell to her. In her heart, however, she knows that she will always record some loss on the art-side for this long interim of practical work.

These tales hint the difference between the approach of men and women to vocational work. A man, as a rule, fulfils his father-office best by choosing wisely one vocation, and holding to it, perfecting himself in it and taking all the opportunities it offers for advancement, and constantly confining to it his faithful effort. The average woman, in ordinary circumstances, fulfils her mother-office best by choosing to make her personal vocation secondary to the duties of home-making and motherhood. Two firsts there cannot be; two devotions occupying the same supreme position at the same moment. And the conscientious mother, of whom there are many more than are numbered among the careless, never fails to put the home comfort and the children's welfare first. Miss Tarbell's arraignment of the "uneasy woman" who sacrifices others to herself is far better suited to the artificial atmosphere of the city, in which the pleasure-loving of every other locality in the United States come to spend their money and make a show, than it is to the average life in America, in which the rarest of exceptions is the woman who serves herself first and best at the table of life's opportunities.[1]   The spinster of to-day, educated and successful in vocational choice and work, is following after men in new fields of individual achievement and playing her part well. The wife and mother of to-day, educated and equally successful before marriage in vocational choice and work, is doing something far more significant, if less picturesque.   She is blazing a new way of life-adjustment.   She is experiencing far more than she understands; is experimenting with far greater success than clearness of interpretation; is feeling her way to the future double "sphere" of womanhood, led by a sure instinct of love and duty.   Her heroism of pioneer adventure in a new way of social service will be appreciated only after the "woman movement" becomes past history.

The approach of man to vocational effort is single. Into the life of every woman who attains full experience of the possibilities of her nature there comes a vocational divide.   On one side is the road leading to uninterrupted advance in her chosen career or accepted work; on the other side is the road leading to the hearth fire which most often she must tend if it is to be kept bright; and to the voices of children clamoring for admission to the gates of life she alone can open.   At the upmost reach of choice on that vocational divide, she must balance the claims for self-

---

[1] Ida M. Tarbell, *The American Magazine.*

expression on the one side, for family service on the other. Physical motherhood itself, among healthy women who live wisely, presents small obstacles to continuous vocational work. As a distinguished sociologist, a man, has said: "These experiences need cause no more interruption than the occasional illnesses or need for occasional rest on the part of men."[2] Most women of to-day are not invalids, and child-bearing is a natural process; and the present attention to the muscular development of girls and the checking of tendencies that make for "nerves" will, and do now, insure for the average woman a safe and comparatively easy maternity. The pathological conditions of much manual work that still give women disease and prevent healthy motherhood do, indeed, present social problems. But it is not physical motherhood that makes it difficult for the teacher or other professional woman, or the woman in the counting-room or secretary's position, to keep on with her chosen work after marriage and maternity. Several reasonable "leaves of absence" would adjust that matter. What constitutes the difficulty is not getting the children here, but taking care of them properly after they are born. Neither are the most serious problems of adjustment, in this country at least, those that concern the willingness of the husband to have his wife retain the freedom and joy of her own self-expression and its convenient reward in cash. The American husband, at any rate in educated circles, is usually more than willing that the wife should adjust

[2] William J. Thomas, *Sex and Society.*

her life to life's demands according to her own choice, as he claims the right to do for himself. The difficulty inheres in the fact that neither parent can choose honorably any way of life that does not place first the economic and the social and the spiritual well-being of the family as a whole, especially as that concerns the offspring. In present conditions, and in those of any future in sight, and in the case of the average family, the economic and professional advance of the husband and father is the chief consideration; and the economic and professional advance of the mother secondary to the personal care of the home and children.

There are but two sets of conditions in which the wife and mother can pursue her own career as uninterruptedly and as independently as can the husband and father. These are, first, the condition in which the man has a large fortune or a large and secure income. In that case, he can rightfully supply, and she rightfully accept, the substitute care of foster-mothers within a home which conscientious attention keeps to right standards. She can thus be free to sing her songs, paint her pictures, teach her lessons, write her books, organize her social service, or minister to the needs of the world. Such instances are becoming more and more common; they show alike the growing sense of justice in men that can recognize values in women's work, and the growing administrative power of women that enables them to manage others' work instead of doing everything for themselves. Whether this arrangement leads always to the finest permanent relationship between parents and children is another question. It sometimes does, and sometimes does not; and the reasons for the differences do not now fully appear. The other set of circumstances that leave the wife and mother as free as the unmarried woman to pursue a career is that in which her genius is so strong, and so in the line of public demand, that she can and does receive large compensation for her work. A prima donna, with a voice that is liquid gold to be coined into great fortunes, can be a prolific mother and manage a big and comfortable household, easily securing so many "assistant mothers" for her household that no one questions her right to sing her way into the hearts of the whole world.

There is another condition of family life, not so uncommon as one could wish, in which unusual burdens of care for others than the husband and wife and children necessitate the continuance of paid work by the wife and mother and a constant and difficult adjustment of seemingly contrary claims upon her strength, in order that the united income may meet the claims of filial duty or other relationship of birth. There are also the conditions, now not so rare as to be negligible, in which the wife earns easily a larger income than the husband can earn and in which economic security and advance for the family itself make it right and wise for the vocational choices to revolve about her work rather than about his own, for a part of the time at least. In these cases, however, the man suffers at present from the gross injustice of inherited standards, developed at a time when women could not earn at all, and he is falsely supposed to be a "no account person"; when, if he had an earning capacity of exactly the same restricted order, and had for a wife a woman who could only "keep house," they might live far below their present standards, and he be considered worthy of honor! The fact is that the adjustment of the family life to "Two heads in council, two in the tangled business of the world" has proceeded but a little way toward full and satisfactory issue. The process of adjustment is not at present easier for the conscientious man than for the woman who desires to do her full duty. The man of to-day has a feeling, born in him from a past in which "husband and wife were one, and that one the man," that he is not doing his full duty as a husband unless he can make his own income provide as much comfort and happiness as each enjoyed when he and his wife were both earning. The world, composed mostly of people who are conscious only of inherited prejudices and ideals, ranks him as a failure, or at least as deficient in manliness, if his wife "has to work." She is conscious that in carrying on a chosen career after marriage she may often place her husband in a false position. And, more than all, there must be choices made when the decision as to which of the two shall keep on in an advantageous position and which shall give way for the other's career must be settled.

The new and finer quality of married life which the new freedom and personal development of women have given, the higher and sweeter comradeship in the larger world of affairs and ideals which husbands and wives now enjoy, enable the moral and intellectual élite among them to settle these problems as they arise with mutual satisfaction. It is not easy, however, for even the moral and intellectual élite to live now in the way possible to the majority of men and women only in some future age, and to be wholly at ease in the presence of the common misapprehensions of their motives and their ways of life. All honor then to the men as well as to the women who live in the present what others may attempt in the future.

Some of us are sure, however, that the solution of difficulties involved in the vocational divide in the modern woman's life does not lie along the line of such development of supreme specialization in all women's work as Mrs. Perkins Gilman and her school advocate.[3] All such theories presuppose that because with a race of healthy women motherhood would be but an incident of not serious physical experience, and because modern industry has taken from the home a large share of the work that handicraft once made its economic concern, therefore home-making and motherhood are so lessened in their demands upon women's time and strength as to present in themselves small obstacles to the continuous pursuit of vocational work by married women with young children. There has been no such diminution of the burden resting upon the wife and mother as that idea indicates; and there is no future in sight when such radical and universal lessening of that burden appears either economically practical or socially useful.

[3] Charlotte Perkins Gilman, *Woman and Economics.*

The fact is that the same process which has carried out of the home and specialized in the shop and factory the spinning and weaving and most of the domestic industries of the older time has changed the centre of gravity in the approach of women to family duty, but has not appreciably lessened its demand on time and strength. The private well gives place to the public reservoir; but eternal vigilance is still the price of good water. All the sanitary conditions of the household are now at the mercy of the public intelligence and public conscience and each household must contribute a perceptible quota to that common stock. The place of work for the girl-child and young woman has changed indeed from the home to the shop, the factory and the counting room, but that very fact necessitates a care and a knowledge on the part of her natural guardians which the old inherently protective work did not. The school has left the hearthstone and set up its own institution as an arm of the Government; but that means that every careful and intelligent mother must learn more and not less about education; and not only about education in general to fit her to vote for members of the school committee, but more about education as applied to Johnnie and Katie and Susie and James, if she is really to do her duty by them. The world is no longer fenced away from the home by the isolation of the separate household, but has free approach, with all its standards and its incitements, to childhood and youth, as never before. That means, not that parenthood is a less onerous, but that it has become a more difficult, function. The

inference from the facts of modern life which seem
to indicate that individual parenthood is no longer an
exacting and an exhausting functional service, but
rather a small share of the public duty of social control of that functional service, is fallacious. The facts
that indicate the socialization of the home do indeed
create a demand for women to participate actively, and
with full power of citizenship, in that social control
of the home. It is an anachronism most stupid and
socially retarding that, in an age in which the Government has actual direction of the conditions of home
life and of education and all the social services which
have been women's share of action and responsibility
since society began, women are held back from the full
citizenship which can alone restore to them their ancient and honorable and well-used prerogatives.

All that can be said by the most radical thinkers
concerning the justice and expediency of the movement
for full freedom and equal citizenship for women cannot emphasize too strongly the truth—that the inconsistency of woman's present disenfranchised position
in the United States is a moral dislocation in thought
and involves a serious retardation in the growth and
application of democratic ideals. The "rights" of
women should have been attended to as completely as
the rights of men in the eighteenth century, when the
just basis of government was up for world discussion.
As it is, the belated task should be got out of the way
of human progress at once so that we can give full attention to duties, with rights taken for granted. This
fact does not prove, however, as many seem to think,

that the vocational specialization which has been an
accompaniment of the development of democracy is a
necessary part of it alike for all women and men.
We are suffering in our thinking in many ways from
the juxtaposition of the vast changes in modern industry induced by the invention of power-driven machinery, and the political evolution which has established the rights of the common man, and is establishing the rights of the common woman. They are not
the same movement; and the arguments demanded by
one are not necessarily suited to the other. Miss
Tarbell's strange confounding of the "Business of
Being a Woman" with the business of being a house-
mother is but one of the many instances of the confusion of thought which two tremendous changes, hap-
pening together, have caused.[4] The business of being
a woman is precisely like the business of being a man;
namely, the development of the highest and finest and
noblest personality possible with the "raw material"
of evolution handed to one at birth and in the circumstances in which one finds one's self. The business
of being a house-mother is quite another thing. That
is a functional service which makes single-eyed vocational choice and pursuit impossible to the average
woman, in the sense that such a single devotion is possible to the average man; and this for the most obvious
of reasons, namely, that the wife and mother (or some
competent substitute under her constant control and
guidance) must live so much more closely to the de-
veloping life of childhood than can the average hus-

[4] Ida M. Tarbell, *The American Magazine.*

band and father that the obligations of family life for a considerable period of her life must be her first consideration.

The choices of life now take a more serious hold upon the enlightened woman's life than in more primitive times. When there was nothing for women to do but marry for the means of subsistence, the demand was only to get the "best provider" one could secure or one's parents could choose. Now it is for the woman herself to decide whether she loves the man more than her "pay envelope." In the past, the major part of the discipline, the ordered and useful activity, the real education of the children, was carried on in and through the family industries. Now it is a difficult problem to prepare the child for his or her rightful place in the world of work. Then the school was but a slight addition to the forces which were training the child for useful and efficient and moral life. Now the school is burdened more and more with the application of social standards to the life of the individual, and its quality and efficiency are vital to human development as never before.[5]

The functional services of home-making and motherhood have therefore not lessened, but increased, in their cost to women's time and strength during the years when the children are in minority. They demand a deeper experience because they are the result of more conscious choices; and experience costs sometimes more than mechanical activity in strength and constitutional vigor. A closer and closer contact with,

[5] Edward H. Griggs, *Moral Education,* Chap. 12.

a finer and finer appreciation of, child nature is demanded by the new applications of the democratic ideal of the government of the family; and close contact with a nature for the development of which one is vitally responsible costs in time and effort. The outer influences which contend with parental control, and often submerge it, demand a general knowledge of social conditions which in itself militates against the entire specialization of vocational work. All this nullifies the notion that, now that industry has gone out of the home to so great an extent, the house-mother has an easy job, and can go on with her own business outside the home, with only slight interruptions.

It is said, Of course she can't now; but when we get all women rightly placed in specialties, and there are enough "substitutes" and "assistant" mothers to go around, and they are all well trained and morally dependable, each woman, like each man, will be able to find the home a place of rest and not of work, and there will be no vital difference in vocational experience between men and women. The answer to this is both economic and social; it deals with both the mechanism of living and the sources of life itself.

In the first place, the economic value of the healthy, competent, expert house-mother has never yet been properly estimated. "Woman's work" has been despised and, therefore, its value unknown because, and only because, women for long ages have themselves been considered inferior to men and held in law and custom as perpetual minors. Just as the position of disadvantage which Afric-Americans hold in the

United States is due, not to the color of their skin, but to the fact that they were once held as slaves, with a Supreme Court decision that they "had no rights which a white man was bound to respect" scourging them like a whip, so the real cause of the disrespect shown toward the house-mother's task is due to the fact that the house-mother herself has but just emerged to the position of independent personality. All the fine talk about the "sacredness of motherhood" and the "inestimable value of the woman in the home" has but added hypocrisy or *unthinking* compliment to injustice, so long as men were ashamed to be caught tending their own babies, or washing dishes or clothes they had themselves soiled, because such things were "women's work."

An article by an able writer in the New York *Times* alludes to the fact that it is only as a daring figure of speech that a man cook is sometimes called an "artist"; since "men cooks, however well paid or useful, have always been considered the social inferiors, not only of those whose appetites they gratified, but also of every tradesman and artisan not engaged in the rendering of distinctively personal services." This writer continues: "It is not that men cannot cook well or cannot make clothes well or are not good domestic servants of every kind; it is only that these are not 'manly' occupations and instinct insists that there is something small, something low or mean in the man who does not make successful efforts to get out of them." It has taken extraordinary social demands to lift even nursing out of this position of disrespect. The lever of patriotic

service to soldiers defending national honor alone gave
Florence Nightingale power to make over this art of
personal service into a profession.   And it has taken
all the power of religious devotion in philanthropy,
and the demands of the medical profession for intelligent lieutenants in their important work, to keep it
in honor.   It is not alone or chiefly that woman's work
has been so general in character as to be really amateur that it has failed to secure respect and that there
has been "no money into it"; for the majority of
house-mothers, in most enlightened lands, have done
their work in the home so well that they have doubled
the purchasing power of their husbands' earnings and
made a unique contribution to the well-being of those
they served.   The real reason for the lack of appreciation is that men, as they have stepped ahead of women
in industrial organization, have been able to choose
what they liked best as their share of labor and have
left the rest to women; and have called it an "instinct"
that made what they did not like to do "women's
work."   Not only that, but the personal service of individual lives is in itself not enticing; it is often hard
and unpleasant.   It is only glorified by affection and
the need to give the loved one the best one has.   Men,
having first and most fully attained the position where
one can serve the loved one in a chosen single task,
instead of by a congeries of general services, have
never learned the value of those services.   A poet says
of a woman: "The charm of her presence was felt
when she went."   The economic value of the competent housewife is felt only when she dies, and the

cost of her hired substitutes shows the manual worker with young children that he "must marry again" because he "can't afford to do without a wife."

A finer and more just appreciation of the value of personal services in the household is being developed. It is now being hammered into the average consciousness by the domestic servant problem. This problem is, in the last analysis, the result of the determination of all women who have had the democratic public school for teacher not to engage in "low and mean personal service" if they can make "successful efforts" in some other form of self-support. We shall use up relays of foreigners of manifold races and hues in the effort to stem the tide of democracy, as, like Mrs. Partington with her broom, we take stand at the kitchen door and declare "thus far and no further." But we shall all at last, or our children's children, have to face the fact that no work considered "low or mean" can have the permanent service of free women, any more than of free men, for *money*. Love alone will buy it.

Meanwhile the house-mother and her sympathetic spouse of the refined, cultured and conscientious class of small income (a most imposingly large class in the United States) are in the very trough of the wave in respect to the economic problems involved in the house-mother's duty to her family. The cost of getting a "trained nurse" for the children is prohibitive for any but the rich. A "nursery governess" is a luxury outside of dreams. The "working housekeeper" is a fiction, for the most part confined to solutions of the domestic problem found in books of writers who have no invalids or young children in the family. The competent "general housemaid" is rare, and when found cherished as a jewel beyond price; often beyond the price the rejoicing family can afford to pay! The fatal facility of early marriage which wins from the housewife all the "good girls" she successively trains, and the more sure fatality that makes the kitchen of the competent woman of small means the training-school for the kitchens of her neighbors who can offer higher wages—all these things combine to make the responsibility of family life, even for the minority who can afford some domestic service, a serious matter. Below this economic line, at the plane of living where no "hired help" can be had except in direst emergency, there is a point in the standard of living where no substitute of any kind has been found, even on the basis of economic well-being, for the all-round service of the house-mother. In a careful study of many families occupying a plane of living just above the want line, the plane where self-support and some slight saving are possible with hard and constant struggle, it has been found that the difference between poverty below the demands of health and work efficiency, and poverty above that line, depended chiefly upon two factors, namely, the *faithfulness and good character of the father*, and the *competency and thrift and good temper of the mother*. That vaguely stated economic factor, the "efficiency of the wife and mother," covers a vast area of service to health, and to work power, and to economic security and advance; a service that knows no "hour law" or "minimum wage." If, in such a laborer's family, you undertake to make good that woman's contribution during even a short illness, you leave a deficit in comfort and in purse that halts the economic progress of the family for a long period. This is not solely a proof of the actual work-power of the woman. She could not perhaps earn elsewhere what she saves and makes good at home. It is proof still more of the family benefit of having family concerns of personal service in the hands of the one most eager to have it done well, and nearest in sympathy to the individuals served.

Still further down in the social as well as economic scale, we come to the plane of living where the housemother does outside work to piece out the low wage of the father, and where for the children there is the dire choice of early entrance into wage-earning or inadequate food and clothing supply; and here you reach a deeper problem. The wage-earning of married women with young children, under present conditions, gives such families less stability, less comfort, less moral protection, and less home feeling, than those families of very small income in which the father earns just enough to pay for the household expenses and the mother gives herself to the family work. Moreover, the husband and father in such cases is more easily tempted to shirk his family duties. Among a large section of the colored population, in places where race prejudice makes it hard for men to get work, the wives and mothers often support the entire family by laundry work or other personal service, and the man grows flabby in character and lazy in habit because it is easy for him thus to depend upon his wife. It must not be forgotten by any student of domestic problems that the father settled down to steady work for the family long after the mother had been drilled in self-sacrifice for the child. If the type of man is still far down in the scale of being, it is a dangerous thing to release him from obligation for the family support. If, on the other hand, we jump across the social field to the most privileged classes, we find difficulties there. Not the superficial ones that inhere in the complaint of the languid and self-indulgent lady that "there are no longer any good servants" or those who "really know their place," but those that harass the conscientious mother in the administration of a large household in which the servants know what used to be held as "their place" too well. If there is anything worse for a young child, morally and physically, than to have a set of grown people around hired to wait upon him, studying how to please him in order to be retained as his servitors, the social condition has not yet revealed it.

All these difficulties, from those of the slums of the tenements to the palaces of the rich, are supposed by many modern writers to wait for solution only until we get the coöperative kitchen and the "hour service" for domestic work and for nursing; the glorified day-nursery and the omnipresent kindergarten, the enlarged public school, and the supervised play-centre; the "Summer Camp" and the "Winter Story Hour in the Library," well established. Then all will go well, and the woman go to her work in the morning and stay as long as it demands, and come home to the refreshment of a house well kept and children glad to see her as a welcome change (and not using her as now as their born slave), and all will "live happy forever after." It is indeed claimed by these solvers of the difficulties involved in the vocational divide in the modern woman's life that mothers of young children should be supplied with half-time work, under easy conditions, and yet secure an equal chance in the labor world. Until we get further away from the strikes and labor difficulties which are one obvious result of trying to get for women a shorter day than is secured by law for men, we cannot have high hopes of speedy arrangements that would make women, in the lower forms of manual labor at least, able to hold their own as specialized workers, and yet be under the peculiar protection of the State as mothers.

This all brings us to the consideration of those deeper social interests involved in the house-mother's relations to specialized industry. Those who have studied the dark problems of prostitution and inefficiency and undevelopment are agreeing that all girls should be secured either in the possession of sufficient means of support or in the power and opportunity of self-support. Most radical social students agree that married women, even with young children, who can, by means of their husband's, or their own, or the combined family income, guarantee to society expert and suitable care for and nurture of the children, may elect their own way of life by mutual consent of the parents involved and with the parental obligation always in

sight. Many are sure that some compromise position,
between extremes now advocated on either side, will be
reached, by which the specialized work-power of all
the women of education and talent and social leadership will be conserved in ways not common now, ways
that will make the years of women's lives after the
children are grown the best of their lives for independent effort. The problem that is now before us—
usually neither solved nor frankly admitted—is that
sharp divide, that inevitable choice, which comes to the
woman who is responsible, as none but herself can be,
for the little ones who make personal appeal to her
as to no one else for close and tender care. The solution of "no children" or "one child only" is no solution at all. Justifiable as such a choice of life may
be in many cases, a sacred duty as it may be in others
where taint of blood or constitutional weakness or
peculiar difficulties of family adjustment make their
demand, the normal family of several children for the
normal parents in usual condition is the crux of the
problem. Here we must pass beyond the mechanical
arrangements of income and labor conditions into the
realm of spiritual and social life.

The tremendous importance of the family as an
agent in the development of human personality is much
talked of but rarely perceived in its true values. That
mysterious process which gathers universal elements
of being into a creature that can be called "I" or
"You," which can be nurtured, educated, individualized, into a conscious, purposive being, able to react
upon the environment which has shaped it, and thus

to create an ever-renewed and progressive environment —how difficult a process this has been! Think of the cosmic cost of will, of unselfish affection, of articulate aspiration! Think how the germinal human being passes rapidly through many of the age-long processes that have thus created human personality; and how many times Mother Nature makes a slip and the human creature remains an "unfinished infant" all its life. And when the baby is well born and fairly started upon the way of life, how difficult it is for it to keep its footing on this slippery ball of earth and really become "somebody." This achievement of the ages does not work automatically. Feeble-mindedness, physical weakness and degeneracy, moral incapacity in manifold forms witness that the cosmic struggle to make human beings out of the travail of elemental forces is not completed *for* humanity but *by* humanity.[6]

Up to date, the family has proved the best and most effective agency for the development of personality. It has so far furnished a breakwater, most vital and helpful, against the non-social forces that work against human progress. So far, that breakwater has consisted in large part of exclusive affection, selective and partial love, reserve of intimacy, and a preëminent devotion to the nearest beloved. The attempt to bring up children outside of home life, even a small class for a definite end, as in Sparta, has resulted in a few better soldiers or more expert workers, but not usually, if at all, in a finer personality. The

___

[6] See treatment of the sacredness of the individuality in Felix Adler, *Moral Education of Children.*

methods of child-care in institutions, even good ones,
generally dull originality and the power of the will,
even if effective for special purposes of conformity to
life's demands.   The care of babies left without
mothers is now seen to demand the personal care of a
foster-mother for the best results.   Babies persistently
adhere to the illogical position that "science" alone is
not enough, but that "cuddling" and personal pride
must be a portion of their "modified" daily food.   The
child seems to need, as a buffer against the indifference
of the world at large, a certainty that he is an essential
element in the social order; and such a certainty has,
so far, not been given save through the parental partiality of affection.   Moreover, so far in human development, this function of the family in the protection and development of personality as it struggles
toward expression in the young child has demanded
that some one in the family shall have and shall express
a type of individuality which is not primarily concerned
with, or showing itself through, specialized forms of
vocational work; but is rather devoted supremely (at
least for the time being) to the family unity and to the
varying wants of members of the family group.   If
children are to gather themselves together "out of the
everywhere," it seems necessary that some one should
be close at hand, when wanted, to help in the process.
It has not so far worked well to have long "hours" or
seasons when the child cannot get at anybody to whom
it *knows it belongs*.   So far, in the organization of the
family, the mother has been the person readily at hand
when the child's needs, physical or spiritual, have de-

manded the steadying influence of a companionship on which it felt a rightful claim. This has been thought to be a natural arrangement, because the child is closer to the mother physically than to anyone else in the Universe.

There is a deeper reason, however, underlying that physical relationship which determines the social value of the function of the average mother in this development of the child's personality through constant companionship. Speaking generally, the feminine side of humanity is in the "middle of the road" of life. Biologically, psychologically and sociologically, women are in the central, normal, constructive part of the evolutionary process. On the one side and on the other, men exhibit more geniuses and more feeble-minded, more talented experts and more incompetents who cannot earn a living; more idealistic masters of thought and action and more "cranks" and ne'er-do-weels who shame their mothers. It is because to woman is committed in a peculiar sense this function of bringing to consciousness from the "raw material of evolution," through personal nurture and individual care, this personality of the child, that women are and have always been, and must, it would seem, always be, the practical and teaching half of the race.[7]

In the development of individuality, it seems clear that the most essential thing is that the conserving weight of the middle virtues and the mean of powers should be nearest the child and most constantly at his service. It is later, in the more formal educational

[7] See Lester F. Ward, *Pure Sociology,* Chap. 14.

processes, that the highly specialized " variations "
which men exhibit (and which tend directly toward
human progress along particular lines on the one side,
and toward human degeneracy on the other side) have
their functional use as example or as warning.   It
would seem, therefore, that no economic readjustment of society in accordance with modern specialization of effort can make it possible for the average
mother of several young children to pursue a specialty
of work with the same uninterrupted effort that the
average man can do. That all women should be educated for self-support at a living wage is a social necessity; that women should be made as valuable now and
in the future as they have been in the past as distinct
economic factors is unquestionable; that women must
reshape many of their activities to suit the general
scheme of industry which has created the factory is
certain; that women should, for their own best good
and for the ends of social progress, keep their hands
on some specialty of work, if only in selective interest,
through the years when they cannot follow it as the
first obligation is clear; that women should hold in
mind steadily reëntrance into their chosen vocation
when the children are grown, in order that life may
mean for them continual flowering of the stalk as well
as the past season's scattered blossoms—this is coming to be perceived as the wise plan for all women who
would achieve for themselves, as well as help others
to achieve, full personality.

This does not imply, however, that the physical
exigencies and the spiritual demands of family life can

ever be reduced to such a perfect factory system as to place the fathers and mothers of young children on the same plane of competitive manual and professional labor. The development of personality is the main business in life, our own personality and that of our offspring; to enrich the world with a unique contribution, made of the universal elements, but shaped to some rare beauty all its own. The old familiar faith, "God couldn't be everywhere—so he made mothers," has its modern scientific translation. The purpose of cosmic effort toward that "one far-off divine event toward which the whole creation moves" cannot achieve its personal work without persons. Personality is not the power to do any specific thing well, although vocational effectiveness is an expression of personality; nor is it a capacity to excel all previous achievements of the human race in some one line of thought or action, although great persons may also be great geniuses. Personality is above all the quality of unity, some individual wholeness that prevents the human creature from wholly losing himself in the whirl of things. To develop this, even in common measure, in the average life, it seems to be necessary that at the point when the child is first making effort to become a person there shall be some quiet brooding, some leisurely companionship of the beloved, a rich and generous sharing of some larger life always near when needed; some life not so much absorbed in its own individual growth as to leave it unaware of the stirrings of another toward more conscious being. For this reason, most of all, the individualization of women within the family may be often rightfully subordinate, so far as vocational achievement is concerned, to the development of that kind of personality which is effective through its breadth and its normal balance of powers, rather than by reason of its technical achievement.

VII

THE SCHOOL AND THE FEMININE IDEAL

PLUTARCH says "Lycurgus resolved the whole business of the State into the bringing up of youth"; the modern Demos is resolving the whole business of society into the education of all persons young and old. The problem of problems in democracy is how to grow people fit for such forms both of self-direction and of social adaptability as this way of living demands. The essence of this interior problem of democracy inheres in the woman question; in that most puzzling of all applications of the democratic principle, namely, how to secure to women full individual development and yet hold them obedient to the large demand of society for service from human beings of the mother-sex. This is the deeper necessity below all superficial questions of women's alignment with the modern political mechanism.

So far in the history of social advance the social responsibility of women has never been shirked by the majority of the sex or ignored by any intellectual or moral leadership. The obligation laid upon women to carry on from generation to generation the sacred vessels of life with contents unstained and unspilled (by their hands at least) and at any personal cost to themselves has been enforced by every religion and has been an accepted element of every code of morals. The common idealism has always demanded of women that at any price of sacrifice of personal ambition, even in the case of genius itself, their chief devotion be given to the family life and through that family life to the State and society.   And whatever may be charged against average womanhood in the past or in the present, whatever of smallness of nature or selfishness of action as relates to the world at large, the charge can never be truthfully made that they have failed to give their utmost, such as it has been, to the business with which they have been specially charged.   Women have come down through the ages bearing double burdens: the burden of sustaining their own lives that they might be of use, and the burden of sustaining their offspring that the social fabric might not rudely end.   This long service has created a feminine ideal of sacrifice and patient devotion to the welfare of others which has ruled human thought and action.   This ideal makes a poet of the Middle Ages say: "Man is made to achieve; and woman is made to appreciate the achievement, and to receive its fruits, and transmit them to the future."   This ideal gave us the aphorism of Swedenborg, the most spiritual of the older contrasts between the masculine and the feminine excellence: "Man was created to be the understanding of truth; and woman was created to be the affection of good."   These and similar sayings give clear indication of the common conception of a positive attitude of man toward

achievement and personal development, and of a negative attitude of woman toward all individualized activity. This is epitomized in the two declarations:
"History is the biography of great men"; and "That
is the happiest woman who has no history."

It must be remembered, however, that aristocracy
in government limited the attainment of this masculine
ideal to a few men at the top of life's opportunities. It
was not until the eighteenth century declaration of a
universal right and a universal capacity that man, as
man, was included in this masculine ideal. The essence
of democracy is its assertion that every human being
should so respect himself and should be so respected in
his own personality that he should have opportunity
equal to that of every other human being to "show
what he was meant to become." Very slowly has come
even partial application of that inner spirit of democracy to women. Class after class of men has
emerged from the obscurity of subservience and ignorance and class-registration to the freedom and dignity of individuality, leaving behind their women with
their children. As, however, it began to be increasingly perceived that a democratic order of society must
be the outgrowth of a democratic family, it began also
to be seen that a democratic family must have two
"heads" instead of one alone. Thus it came to pass
that the most vital element in democratic society,
namely, an equal opportunity for education, began to
be considered a right of women as of men. At first,
as was natural, it was not the right of women as human
beings needing self-development for their own pur-

poses of growth that won the opportunity of education; it was rather because the democratic State needed common schools, and women as the natural teachers of the race must go out from the hearthside training of children into the more formal and better organized system of modern education. The first reasons were, therefore, those of social thrift rather than of justice to women, as was shown so obviously in the inauguration of normal schools. As a distinguished gentleman said, when urging an appropriation for a State normal school before a legislative committee (in the fifties of the nineteenth century) : "Gentlemen, we have all observed the fine manner in which the best and most cultivated women are educating their own children, and by utilizing this gift of women we may put two females in every school to teach at half the price we now pay one inferior male." [1]   On that basis women entered their first educational opportunity above the grammar grades and "female finishing school."

This small crumb of education, and the opening of high schools and academies of a better grade, together with the industrial changes wrought by the invention of power-driven machinery, combined to make it more and more clear that women must be counted in as persons, as well as a class of social servants, and must "emerge," along with all other submerged "masses," into individuality. Democracy means the liberation and development of a wider and wider range of human power. When democracy touched the feminine ideal

[1] See *Women in Our Public Schools,* A. G. Spencer, *History of Rhode Island Public Schools.*

it began "to suffer a sea change into something new and strange." It began to be seen that the incapacity to have a "history" or to contribute to history might not be the supreme and only excellence in women. It began to be perceived that much power of achievement in women waited for the liberation of opportunity, as was the case in the restricted classes of men. The feminine ideal began to include not only ability to meet the demands of a social function, but capacity to share as a person in the larger life of the world of thought and of action. Then came, in a rush of practical answer to the demands of this new ideal, the opening of colleges and universities and technical schools to women, and the entrance of prepared women, not without friction and cruel suffering in many cases, but the successful entrance of women into the learned professions. The upmost reach, both in attainment and in security, in this educational opportunity for women is shown to-day in the United States in the coëducational State universities. These both crown our democratic system of free schools for the people, and also guarantee, past all whim of change, the right of women to equal schooling with men.

Women, as a matter of course, were at first admitted to institutions of higher learning, which had in all cases been fitted for men, and the demands of social life upon men; and they had to join on as best they might, whether the orders of the educational leaders made it easy or hard for them to keep step. Women, however, began to go to college just at the moment when education itself was entering upon the most profound transformation to which any system of inherited ideal and practice has ever been subjected.   The culture of the schools of the past, the "liberal education" of the colleges, was intended for a select class of people who were to be "leaders."   The type has been correctly defined as "classic"; which word in educational fields signifies far more than the learning of Greek and Latin.   It means also, and more vitally, a system of education fibred upon a conception of education as the need of only a small class in the community. This classic education was intended for the training of ministers, lawyers, doctors, librarians, writers, and teachers in college.   All technical preparation for work, even in these vocations, was left to apprenticeship to masters in the several arts; the training was, therefore, wholly "general."

In the nineteenth century a terrible iconoclast entered the Temples of Learning, and right and left he knocked the ancient gods off their pedestals.   His name we call Science.   Then commenced a vast enlargement of the curriculum.   Then it began to be said "that no man could be truly educated who knew nothing of the Universe in which he lived or of the Facts that this new teacher bade us worship as the 'God of things as they are.'"   Then the new teacher turned his attention from destroying ancient idols to serving as a magician of practical utility; and "pure science" joined forces with "applied science" to revolutionize the world of material and industrial and artistic effort.   Then the practical American people began to say: If it is right for us to spend the people's money for the education

of ministers and lawyers and doctors, of writers, statesmen and teachers, it is right for us to spend the people's money also for the training of leaders in scientific
achievement, for securing higher efficiency in industries,
for the perfecting of mechanic arts, for the development of every form of human endeavor and the perfection of every sort of human ability, the outcome of
which may be of social value. Then began the
struggle between the classicists and the scientists, the
end of which is not yet. Women, be it noted, came
into the opportunity of higher education just at the
moment when "the still air of delightful studies" was
being rudely assailed by the voices of these disputants,
each standing for the new or the old in college ideal.
"New people," those who are just "arriving," are always most conservative and orthodox because least
secure of their position; and hence the women's colleges at first gave, and many of them still give, most
loyal adherence to the classic "faith once delivered to
the (educational) saints." Not for worlds would some
of them open their curriculum to questionable scientific
courses on the same terms with mathematics, languages
and the other inherited "courses leading to a degree."

The State universities, as was natural for the people's schools, first began to give full response to the
people's needs that education should be democratized
along with governmental forms. The charge of "utili-
tarianism" brought against the enlarged vocational tendencies of the modernized college and university is
quite absurd, when we consider that all the old classic

education was distinctly a preparation for a few vocations. The only difference is that we are now trying to fit for many, instead of few vocations, and for a range of vocations which takes in others than those of distinctly literary nature. Very few people have ever been to college just "for the fun of it." They went in the past to get ready for leadership along lines defined by the then social need. They will go more and more to get ready for the vastly wider range of leadership that the present and the future social need defines.

In the rapid changes in curriculum induced by this movement for the democratizing of higher education the "special needs of women" began to be discussed, and efforts began to be made for supplying those needs in so far as they appeared clear to the educational leadership. The new feminine ideal, with its double demand both for women as developed persons, and for women as serviceable functionaries in the family life, began to write itself out in courses of study. The still widespread and dense confusion of mind as to which element in the feminine ideal should have first place and which should have right of way in preparation for life has made the whole approach to education for girls and women a confused and awkward process.

Beginning with the general needs of all little girls we at once, as in all elements of the "woman problem," reach into the deep places of the "human problem." The school and the feminine ideal are a part of "education and the larger life." This fact makes the present confusion as to the basic reasons for sending girls to college, or for giving them High School education, or even for letting them learn the alphabet (which is quite a new thing in social economy), and gives us amusing as well as aggravating "remarks" by distinguished gentlemen at educational functions. The common phrase respecting the introduction of courses in "household science and art," in "domestic economy," etc., is: "We do this to make women better wives and mothers and more efficient home-makers." The inference is that these two aims are identical. Incidentally this may be true, fundamentally it cannot. Wifehood and motherhood, like husbandhood and fatherhood, are spiritual experiences and the expressions of personal character. They test and discipline and develop human nature; but only a fine individual can be a really good husband or wife, father or mother. That a woman is the "best housekeeper in the neighborhood" does not, therefore, guarantee that she is a comfortable and charming wife, or that her children "rise up to call her blessed." That a man is a "good provider" and a success in his chosen field of work is no proof at all that he is a desirable husband or a good example for his sons to follow. Moreover, the character of the home life does not inhere in the variety of domestic occupations carried on in the home nor even in the skill shown in those occupations. Were this the case we should have poorer homes now than we used to have when every woman had to make her own "tallow dips." In a large area of life the contrary of this is true; we have better homes for not having them so largely shops and factories. How much of the shop and factory now left in the home is yet to be taken out of it in the process of industrial organization, no one can now tell. But this we know, the world is getting impatient of all slipshod, inefficient work in any field, and all the work that is done in the household, whether much or little, must become standardized.

Meanwhile the confusion of thought that lumps together all forms of domestic science courses of study, from the elementary school to the university, as "fitting for wifehood and motherhood," must be resolved into some clearness. Girls do not need to spend the time of a four years' college course in order to learn what an average housemaid "picks up" without the least attempt to understand the science of her art. "General housework" for a family of two to five does not require such a lengthy preparation as elaborate college courses imply. When the college takes hold of the matters involved, *they become specialities of vocational training for highly paid positions in professional life;* they do not remain mere helps toward a more efficient care of the private household. [2] What happens to farming when the university takes hold of it? It separates into departments of study; study of soils, of varied theories and processes that make of this ancient and general art a variety of sciences and business careers. What happens to "general housework" when the college takes hold of it? It becomes cooking that fits for a dietitian's specialty or a teacher's chair; it becomes applied art, landscape gardening, interior

[2] See catalogues of household science courses in colleges and universities.

decoration, inspectorships of trade conditions for the benefit of the consumer, trained nursing and hospital management;—all manner of specialized vocations by which competent women earn a living and obtain a good position in the professional world. Your "splendid housekeeper" becomes a sanitary expert, and expends upon a community that energy which so often in the past has made husband and children so unhappy! Your woman of exceptional taste and desire for lovely things, whom fate has so often married to a man more appreciative than wealthy, has now a chance to spend much money of other people for beautiful objects which they could not select for themselves; and is thereby made happy even if personally restricted in purse. Your "natural-born nurse" who loves to fuss about invalids, and has so often in the past either annoyed or spoiled her own family according to their temperament, has now her chance to care for the wards of society in a large institution. Your big-hearted, sympathetic helper who formerly engaged in philanthropy at any cost of character to her beneficiaries has now an opportunity to become a "social worker" under leadership that fits her work, however personal and ameliorative, into the general needs of social progress. All this is very fine and helpful to women and to society alike; but extended courses along the lines leading to these specialties of vocation are not essential to, and do not specifically lead toward, that simple all-round training and practice in the fundamentals of housekeeping which are required by, or can be used to the full by, the average housemother.

Unaware of the significance of this fact, however, the educational authorities for the most part go on blindly mixing all manner of vocational training for girls in one indiscriminate mass, and applying any part of that new educational advantage where it is possible to tack it on regardless of any logical plan. For the little children up to the end of the elementary school we rest back upon a little "sewing and cooking" for girls, a little "woodwork" and "use of tools" for boys; in the high school we match the boys' "forge" against the girls' "millinery and art"; and we are beginning to start trade-schools for girls as well as for boys when we fully realize that girls as well as boys must earn their living in the modern shop or factory. The general course, however, in all meetings devoted to vocational training, industrial education and the like is for learned people to talk several days about trade-teaching and work-efficiency for boys and men, and then lamely add at the end of their addresses, "and girls," without any clear idea of what should be done with and for girls. The basic fact of the present vocational divide in the life of the average woman is neither perceived nor stated and therefore, of course, the solution of it cannot be given.

There are three divisions in the problem of the education of girls and women, and its solution waits for clearer apprehension of the significance of those divisions. There is first the preparation of all girls along the general lines that will fit them for all-round efficiency in relation either to their personal needs or to their special social function as women. There is, second, the definite preparation for some trade or specialty of work which will enable them to earn their living in a suitable and morally safe manner, of all girls who must begin to earn money as soon as society considers them physically, mentally and morally fit to do so. This period is now set generally at the ages between fourteen and sixteen. There is, third, the preparation for social leadership which the girl requires who is either to marry and maintain a home which may be a centre of light and direction in the community, or who, if remaining single, or if married continuing individual work, will occupy a position in some one of the learned professions. In all three of these divisions the double motive of the modern feminine ideal, namely, to grow persons of self-directing power, and to develop social serviceableness, must be held firmly in mind.

The first division of girls, by far the largest and hence the division that social well-being demands should have first attention, is that division who must get their chief preparation for the exigencies of life in the elementary school; sometimes supplemented by the first year or two in the high school. Whatever the average woman needs most, therefore, must be put into the home and school training that the average girl can get before the ages of fourteen to sixteen years. The pathology of women's wage-earning at the present stage of industrial organization convinces us that we must have the specialized training for self-support needed alike by the girl who must "get her working papers" as soon as the law allows, and by the girl who can prepare through years of leisurely training for an advanced position in professional life. The pathology of labor conditions in general, and the whole range of philanthropic study and effort, show that the ability to provide a comfortable household into which to put that home-life that is needed for social well-being demands from men far more versatility and more independent power, more capacity to rise above adverse circumstances and more ability to take advantage of favoring chances, than the average man now shows. The same pathological elements of the modern industrial order, the same needs of the household and the home, prove that women, the average common run of women, need two sorts of preparation for life, to be early acquired and more thoroughly acquired than is now the case; namely, the preparation for home demands and the preparation for self-support.

If, then, we accept it as fact that the vocational divide in women's lives constitutes a permanent obstruction to wholly uninterrupted vocational work and must make the approach of the average woman to specialized labor double, not single, her constancy to any pursuit being always conditioned upon her occasional, often her lengthy and exhausting, devotion to making whole people instead of manufacturing particular products of human activity, the school must prepare for both exigencies of vocation and prepare for them in proper sequence.

If women in general, especially women of the poorer classes, must have this double approach to vocational work, namely, that of wage-earner until marriage and

then, if continuing to earn, requiring, for their own
health, the well-being of their children and the good
of the family, special arrangement of industry suited
to their special needs, and if they may usually serve
best by acting simply as house-mothers, it seems clear
that, under present conditions, skill and capacity in domestic work are needed by the majority of women.
These qualities and attainments of the successful house-
mother are not now sufficiently developed for the majority of girls by domestic training in the home. The
average conditions of city life, indeed, make it almost
impossible to secure adequate domestic training in the
private house. Moreover, the changes in our population, the incursion of vast numbers of an immigrant
population ignorant of much that our present civilization requires for health, cleanliness and comfort, create an imperative demand for standardizing domestic
training. The public school is the only medium by
which a common standard of the requisite intelligence
can be taught.

Whatever extension of specialization there may yet
be in women's work, we now need a modern school
substitute for the old-fashioned household training to
fit the average girl, especially in large cities, for the
demand which the average lot makes upon the average
woman, which it is clear is the power to make and
maintain a healthful, tidy, thrifty, comfortable family
life in a private home. For this we must have not a
school-study simply, if we are to rely upon the school
for this training; we need a school *practice* that may
develop a fixed habit, that may become a "second na-

ture." Moreover, the domestic power that the average woman needs most, and often needs for the longest
period of serviceableness, must be gained *first* if it is
to prove for life an easy mastery of domestic skill.   It
must be planted deep in the primary centres of develop-
ing power in childhood itself.   The reason for this is
both pedagogical and social; pedagogical in that the
processes required are general, with large sweep of
activity and yet with personal interest and direct relation to easily understood personal wants.   Socially, because these activities connect the consciousness immediately with the first social groups to which allegiance of service should be won from the child, namely,
the family and the school.

On the other hand, the specialized earning power
which all women need, and which the poorer classes of
women must have for self-protection, should be gained
second, if it is to secure a successful entrance into the
field of organized industry.   The reason for this is
also both pedagogical and social; social because trade-
teaching and definite preparation for specific professions require intellectual alignment with the larger
groups of industry, the State and society, and hence belong to a later development of social consciousness;
pedagogical because the attainment of perfection in
one process means a longer and harder devotion of
study to that process than suits the child.   It is for
the period of youth to learn how to do one thing well.
It is for the period of childhood to linger on each
process of activity only so long as its educational value
continues to inspire interest.   It is for the youth to

learn that he is a part of the larger social whole. It is
for the child to know how he is related to, and may be
a helpful part of, the family and the school.

If these things be true, then our course is clear as to
the sequence of industrial training for girls. First, in
the elementary school, a genuine, not a make-believe,
apprenticeship in simple domestic arts, such as the
simple housekeeping of the ordinary family requires.
Cooking, washing, ironing, setting and serving table,
buying judiciously right kinds of foods, getting to
know by constant use (rather than by charts on the
walls) the right kinds and preparation of foods for
health, strength and pleasure of taste; all this is needed
by the average woman-head of a family. All this fits
in with the average little girl's liking to do real things
and can be accomplished in effective training before
the ordinary girl is 14 to 16 years old. "Domestic
science," fitting for the profession of dietitian, or
matron of an institution, or teacher, may be properly
left for the high school and the colleges. But, before
there was a "household science," there was a "domestic
art," and it is that art in its simplest forms that the
average girl needs to "get by heart" in a constant drill
of "learning by doing" such as the old-fashioned home
supplied. How, in the universal sense now demanded,
and with a uniform standard of excellence and a scientific background to meet health requirements, may this
art be acquired, to some extent at least through the
public school, not as a substitute for, but in addition
to the home training? How give a constant drill in
domestic art in a school-house? The answer seems

easy. We are engaged in a crusade against preventable disease. This leads us to see that under-feeding
or bad feeding of school children is a physiological
sin. Some say give school lunches to those children
who need more or better food; others object on the
ground of possible pauperization. The answer to this
new demand for better nourishment of children seems
to be educational rather than charitable. The need of
schoolgirls is for constant practice in domestic arts.
The daily lunch at school, directed by competent
teachers, but *furnishing real work under sense of responsibility for actual results,* would provide the ideal
pedagogical method of such training. Why not thus
combine the two needs?

Again, we are demanding more "fresh air" schooling, and more outdoor activity for boys and girls. We
are demanding also a longer school day, and a longer
school year, as necessary to give proper life-fitting for
children obliged to leave day school at the end, or even
before the end, of the grades,—and for all children,
many believe, in view of the enlarged curriculum.
These needs all point to the possible municipal use of
vacant lands for "school gardens," to a possible and
needed training of boys in raising the raw material of
food, for use by the municipal schools at the midday
school lunches which that longer school day would
make necessary. If our boys and girls from 10 to 14
years old in the grade schools could thus live over
again in actual experience of daily work, safeguarded
from fatigue and guided by the best instruction, *the
basic training of the race in getting sustenance from the*

soil and in converting raw material into food, shelter, clothing and comfort, they would be able to face the modern world of specialized industry without fear of the tyranny of greed or the weakness of ignorance. Secure against adverse circumstances in the power of mastery over primitive processes to meet primitive needs, the working-man and the working-woman could never be "slaves." There is every economic, every social, every pedagogical, every health reason for giving our boys simple agriculture, our girls simple domestic art, in the grade school instruction; and this in an apprenticeship, an actual long-continued, constantly repeated process-activity.

This is not suggested as an attempt to divide children into social classes. Far from it. The elementary school should give the universal elements of education, the things all boys and girls need most to learn. Many of us believe that the basic historic occupations of the human race indicated above have a universal educational value and, therefore, should be in all the lower schools. Simple use of tools required in many and varied manual activities may well be added to the industrial training of boys and girls alike, in the upper grades of the elementary schools, in order to make "handy" men and women.

For all this educational demand for girls and boys alike, there is a deeper than an economic, a broader than a vocational basis. We have come to understand that, in some sense at least, the child epitomizes the life of the race; and that, therefore, his training for society must embrace in right sequence the stages of human advance. [2] We have begun to see that, as the race has learned by doing, the child's education must be centred around activity, ordered to ends of growing power of self-expression.[4] [5] We have begun to see that useful work within his scope of physical and mental power is a supreme interest to the healthy child and if not allowed to tire or become monotonous constitutes, by that interest, his chosen play. Moreover, we have become uneasy concerning an industrial system that makes the average manual worker seem a mere attachment to the machine and that so ties him to a small part of a vast labor process, whose plan he cannot control and whose ends he cannot see, that he loses all creative joy in his work. We bemoan the helplessness of the man whose labor has been snatched from his hand by a new invention or who has become prematurely aged by trying to make human nerve and muscle keep up with iron and steel. We play at arts and crafts "revivals" and make fruitless appeals for a return to the time when a worker controlled both the material and the process of his labor and could better than now use his intelligence and character as part of his stock in trade. Yet in our talk of "vocational training" for better work-efficiency, how seldom do we recall the basic fact that the manual worker of to-day must know not only how to do some one thing well, but also have power of adaptability to shift his effort to some other labor, should swift industrial changes

[2] See Johann F. Herbart, *The Science of Education.*
[4] See F. Froebel, *Education by Development.*
[5] See John Dewey, Ph.D., *Ethical Principles Underlying Education.*

take away or wholly transform the work he first
learned to do! Nor is the helplessness of a specialist
in the grasp of personal or social crises of change confined to the manual laborer; it is characteristic as well
of the commercial or scientific, the professional man
or artist who faces in mid-life or old age a need for
doing for self-support a new thing, or an old thing in
a new way. The man of to-day does not, indeed, like
the woman of to-day, face a vocational divide when he
marries and has children; but he would often be advan-
taged by some avocation to balance his intense vocational specialty; and he often stands in dire need of an
economic refuge from the tyranny of greed and custom
and the vicissitudes of industrial change. The education of every boy, therefore, ought to provide adequate
economic "first aid to the injured" in economic accidents; and the education of every girl ought to offer a
safe and easy bridge over the vocational divide between
the obligations of the spinster and of the house-mother
by making her more easily proficient in fulfilling both
functions. These fundamental occupations of the human race, which underlie all other labor and which can
alone give true independence in life-choices to the average man and woman, offer the only forms of manual
training suited to the demands of an education fibred
upon "learning by doing" adapted to children between
the kindergarten and the high school years. Such
forms of manual training as they offer alone present
to the childish imagination a glimpse of a "whole life."
Such forms of manual training alone hold the factory
and shop at decent distance from the little child, and

connect the public school with the private home instead of with the market place, with the out-of-doors instead of with the congested city. Such forms of manual training alone place in the foreground that all-round "faculty" of the alert and adaptable person who is equally at home on a "prairie schooner" and in a vast city, and equally master of fate in an ebb or a flood of fortune.

We have much ado now to keep the wheels of the factory from drowning the songs of the kindergarten and in preserving even the first years of childhood from the narrowing influence of "vocational differentiations" in the primary school. This, therefore, does not seem a good time to be trying a wholly new experiment in social advance by making both parents specialists all the time!

"We want not thinkers, but men thinking," says Emerson. Still more we want, not workers, but men and women working. A machine-dominated age of all others must make a stand in the home and in the school for the values of a free and broad approach to life, historically and rationally, as an indispensable preliminary to the specialized drill for the technique of some one element in machine-dominated labor.

Unless we are looking forward to an industrial despotism in which life itself will be wholly subordinate to the means of living, we may well ground the child in the activities that have served and may still serve the whole race, before we teach him how to "walk a tight rope" of infinitesimal specialization. Moreover, the labor war in which we are now plunged, a war whose bitterness grows more and more intense, will not be fully won in the interests of a wage-earning class whose futile weapons of resistance to intrenched wealth are but the hunger-driven "strike" or the desperate dynamiter. *More individual capacity in all the range of common life can,* in the long run, alone compel a juster sharing of the profits won by individual capacity. By the same token, the full and balanced freedom and power of women will never be attained by those among them who are dependent upon others for all manner of personal services, any more than by those among them whose purse is so held by another hand that their very souls are mortgaged. The vocational divide in the lives of modern women, therefore, epitomizes and makes dramatic the great struggle of spiritual democracy, the struggle to grow full and unique personality and at the same time to conserve social solidarity. Repetition on these points is justified by the confusion of mind above noted.

The second division of girls, namely, those who must receive vocational preparation for manual work in shop or factory, for clerical positions in office or counting-room or for assistant positions in such personal service as they may be able and willing to enter, and who must get this vocational training as early as possible in order to earn their living when still under eighteen years of age, is next in importance of numbers and need. The social propriety of giving this industrial education to girls is very nearly conceded even by conservatives in education. It is becoming clear that since girls are doing the work which young women have always done between the period of formal schooling and marriage, they must in the new industrial conditions learn how to do this useful work in the manner now demanded. The trade school for girls has entered the field of education and it has come to stay. It is not yet, however, adequately correlated with the rest of the schooling which girls receive, and there are sad duplications and sadder chasms in the education of which the trade school is but a part. Some time we shall be wise enough, both in the interest of boys and of girls, to work out a general plan of education which will fit for no one class condition exclusively or demand that one know in advance just what one wants to do in order to get the best of the school opportunity. Some time we shall be able better than now to determine what elements of education are so universal that all children must have them, what so specialized that only certain classes need them, and how to fit the specialized elements of training into the general scheme in order that the same person can profit by both equally. Meanwhile, as we stumble along, in a few experiment stations of the new education an industrial training is now given to girls which tends toward the general home usefulness outlined above, and which gives that tendency at the early period when it is most required. Where this is being attempted with any success it is already clearly seen that such process-activity is a valuable central interest around which to group arithmetic, language, the art-side of education, history, and ethical suggestions of self-control and social usefulness as well. Just in the same way agricul-

ture in its simple forms, and the care of domestic animals, have already proved master interests in the early
training of boys, around which to correlate all the
studies of the elementary school.

Meanwhile, also, the growing attention to trade-
teaching and vocational preparation of girls for self-
support has started currents in education which, when
not confused (as they so often are) by leaving until
too late a period the general process-activity which
leads toward domestic life, promise to make it vastly
easier for all girls to earn their living in better ways,
under better conditions, and for better pay, within a
generation of American life.

More and more, as we are working out a consistent
theory of education in general for boys and girls and
for youth of both sexes, a sure instinct is enriching the
curriculum of colleges and universities in which women
are students by the insertion of courses which are intended to fit them both for the position of woman-
head of a family of social leadership, and for those
professional careers which lie nearest the home life.
Books are being compiled to show how educated
women may fit themselves for other employments than
teaching, and the courses in household science and
economy are now made to cover a wide range of vocational training for many important professions. Perhaps the most important sign of the times in this direction is the recent action of the Association of Colle-
giate Alumnæ commending this enlargement of the college curriculum.

In regard both to the vocational training of girls

which must follow immediately upon graduation from the elementary school, and that which can be obtained through the high school and college, certain main points of guidance may be noted. If women as a sex are generally to be confronted with a vocational divide at marriage, then it stands to reason and common sense that they will choose, and their parents for them (where no special talent is indicated), such training as will serve best for both personal self-support and family usefulness: that is to say, the trades needing shortest preparation for wage-earning, and the professions most nearly allied to general culture, will be the most popular in the educational choices for girls. This is understood in the case of the girl who must begin wage-earning early in so far as it relates to preparation for factory and shop work in the occupations nearest in locality to her home and demanding least time for acquiring technique.

We have not yet reached the point where any well-considered plan is being wrought out in school experimentation for the training of *girls for specialties of wage-earning in activities required by the home-life itself.* If the domestic help problem is to be solved we must solve it along the lines so well and thoroughly outlined by Professor Salmon in her valuable studies; [6] that is to say, we must put the help within the family on as democratic a plane as service outside the family, and adopt, as far as the exigencies of family life allow, the "hour-system" and the "out-living" instead of the "in-living" of domestic helpers. If we are to

*Lucy P. Salmon, Ph.D., *Domestic Service.*

get for domestic service the same type of girl who
now enters the shop or factory, the counting-room or
office, we must make the conditions equally attractive
to the self-respecting girl who has had some education
in the public school. The belief that any system on
such a basis can regulate the family life as the factory
and shop may be regulated has been already disclaimed.
The woman-head of the family must be able and willing, in the overwhelming majority of cases, not only
to organize, but personally to do whatever work is
necessary for the well-being of her family. No
woman-head of a family of average means and condition can utilize an hour system or any form of domestic service which can be adjusted to the demands
of educated and self-respecting helpers, unless herself
both competent and ready to serve in similar ways.
The tendency of the world of organized industry is
to lessen the amount and variety of household work
by the outside preparation of foods, the mechanical
inventions for cleaning, etc., and the easy access to
supplies of all sorts. The burden of the house-mother
who does not and will not shirk her main responsibility is thus much eased. The need for some assistance
and in many cases for much assistance to the house-
mother during the years when her children are young
still remains and grows to a condition of acute suffering and mal-adjustment in country districts and in
manufacturing towns in which "hired help" is beyond the reach of most women in the years of married
life when they need it most. We have accepted too
supinely the alternative of no help or help all the time.

We have neglected to consider the middle course of partial help from younger girls which might be made both efficient and suitable for the worker, if we but added to our trade-teaching some specialties of child-care, house-care and sick-care, such as a healthy girl of sixteen to eighteen years could well do if only she knew how. For the average house-mother of small means but good intelligence and willingness to serve her family at first hand, two to four hours a day of competent help from those whose breeding made them fit companions for her children would be a greater assistance than a longer period from those whom she had to watch and direct at every moment. When the managers of modern trade schools for girls have been asked why they did not fit for family service, they have usually had in mind in their answers the ordinary "going out to service" which is the inherited form of domestic helping. What we need now is an extension of the general tendency toward home-usefulness which may be given in the elementary school along lines that are sufficiently differentiated for technical training, and which would fit the girl of fourteen to sixteen to do some one thing needed by the household well, and for pay, on terms as carefully outlined as those which underlie employment in the shop and factory. This extension of trade teaching, when tried in even the smallest experiment by Young Women's Christian Associations and like volunteer efforts in the educational field, has shown that it is not the work in the home that drives the "best girls" from it, but the lack of democratic organization of household labor and the lack of business management of the ordinary household. When we get along a little further, we shall see better how to add to the training for specialties of self-support in the shop and factory and counting-room such specialties of household aid as are most susceptible of this organization and business management. Then it will be quickly perceived how many girls, and their parents as well, choose these instead of specialties more remote from the home life.

Mrs. Richards, whose inestimable service to the women of the United States makes her recent death a public calamity, once said that "the old family life took the dining and sitting room into the kitchen; the new family life would take the kitchen into the dining room and the sitting room." [7] It was a fine way of stating a fact, more and more apparent, that mechanical invention and modern industry are so refining and easing the processes of household labor that the woman-head of the household can more and more dispense with kitchen paraphernalia of the inherited sort and do her work in the daintiest surroundings. When she can and does so manage her own supreme share of the household demand, she can begin to utilize to its utmost efficiency, the hour help of the well-bred and educated woman and girl who will then be ready and more than willing to aid her. This, of course, does not apply and will not for a long time, if ever, to the rich family of many servants, or to the needs of those women who should be emancipated from even the usual

---

[7] Ellen H. Richards, former editor *Journal of Household Economics,* Professor in Boston Institute of Technology.

burdens of the home life by reason of special talent and social usefulness which make it well worth while that society should release them from the general for the sake of the special usefulness.   This discussion is dealing with the average condition and the average need, not with the exceptions either of circumstance or of individual genius. The fundamental need in the reorganization of this average household is to democratize the home in all its relationships. The extension of the trade-teaching of girls along the lines indicated will prove a great help in hastening that reorganization. The extension of the college curriculum along the lines of domestic economy and the preparation for professional work in lines near the home life will be the great leading influence toward that extension of the trade-teaching of girls and the better organization of domestic labor. Already a pronounced and healthy guidance along this line is shown by college graduates and other cultured women of democratic tendencies and of high social ideals.

To this end, as well as to the ends of social progress in every direction, one study has contributed more than any other; and that a new study, and one especially capable of forming the more philosophic element in the preparation for life work given by the new courses for women in high school, college and university. Reference is here made, of course, to the new science of sociology.[8] Sociology is so new that it is still in its callow youth and denied the honors of the older and

---

[8] See Lester F. Ward, *Outlines of Sociology.*

more definitely outlined disciplines of the mind. Its very title of "science" is contested by many educational leaders. Yet at least sociology is a daring and masterful combination of accepted sciences; of biology, ethnology, psychology, history, economics and politics. As such it is offering its new explanation of many ancient riddles of life and its still newer gospel of social control in the interest of a purposive human progress. It not only boldly shows "why we are so," but why and how we should become something different, in social relationship. In its forms of theory it has proved most congenial to the feminine truth-seeker, and in its forms of practical suggestion still more the very bread of intellectual life to women desirous of doing their duty. Abstract philosophy has never been close to the feminine genius; that is why philosophers have been so prone to believe in the hopeless inferiority of women! For a human being to sit down and evolve a theory which he called "universal" and "ultimate" has always affected the sense of humor in women! It has seemed to brilliant and clever women a bit absurd for the finite to be so sure about infinite truth. Also the incurable practicality of women, which has often enough made them poor helpmeets for the idealism of men, has made them query "what's the use" when the philosopher painfully evolved some "camel" of theory from his inner consciousness, and never thought to test at first hand the real things of daily living. This has been at once an advantage and a disadvantage to woman: an advantage in keeping her mental tendency close to facts and useful work; and a disadvantage in depriving her of some of the delights of mental aviation. The new ways which sociology has inaugurated of making explanatory notes of the universe, the new ways of dealing with the age-long riddles of the existence of evil and the way of escape from it, which sociology offers, the new ways of going directly to the facts of environment for the reasons for social ills, and the still newer ways of demanding radical changes in environment for the benefit of the social whole, exactly suit the feminine mind, and are in direct line with the special sex-development of women. Naturally the new sociology is furnishing, along with other fresh explanations of life, the most complete solution of the old puzzle, What are women and what are they for? which any science or philosophy or guess of the human mind has yet offered. Naturally, also, although the fact is not yet clearly perceived in full significance, we find that those colleges and universities which develop "courses suited to the special needs of women" also offer the most advanced and varied courses in social economics. In many of these the attempt to suit educational opportunity to the new feminine ideal has definitely linked itself to the attempt to incorporate the new social philosophy and the new tendency to social service into the new education. This is true not only in the colleges and universities, but also in the secondary schools, where it is already a pressing question,—What elements of sociology may properly and usefully be taught in the high school, and where shall we insert them? In this connection let us note that training in household economics and home-making is now given in at least four kinds of educational institutions of grade above the elementary school, namely:

I.   As a department of high school instruction; often the extension of a course in manual training in the grades below, and in any case conceived and treated for the most part as general preparation for life, but having an increasingly distinct bearing upon vocational choice and business training.

II.   As a department of normal schools; chiefly as a means of preparing manual training teachers for the grade schools, the courses being technical and practical and attempting to deal only with such processes as children can understand and practise.

III.   As a department in colleges and universities attended by women and with the double purposes, seldom differentiated in the consciousness of the teaching body itself: one to fit undergraduates for the home, and the other to aid toward vocational usefulness and success.   As has been shown, increase in these courses is called for by three classes, those that demand enlargement of the inherited curriculum of men's higher education for purposes of general feminine culture; those that desire a more varied training of women for self-support in professional fields; and those who see the need for better training of women for philanthropic service.

IV.   As a specialty in a separate technical school, like Pratt Institute, for example; [9] or as a distinctly defined technical department in a university, like the School of Industrial Arts of Teachers College, Co-

[9] Brooklyn, N. Y.

lumbia University;[10] or like similar departments in many of the State universities; or as a special department in a post-graduate training school like that of Stout Institute in Wisconsin.[11] The purpose of such schools and departments is distinctly to give high-grade preparation for professional work in teaching, in philanthropy, in social leadership, along all lines of child-care, sanitary housing, preparation of nourishing food on a large scale or teaching how it should be prepared, more healthful and artistic dress, and the instruction of the poor and ignorant. If these technical schools help to standardize the private home, and they surely do, it is mainly by and through the professional leadership they train and help to secure in paid positions, rather than by the individual teaching of the house-mother.

In the technical schools of household science, however, we have a sharp division of pedagogic need and direction; for in some of these schools we find large classes of very young girls, many of them not having received any high school instruction, who are seeking trade-teaching in dressmaking, millinery or similar kinds of work; or else those just learning how to help at home in a small family of restricted means. The teaching body of such schools need to be masters of that triangle of knowledge required for vocational guidance of young girls going into manual labor; namely, general information concerning work-opportunities for girls in the locality, special knowledge of

[10] New York.
[11] Menomonie, Wisconsin.

the capacities of their students, and some idea of the social condition of the families from which they come. All this requires some measure of applied sociology in the teachers as that is sharpened to economic conditions and possibilities; but does not constitute, of course, any part of the study of the girls themselves.

On the other hand, those technical schools and college departments of household science that minister to the needs of more mature students, of women who are in training for higher-paid and more responsible positions,—professional, commercial, mechanical, philanthropic,—should offer to their students thorough courses in sociology. Theory of social development, social psychology, social ethics, social uplift, and the history of social institutions lead toward intelligent mastery of social problems and are a guide to practical service. If such a high-grade technical school is attached to a university it can now easily secure the needed instruction along these lines; if it is an independent school it must provide its own instructors in the science of human development and the art of conscious and purposive human progress. Psychology, personal and social; physical development on a well-defined biologic foundation; the history and meaning of social institutions; the social aspects of education as a "process in the spiritual evolution of the race";—these are essential studies for all men and women. The evolution of the family and its vital place in the socialization of the individual; the racial, political and economic factors in civilization; the control and abolition of social ills, such as crime, vice, disease, poverty; the community ideal in general, and in particular as related to one's own locality; the essential next steps in social progress and how to attain them; these are vital necessities of study, especially for women of light and leading, whether in vocational positions or at the head of private homes of social influence. It seems clear that educational institutions and departments of colleges dealing with the mechanism and the economics of the home life might well lead in emphasizing these social values of the home life and of the society of which the home is the centre. It should be added, and pressed home to the consciousness of men at the head of institutions in which sociology is made a strong study and in which many women take its courses whether or not in connection with household science and art, that the *ethical content of applied sociology must be clearly and inspiringly presented,* if these courses are to make to the women students the strongest and most effective appeal. Not only is it true that the genius of women is practical, and the organic function of women is teaching, but the drill in motherhood's devotion to family life has given women an unconquerable tendency toward personalization. This may be overborne temporarily, or seemingly submerged under the sweep of influences that are pushing us toward impersonal environmental changes; but after women are accustomed to equal opportunities in education and in work they will right the balance again; and now they need always the appeal to the individual conscience and the claim of the individual need upon the social organism to make sociology vital to them. The law of

human development must be translated for ardent and
sensitive youth of both sexes in terms of social service
and social uplift if it is to move the inner sources of
mental and moral power. In the case of the average
young woman it must also be translated in terms of
personal care and help for the exposed and abused
child, for the neglected aged, for the oppressed weak,
for the defective and incompetent needing protection,
for the heroic struggler on the labor field defeated for
want of social justice. This translation of applied sociology in terms of enlightened philanthropy and moral
reform is what the average young woman needs, and
many young men would profit by, as well.

The normal schools are the weak point in our educational system, and here we come upon a waste place
which the right kind of sociological study might make
to blossom as the rose. The social aspects of education, the relation of the modern school to the family,
the State, the industrial and the social order,—this is
a study which would vitalize the present preparation of
teachers for the elementary school. The fact that
the common school in the United States is the real
"melting pot of nations," and that the school is in
closest touch of any of our social institutions, with the
bewildering variety of ethical ideals emphasized by
the home and church influence, makes the school the
one place in which a possible minimum of ethical agreement to guide the common social life might be developed. The greatest of social needs in our country is
some common denominator in personal and social morality which can bring the community together in one

common aim in matters most imperative as to individual conduct and as to social well-being. Herbart declares our chief need in education to be "character training, based on an irrefragable foundation of morality." Where shall be found that irrefragable foundation, one which can be accepted as such by all religionists and all non-religionists, save in the testimony of human experience deduced by searching and fearless inquiry into the social results of motives and of acts as these are interpreted by the trained reason? Only an irrefragable foundation of morality of this sort can develop a national morality, united and strong enough to control vagrant and unsocial impulse, to dominate education and to give method to social action. If it is true that we need this minimum of commonly accepted ethical standard, and must depend for it chiefly upon the school as that affects character from the kindergarten to the college, then we must grow teachers of the elementary schools (in which alone the vast majority of children get their school influence) capable of the high exercise of mind this inquiry into the verdict of the nature of things and the course of human development demands. How can we do this unless we have not only courses in sociology, pure and applied, in the normal schools, but also an atmosphere of valiant truth-seeking and scientific veracity equal to that which any college or university can boast? This is a matter near to the feminine ideal and its representation in the school, from the fact that the overwhelming majority of teachers of the elementary schools are women.

No problem in public education pleads more eloquently for solution, however, than that of the social and moral instruction of the high school. Since but a small fraction of young people go to college, and since attendance at day and evening high schools is becoming an increasing custom among children even of the poor and since the reaction of the school upon the home often reaches its strategic point when the boy and the girl at the period of growth in which their sense of personal choice becomes keen take from the high school to the home the standards they have gained from the teacher, this question is of deepest importance. The college man or woman, moreover, if profiting by the opportunity given to gain command over culture-tools, can easily make good deficiencies in the college course as these are revealed by ripened experience; while the boy or girl who learns so little of so many things in high school is likely to fail in knowledge of ways of supplementing school instruction.

If then sociology, or a knowledge of the laws of human society, needs to become a part of high school training, how may it be accomplished? Not surely by text-book instruction in pure sociology! To see youth struggling under abstract statements of social laws and conditions, or confused by much descriptive treatment of the remote and strange in human existence, is a sorry sight. Civics and philanthropy, however, based upon right understanding of group relationship and political and social structure, the social institutions, especially the family and the school, and the State which gives us our sense of human solidarity, —these are vital and inspiring to youth. Vocational ethics in choice and standards of work, including such study of economic history and its social interrelations as may throw light on personal problems, or lead to large views of human industry and achievement, these are vital themes for the young. The sociological basis for self-culture, mental, physical, moral, the cosmic reasons for making the most and best of oneself as a part of the social whole, all that constitutes what Dr. Ward calls the "ethics of applied sociology," this is a much needed appeal for modern youth. The young question all things with an imperious, What have you for me? It seems clear then that in a time when ethics is becoming socialized, certain universal standards of choice and of action in the conduct of life must be gained by them, if at all, along broad lines of social necessity. Hence if sociology has any moral guidance in an hour of radical change of thought and of life, by all means saturate the teaching influence with it in order that the young may profit by the new way of outlining human duty. And still more, if sociology has any special guidance for womanhood in an hour of profound change in outward circumstance, any fresh sanctions for established codes of morals in marriage, any new readings of social responsibility for the home in a time when the old admonitions and restraints fail to command, in the name of social health and social progress send all the women and girls to school to the new science! And if they will take it more eagerly, as seems to be the case, when mixed with special ingredients called "household economics" or "domestic art," by all means let us make the combination.

Perhaps of all the new educational opportunities open to women the establishment of training schools for social service, schools for fitting men and women for ameliorative and constructive work in philanthropy and civics, has proved the most satisfying and help-ful.[12] Women have been accustomed throughout all the past to bearing in a peculiar degree the social burden of the weak, the undeveloped, the incompetent and the infirm. These new schools show them how to help bear these burdens, not only in ways more humane for the individual, but also more wise for the social whole. There are men in these schools of civics and philanthropy, it is true; a few, gained by dint of much earnest work on the part of the Directors; but the over-whelming majority of students are women, and doubt-less the disproportion will be slightly, if any, decreased in the days to come. Some specialties of legal and political aspects of the social movement, some leader-ship of the labor struggle, some few large administra-tive offices, some institutional superintendencies, will call for and will hold men; but the great task of taking care of the socially backward, and the ever-changing but never-ending ministration to individuals which every form of social helpfulness yet devised has in-cluded within its programme, will in the future, as in the past and in the present, send ten women to every one man as students to these schools. The sort of in-

[12] Pioneer "School of Philanthropy" opened in New York City un-der the auspices of the Charity Organization Society in 1898.

struction given in these new technical schools is precisely along the lines of the socialization of the family life and of the feminine ideal for which the times most loudly call. Hence their significance is not alone for the social movement as a whole, but also for the specific development of women in the larger and more complete citizenship to which they are called.

Back of all these changes and developments of the educational ideal and practice as applied to women lies the stupendous fact that humanity, at least in its centres of enlightenment, has come to realize the worth and value of human nature as a whole. Not yet is it clearly seen that women, as women, have still to make a distinctive contribution to the human commonwealth on the intellectual as well as on the moral side; but it is already becoming apparent that those human qualities which men and women have in common should not be wasted, ignored or misused because embodied in a woman's form. The ways in which the school must be modified, now that all boys, instead of a few selected boys, attend it, take long to tell and longer to work out. The changes in the school which will follow the further admission of all girls, with all boys, require profound study and detailed description. But the master fact that has opened the door of kindergarten, primary school, high school and college to girls and women can be told in a sentence: Humanity has at last conferred on women the franchise of the mind. Henceforth not the "affection of good" alone is the ideal of womanly excellence; the "understanding of truth" is also her high privilege and her conscious duty.

"He for God only, she for God in him," can no longer represent the relationship of man and woman to each other and to the universe. As at the beginning of the Christian era came a call to women to own and save their own souls, not as members of a particular family, but as individuals, who must singly and alone "appear at the judgment seat"; so at the beginning of the twentieth century women are called upon to "make up their own minds" on all the vast and terrible issues of life, and to see to it that they have the mental equipment necessary to that difficult process. For this end the school has at last opened its doors to women,—in order that every atom of the social whole shall feel the currents of the mind, as well as the pulses of the heart, of creation, moving them all alike in response to "whatsoever forces draw the ages on."

VIII

THE SOCIAL USE OF THE POST-GRADUATE MOTHER

OF all the dark pages of human history, none is quite so black as that which records the treatment of "witches." A few of these victims of superstition were men, but the great majority were women; so that the very word witch has come to have a feminine suggestion. As Lecky truly says: "It is probable that no class of victims endured suffering so unalloyed and so intense" as that of those condemned to torture and to death as sorcerers and sorceresses. The martyrs for religious belief died rejoicing in the faith of a compensating and eternal heaven. The victims of popular ignorance, who suffered because freer in thought and more intelligent in action than their contemporaries, were sustained by the dignity of conscious rectitude and a superior perception of truth. The sufferers from political oppression, and from racial prejudice and the cruelty it has engendered, have generally possessed some relief in the loyalty of comrades and in the affections of family life. But witches were usually persuaded by the terrible ordeals to which they were subjected that they deserved their fate. The disordered condition of the public mind reacted upon their own consciousness to make them feel accursed of God and bound slaves to Satan, and horribly sure that they must go from the tortures of court and of church on earth to the everlasting torment of hell.

Why were middle-aged and old women, with a few young maidens, singled out as the special victims of that terrible mania of superstition which for fifteen hundred years lighted lurid flames of burning humanity on innumerable hilltops and inspired a malignity and ingenuity of torture unmatched in the whole realm of cruelty? There were two reasons. One, and the chief reason, was that hatred of women which asceticism developed. When Cato declared that "if the world were only free from women, men would not be without converse of gods," he but expressed the general if rather good-natured contempt for women which the masculine classic civilization engendered. But when the early Fathers of the Christian Church denounced women as active centres of evil influence, they added hatred to contempt, and fear to indifference, and hence placed themselves in the realm of maniacal delusion respecting women. In Chrysostom's famous saying, "Women are a necessary evil, a natural temptation, a desirable calamity, a domestic peril, a deadly fascination and a painted ill," he softened by oratorical phrase that horror of women felt by the ascetic monk. To that unclean and morbid creature, who inflicted torments upon himself in a nightmare of inverted morality, "woman was the door of hell" and the "source of human ills." To that ascetic monk who believed that to be most miserable was to be most holy, all the charm and joy of womanhood was a delusion and a snare. So far did this hatred of woman extend that in the sixth century at least one provincial Council of the Church forbade women to receive the Eucharist into their naked hands on account of their impurity! By reason of this strange perversion of religious doctrine the beneficent ideal of woman's spiritual freedom, as attested by the early Christian Church, was later on almost nullified. Woman escaped from the bondage of ethnic faiths, by which her heirship to spiritual responsibility and spiritual advantage was made to depend upon her family relationship, when Christianity made Jew and Gentile, patrician and plebeian, master and slave, man and woman, alike equal at the Altar of the Church. This Magna Charta of spiritual liberty which gave woman a soul of her own promised a new freedom and privilege all around the circle of human rights and powers. But when asceticism began to dominate the ideals of holiness, woman again passed under the yoke of bondage and became subject to a new and more terrible form of restraint. It was this feeling against womanhood in general, only softened by the attitude of the Christian Church toward the women who served its own interests outside the family life in Religious Houses, that made possible the torture and execution of so many helpless old women during the dark and middle ages. Feeble, often seriously diseased, generally past the time when they could demonstrate their usefulness to the common sense, these old women were peculiarly susceptible to the suggestion of hysteria and morbid fear which marked the witchcraft delusion. We read that over seven thousand victims

were burned at Trèves; and that a single bishop of
Germany, in a single year, ordered the execution of
more than eight hundred poor creatures. In France in
one execution four hundred witches suffered death; and
in Italy a thousand were thus murdered judicially in
one province. The Reformation did not end this
form of persecution; in many cases it increased its violence. In Geneva five hundred victims perished during
three months; and Luther declared he would "have no
compassion upon these witches, he would burn them
all." In Scotland, mystical and theology-mad, the per-
secutions were peculiarly atrocious; and it is common
knowledge how the superstition crossed the seas and
gave the shame of Protestantism to New England.
Even the reformer Wesley believed both in witchcraft
and in its severe punishment by the saints of the Church
declaring that "the giving up of witchcraft is in effect
the giving up of the Bible." Not until the first quarter of the eighteenth century did the rational sense of
mankind do away with this monstrous inhumanity. So
great and wise a man as Sir Matthew Hale hung two
witches in 1664, and the last execution in England oc-
curred in 1712, thus linking bigotry to the age of
reason.[1]

The belief in magic, however, dates far back of
Christianity and belongs to an almost universal tendency of the human mind to ascribe to supernatural
causes both personal and social calamities. In this
tendency to supernaturalism women have had their
share not only as believers, but as active agents of

[1] See W. E. H. Lecky, *History of Rationalism.*

supernal powers.   Among undeveloped peoples, although there may be no women priests, there are women prophetesses, and sorceresses divide fearful honors with sorcerers.   The proportion of witches to wizards is indeed far more equal in primitive life than is the balance between the sexes in the later period of witchcraft.   As Otis T. Mason well says, in ancient times [2] "women were thought to be more persuasive, acute and dangerous than men for lobby work between worlds."   Hence, in the early days, witches were spoken fair and honorably entreated to use their powers for the benefit of mankind.   Dr. Mason adds: "Women hear better, see better, are better talkers than men, and can therefore become successful conjurers of fate."   Inasmuch also as "they cook better," or more frequently, than men, their witch's cauldron may contain, beside "toil and trouble," some special concoction for the aid of faithful friends.   The Zuni Indian sings:

> "The Sun is the father of all,
> The Earth is the mother of men,
> The Water is their grandfather,
> The Fire is their grandmother."

And the picturesque personalizing of nature by the child-mind of the race gave to women a place among the gods equal to that of men.   Hestia, the sister of Zeus, was the special protector of the domestic hearth and worshipped with most sacred rites.   The Roman Venus, the Greek Aphrodite, the Phœnician Astarte,

[2] Otis T. Mason, *Woman's Share in Primitive Culture,* chapter *The Patron of Religion.*

the Assyrian Istar, the Egyptian Hathor, all celebrate the power of romantic love that binds the sexes together and slays antagonism between them. The Demeter and Athena myths all lead to a reverence for womanhood as embodied in the fruitfulness of the earth and in the peaceful order of social life. The great Egyptian goddess Neith, the Weaver, whose hieroglyph is the shuttle, passes down even to our own civilization the recognition of woman's value in the industrial arts. The Chinese female Buddha, Kwan-yin, the Mother-goddess, may be responsible even at this late day for some of the new freedom and power of her sex in that suddenly awakened land. Everywhere in mythology, and in the story of human life before formal history began, we find traces of a reverent appreciation of the woman-spirit as symbolized by goddesses. The classic Fates make women preside over destiny; the spinner of the thread of life, the mysterious power that determines its length, and the dread agent of its ending by death, are all portrayed as the genius of womanhood. The energy of women and their constant usefulness were fitly symbolized by the activity of the women-worshippers who in the Temple of Athena spent nine months of incessant labor in weaving the peplos which was carried in the sacred procession and was the annual gift to the goddess.

In all these hints of the past the woman-spirit is honored; and although "hags" and evil-working old women are not wanting, the general tendency of primitive and of classic faith and worship was respectful if not reverent toward elderly women. The ancients believed in magic powers intensely and universally, but not that such magic powers always or usually denoted evil spirits. Christianity, when it entered upon its mania of asceticism, turned all the spirits of the air, even to the lovely fairies and the helpful "Brownies," into emissaries of Satan, the arch-king of evil. Minerva, the air goddess, symbol of light and wisdom, became transformed with all her kin into witch-creatures who spent unholy Sabbaths in secret converse with the Devil and came back riding their broomsticks through the air to seduce and ruin mankind. In this connection it must be remembered that the natural tendencies of the woman-nature are wholly against asceticism. The nearness of the mother to child-life forbids the average woman from really believing, whatever the theologians may make her say in church, that this world was meant to be a "living tomb" or a "chamber of death and misery." Children bring with them an ever-renewed and ever-renewing sense of the gladness of life, and not all the morbid priests or abnormal theologies have ever been able to persuade women in general that the laugh of a child is a lie! Nature, indeed, having in view the perpetual adjustment of adult life to the child's demand for freedom and for joy, has, as Havelock Ellis finely says, "done her best to make women healthy and glad." The false view of life and duty which asceticism held and realized made this natural union of the woman-nature with the child's charm and gladness seem a wicked thing. Nothing but such a hatred of womanhood and such a fear of her as the embodiment of the natural attractions upon which the home is builded could have made possible the tragedy of the witchcraft delusions and its untold miseries.

The second reason why, as a rule, women were the special victims of this witchcraft horror is the fact that women, while suffering less than men from serious and fatal disorders of the brain and nervous system, are peculiarly susceptible to slighter disturbances which produce irritability, abnormal excitements and diseased manifestations of energy. This tendency is being corrected in rapidly increasing ratio by the better physical training of girls, by the wider intellectual interests of women, and, above all, by the new opportunities for congenial work in later life which are now the common privilege of the sex. In the earlier days, however, when witches paid the penalty of superstition through the tyranny of false doctrine, the lot of the majority of women was extremely hard. There was no limit to woman's child-bearing except nature's failure to add another to her cares; there was no limit to her household drudgery except nature's failure to give her strength to rise again to her daily task. She was socially denied, except in the case of a few "ladies" at the top of life's opportunity, any share in the intellectual stimulus that is so therapeutic, and she had no ability to secure those pleasant diversions that balance work for the benefit of the nervous energy. After thirty to fifty years of overwork, under most adverse conditions for the preservation of health and strength, the wife and mother could be left to an idleness most harmful; or else be pressed still to a form of hard labor least satisfying to personal desires. It is not strange that the prevalence of nerve troubles of various sorts among old women thus mistreated has made them pass down in art and history as "uncanny," and also made them, during the nightmare of the witchcraft delusion, seem the natural prey of Satan as he sought "whom he might devour." Men and women alike age prematurely under the hard conditions of primitive life; but old women have been thought to be either wholly useless or else made to work in narrow lines of activity, while old men have been more often favored as still "good for counsel." This hard lot of the old woman was modified in the patriarchal family by making the oldest mother a sort of sub-despot, a deputy ruler over all the younger women and girls. This has helped her in dignity of position, and in stimulus to effort, to conserve her powers in old age; but, lacking education and true moral discipline, the mother-rulers of more primitive forms of family life have often perpetuated the most archaic and socially harmful usages of domestic order. This personal alleviation has therefore not been a social gain.

Of all the wastes of human ignorance perhaps the most extravagant and costly to human growth has been the waste of the distinctive powers of womanhood after the child-bearing age. The absurd mistake of supposing that a woman's usefulness was ended when her last baby grew out of need for her personal ministrations was natural so long as women were held subject and inferior, and denied all mental training;

but its lingering remnants in the modern mind are grotesque. Only recently a political orator, wishing to characterize his opponents in the most contemptuous of terms, said "they were a set of old women." This phrase as an expression of utter futility and weakness has come down from times in which women's strength of mind and body was so shockingly exploited that in old age they were very often diseased and abnormal, helpless, and a family burden. From this fact, due not to natural limitations, but to social conditions resulting from the misuse of womanhood from childhood to old age, has arisen the false conception of women as semi-invalids in the earlier part of life and incapable of any efficient labor of mind or body in the later years. Nothing could be further from the truth as now revealed and demonstrated by scientific study. In point of fact we now know that so far from men being the favorites of nature as to health, strength and longevity, and women (like stepchildren) a denied class, the contrary is more nearly true.[3] It is women, as mothers and potential mothers of the race, whose life and health the cosmic forces most concern themselves with, and longest sustain in activity. Inquiries into facts are now taking the place of theories, whether of poets or theologians, and facts prove women capable of more than holding their own in the balance of sex-relationship and in the work of the world. Facts show that more male than female children are still-born, and that more male infants succumb to disease before the third year. Facts show that more

[3] See Havelock Ellis, *Man and Woman*, Chap. XVII.

boys than girls are abnormal or deficient in mind or
special sense, and that more boys than girls suffer
premature death from many of the ills that flesh is
heir to. Facts show, above all, that more women than
men live to a ripe old age, and not only thus survive,
but have a good chance for health and strength. It
is declared by experts that mental derangements are
more common in old men than in old women, Dr.
Wille setting the ratio at ten per cent. males to six
per cent. females. The specific gravity of the blood,
as Lloyd Jones has shown, is found higher in old
women than in old men; and there is far greater constitutional youthfulness among old women than among
old men, which is in itself a sign of greater vitality and
later conservation of work-power. The liability to
death is about the same in the two sexes between the
third and thirtieth years, and there is a special danger-
period for girls between the fourteenth and twentieth
years; but when we get above thirty-five the chances
are better for both life and health for women than
for men. This is not alone a peculiarity of civilization, for we are told by those who have especially
studied the matter that among some savage tribes
fully two-thirds of those surviving the sixtieth year
are women. It is true, however, that the conditions
of civilized life, especially those easier domestic conditions we now have as the result of inventions of all
sorts, are especially favorable to longevity in women.
Dr. Langstaff says: "It is quite plain that the recent
fall in the death rate favors the accumulation of surplus women." The result of all the recent studies of

sex-differences and sex-conditions leads to the conclusion that under most of the conditions of social life, in
a wide range of varied forms of human society, we
have proof of the "greater physical frailty of men and
the greater tenacity of life in women." As Dr. Campbell says: "Women possess a greater innate recuperative power than men," and, although more often
slightly ill, make easier recovery. The facts make the
phrase "the weaker sex" as applied to women a little
misleading.

Men, it is true, are able to summon for emergency,
or crisis-effort, far more muscular power than women.
They have a steadier nerve, and a greater capacity for
putting all the strength and vigor they possess into a
short term of effort for a distinct end. This gives
them efficiency of the highest sort in the regulated industries of the world. This makes men far better able
than women to keep pace with the modern machines, to
hold their even share of the burden of business demands, and to fill the larger and more exacting offices
of the world in public affairs. Moreover, men have,
through all their earlier years, "a straight line" of
progressive power up to the period of the slowing down
of age; while women have for years "a curved and
variable line" that requires consideration each month
at its weakest point. Men can go from strength to
strength steadily until they have reached their merid-
ian of power without a break. Women have periodicities that often hinder regular advance. Men also
are relieved from the physical cost of parenthood. A
man who is married and has children has, indeed,

"given hostages to fortune" and must work the harder and serve the more unselfishly. But women, in addition to the economic burdens which parenthood imposes, must also contribute a measure of physical force, a determination of bodily strength both in child-bearing and child-rearing, which means often a heavy price paid for social serviceableness. A childless woman once said to a mother whose splendid family of five children were all that any parent could desire, "How I envy you! I would give twenty years of my life to have such a family as that." "Well," answered the mother, "they cost about that." All that is implied in the curves and periodicities of women's lives makes them more dependent upon men during the early period of life than men are upon women, and gives a sound biological reason for the social demand for "chivalry," and for the saving in all possible ways of women's strength and health while they are about the social business of motherhood. This it is which makes the father in duty bound to carry the heavier economic load all through the child-bearing and child-rearing period. This it is which made our Saxon forefathers in an ancient statute give "a married woman, with child, free range of the forest for wood-gathering," and a generous "share of the harvest." This it is which has made all progressive and successful civilizations guard both the young mother and the potential mother from excessive labor; guard such both by the personal devotion of their men relatives and by the social consideration of laws and customs.

When, however, the climacteric of middle life is

reached, nature gives a new deal and starts a fresh balance of power between men and women. When the child-bearing age is passed woman's line of life becomes as "straight" as man's, and the "curves" that have required consideration at their weakest point are no longer a part of her experience. Moreover, at the point when the change comes in women's physical condition, there may be, and now increasingly is, a fresh start given to the mental and emotional life. It cannot be too soon realized that in the lives of women there is capacity for a *second youth*. A second youth, that holds in reserve full compensation for any expenditure that a reasonable motherhood may have demanded. A second youth, when new thoughts blossom, when wishes and tendencies of personal development may flower into realization, when all that has gone into the sacrificial service to family life may add a peculiar flavor and a special wisdom to personal achievement or to enlarged social service. This is the meaning of the "Women's Club Movement" and of the many forms of associated action by which mature womanhood, now that it is at last educated and free, takes up its own self-culture and its own chosen activities for the common good. Asked once to describe the Women's Club Movement one answered, "Women's Clubs are the great non-academic university-extension movement of the nineteenth century for women in their second youth." A wit hearing the answer asked if a "second childhood for women preceded their second youth?" Not a bad hit, and not simply a jest; for, if an undisciplined woman, bound to make a fool of herself, does not accomplish that unhappy distinction before she is twenty-five, she will surely do it between forty-five and sixty to astonish her friends by her extravagancies of behavior.   The trained and disciplined woman, however, is eager for work and for large enterprises at this period of life as never before. She seeks activity of whatever sort as native to her own desire, and if she is not sufficiently well educated or sufficiently in touch with the things best worth doing, in the lines most congenial to her natural capacity, she is likely to rush about from one to another busyness of interest, without plan or effectiveness and to a distraction of energy. To many women, also, whom life has used hardly in circumstance or relationship, there may come a childish restlessness before they can "settle down" to the true rejuvenescence of thought, of feeling and of power which is theirs by right. The old theories of women took no account of this rich and large possibility of later life. If the fact that more women than men lived to old age, and that more women than men seemed to relish life and want to engage in activities of moment after they were old, was at all perceived, it was laid to the natural perversity of women that they thus hung on to life when no longer desired and put themselves in the way when they could no longer do that for which they were made! As Professor Sheavyn well says: "The disadvantages of being a woman have been better understood than the advantages." [4] Now, for the first time, we are learn-

---

[4] Phœbe Sheavyn, Ph.D., *Professional Women* in *The Position of Woman.*

ing how great are those advantages; or may be if the woman's life is lived sanely and wisely; advantages physical, psychical, and vocational, personal and social.

Nature has indeed conveyed to us in no uncertain manner her determination that her gifts shall be shared with an absolute justice between her men-children and her women-children. The boy has his long, straight path of progress, passing on into youth, and later manhood, up to the point where senile decay threatens; which point clean living, noble purpose, intellectual activity and wise physical, mental and moral hygiene of every sort may push far into the seventies or eighties, or even beyond, if the prophets of a longer term of life for mankind may be believed. This long straight pathway gives man his preëminence as a special worker and vocational expert. The girl, on the other hand, has her better start in constitutional vigor and her surer normality and balance of faculties; and the woman, throughout early and later experience, possesses her stronger recuperative power, her greater capacity for constant labor if free from excessive strain and varied in sort; and her curving line of muscular and nervous power, while giving more variability and less dependable response to highly organized labor, insures her a finer and more flexible adjustment to the general demands of the social order. If she marries and has children she has her longer "curve" of recurrent need for special consideration, protection and care. At last she emerges from the variability which is the price of her special sex-contribution to the social fabric, and becomes in a peculiar and a new sense a citizen of the world; a *Person,* whose own relationship to the social whole may now of right become her main concern. The audiences composed of professional workers and members of reformatory organizations and leaders in philanthropy are often a striking testimony to the as yet half-conscious response of women to this call of their second youth. The faces of women of sixty years and over, lined with marks of many emotions and much lore of life-experience, are alight with an enthusiasm and a hope, a strong and vital interest in life and its meaning, which loses nothing in attractiveness when matched against the groups of college girls as they leave their Alma Mater. Indeed the mothers are often younger at the moment than their daughters just graduating, because love has taught them as well as books, and contact with child-nature has kept them hopeful as well as made them wise, while the student, still in the period of acquisition, is always in danger of mistaking words for life, theories for realities. Moreover, women who have had a true marriage and a welcome discipline of family service have had what no young women, and few if any unmarried women possess, the constant help of the masculine way of looking at things to balance and keep sane their distinctly feminine approach to life. They are therefore able, if they have used well their opportunities, to understand men and women alike and to work for and with both impartially. This is a point of far more social importance than is at present recognized. If there are any dangers of "feminization" threatening us in the school or in society at large, any real overplus of specially "womanly influence" in our present civilization, those dangers inhere in the large celibate majority of intellectual leaders and representatives of womanhood in the field of expert knowledge and work. There is a "finicky," over-precise, ultra-refined morality and idealism which women develop by themselves, and which is difficult to adjust to the larger, looser, simpler, but often more vital ethics and aspiration of men. The rounded wisdom and experience of the post-graduate mother (who usually has to practise her motherhood on her husband as well as her sons and thus learns tolerance and breadth of view) will come to be prized at its full social value, therefore, when more women qualify for its highest potency and the world learns at last what "old women" are for, and what social end they may serve. Then it will be at last understood why nature preserves so carefully both the life and the health of women; why she gives them a new strength of body, a new youthfulness of purpose, a new capacity for spiritual adventure, so far in excess of men, when the time comes that their whole life may rightfully become their own in a more complete sense than ever before.

It is said of the high-caste Brahmin that he has three stages in life, three grand divisions of duty and of experience. First he must be a learner, devoted to acquiring the knowledge that a leader of men should possess; next he must be a father and householder, paying loyally his debt to society by rearing offspring who may connect his ancestors with his descendants in worship and family continuity; last he may become a pilgrim, a solitary seeker for truth, enjoying at will the high communion of those who live but for spiritual ends of being. The modern woman has now outlined before her, faintly as yet but growing in clearness, her own "three-fold path of life." First, the learner and the doer fitting for self-support and self-direction; next, the devoted servant of life's most intimate demands upon human beings of the mother sex; last, a conscious sharer, in a new and more inspiring sense, in the larger life of the race.

There can be no general clearness of vision as to this three-fold path of womanhood, however, until more educated and competent women prepare for their last and splendid opportunity of service by a better use of the leisure hours of that period of life which is given especially to family interests. The vulgar phrase, "She does not need accomplishments now, her market is made," only emphasizes the too frequent undercurrent of women's attitude toward personal achievement. If one must earn a living outside the home, ambition now makes most women seek to do it in the best way they can and to the highest results of financial and social return. But the average married woman, with or without children, is too prone to look upon her life as ceasing to afford or to need new or continued modes of self-expression. There is an almost fatal tendency among young married women of average education and circumstances to give up wholly the vocational interest which was theirs before marriage. "No, I don't play now, I gave up practising

after John was born." "No, I don't paint now, the
house takes so much time and Mary is a great care."
"I never think of reading a book now, the magazines
are all I can manage with the house, and no maid."
"I can't work at my trade or my clerical work now, of
course, for I can't be gone from the house all day."
How often these and similar expressions are heard!
It is true, of course, that competitive industry being
arranged for all-day service most married women are
unable to engage profitably or properly in the work
they did before marriage. But there are few women
who cannot keep at least a selective and constant interest, and some small practice to "keep the hand in,"
that will stand them in stead if there should be need
of earning in case of widowhood or financial calamity,
or when larger leisure from the upgrowing of the
children makes it well for them to have some special
interest of their own. Moreover the period of life
when a woman has the largest end of her activity fastened to the family need, and her economic position,
therefore, properly secured by her husband's work for
the family, is precisely the period when she may use
her leisure, be it much or little, in preparation for some
kind of work she wants to do but was not trained for
as a girl. How many men find themselves in positions
where they are kept doing what they would so gladly
exchange for another sort of labor no one was wise
enough to fit them for in youth! The tragedies of
misfit industry, the heroisms of men who stick at a
hated task because it is all they know how to do and
they dare not leave it for the sake of wife and bairns,

—these are material for great dramas. How rich an opportunity many women waste, an opportunity to prepare in a leisurely way, through years of security of home protection and care, by use of the bits of leisure almost every day affords, for the work nature intended they should do. Women have but just begun to see and use the advantages of their three-fold path of life and only those most clear-sighted and brave can as yet do so.

One thing stands in the way of women's realization and appropriation of these advantages, and that is the aristocratic attitude of both men and women toward "paid work" for women. So long as it is thought unfitting for a married woman to earn money inside or outside the home, so long as it popularly discredits a man if his wife thus earns as a result of her own labor outside domestic work, we shall have a majority of women unwilling and unable to use to best advantage the leisure hours of their earlier married life and hence unable to use most effectively their third stage of opportunity. Enough has been said in this discussion to show that it is intended to strengthen rather than to weaken the demands of family life and child-care upon women. It remains to insist that until women themselves outgrow, and teach their "men-folks" to outgrow, the notion that it is honorable for men to earn money in useful labor but dishonorable or a dire misfortune for women to do so, the right personal and social use of women's lives cannot be accomplished. It is now considered right and highly proper for a woman to earn money if unmarried and her "father can't take care of her," or if a widow whose "husband did not leave enough to support her," or a wife whose husband is disabled, ill or incompetent. It must become natural and common in the public eye for any woman to earn money who wants to and can. At present we have advanced little beyond the period when the "wife of Thomas Hawkins" was granted by the selectmen of her town, in the seventeenth century, the "right to sell liquors by retayle, considering the necessitie and weak condition of her husband"; and when widows were "approved" by the church trustees to earn a pittance in "sweeping and dusting the meeting house" because they had no "provider." [5] The great city of New York still requires its married women teachers to swear that their husbands are morally, mentally or physically incompetent in order to retain their positions!

The adjustment in plans of living to home needs and obligations is a private concern of each married pair. The only social claim is that the children, if there are any, shall be well-cared-for in all respects, physical, mental, moral and vocational. The adjustment of each woman to her own vocational desires, capacities and opportunities is a matter for herself and her husband to settle between them; it is not even the proper concern of either mother-in-law! The more exceptional women earn in art and literature, in singing, painting, acting, on a plane where it is clear they are conferring social benefits and hence have a right to financial returns which do not degrade but give distinction, the more nearly we approach a time when common women

[5] Early Colonial Records.

may earn money by any sort of labor they can do well enough to be paid, and whether married or single, without injuring their own or their husband's social position. We are, however, a long way from that day now, when even the law penalizes the marriage of teachers and custom forbids any organized adjustment of labor to the special needs of the house-mother. The choice for the manual worker is sharply made, "labor all day and leave your baby at the day-nursery or stop at home and starve." The choice is almost equally difficult for the clerk, the stenographer, the telephone operator, the professional woman, the business manager. The Utopias in which all these difficulties vanish with a "presto change" are interesting to read of in books; but what is really helping the actual situation is that men and women, richer or poorer, but of the moral and intellectual élite, are now working out for themselves many modifications of the rigidity of modern industry as it relates to the married woman and the mother, in a most difficult but a most useful domestic experimentation.

Meanwhile the average young married woman, and especially the average young married woman of good education and fairly good financial circumstances, needs most of all to see and to use her fine chance for preparation for vocational achievement, or for social usefulness, after she has become released from the heaviest duties to her family. Everything done by such a young woman in a professional manner and for pay on a business basis, helps to democratize the industry of women and to place the whole relationship of her sex to industry on a truly social plane. The aristocratic notion that it is a dire calamity for a married woman to have to earn money can only be outgrown by having multitudes of married women who do not have to earn money for personal comforts or family well-being do something that the world wants to pay for and take their compensation naturally as men take it for worthy service. Whether or not, however, women earn money in personal labor outside the home during the years when their chief devotion must be to the family needs, they can keep interest and study and acquaintance open toward the free time of their second youth, when they will need and want to do something for and by themselves to round out their own personal lives: whether that something shall be a paid or an unpaid service. All this presupposes that women shall have had needed care and protection and support in their distinctive function of motherhood and thus have escaped that too common tragedy of overwork and neglect which now leaves so many women helpless and invalid in middle life. The majority of house-mothers among the wage-earning class are now overworked and underfed; overburdened with care and denied all the diversions and rest that enable women to keep well and happy and able to enter upon their third stage of life fitted for its opportunities and its joys.

Moreover, it must be pressed home to the public mind and conscience that the waste of womanhood in its later life has been throughout the ages, and now is, the result of an ignorant and careless treatment of girlhood. The same scientific inquiry which proves the eligibility of womanhood to a ripe and useful, a vital and youthful-hearted old age, demonstrates beyond cavil the social crime of ignoring the special danger-point in the physical life of woman. We learn from every quarter of science that the weak point in womanhood is between the ages of thirteen or fourteen, and nineteen or twenty years. At that time and that alone death and disease stand nearer and more threatening to the girl than to the boy. At that time and at no other, save during actual child-bearing, the womanhood of the race stands in greater need of special protection and help from society and from parenthood than does the manhood of the race. Mature women may always need social protection against long-continued, monotonous and uninterrupted labor. They may always be less able than men to survive shocks of accident or to sustain hardest trials of muscular effort without permanent harm. As Professor Thompson says: "Men are stronger in relation to spasmodic efforts and isolated feats." Hence the rule of the sea in shipwreck, or of the land in any terrible disaster, the rule of "women first to be saved," has a reason in the nature of things, since men can summon so much more special power for the special demand. The greater tenacity of life among women, however, their greater resistance to disease, their larger capacity for continual, sustained effort if that is varied in form and not too severe, are ample proofs that women need not be invalids or "weak," and that it is a social mistake or a social crime, or both, if they are so in any prevailing numbers at any period of life. The reason that the old age of women is so often pathological in condition, the reason that marriage and maternity mean so often extreme suffering and disease, the reason that so many women fail of the second youth that is their birthright and have instead a long decay of life in depressing helplessness and futile longing, is more than all else because the first youth of women is so generally misused. Those years between fourteen and twenty when death and disease stand nearest to womanhood are the very years when in many civilizations marriage and child-bearing have made their heaviest demands upon the young life. The physical weakness of both men and women in India, their lack of stamina, their easy yielding to all manner of diseases, their quick fading at the touch of hardship, this is the price India has paid for her child marriages. And not this alone, although this is so obvious that all mark its terrible consequences of social mistake. There is another price paid, the very life-portion of nature's dower to the women of India, nature's dower of health and happiness. Nowhere do women so age in mid-life, so suffer with all manner of maladjustments of physical, mental and moral condition, as in countries where girlhood is thus sacrificed, and the time of all others when womanhood most needs care for the upbuilding of the individual life is misused for a premature devotion to other lives. The sadness of the women of India, who have become conscious of their lot and its contrast with happier lives, is only understood when we see clearly what an outrage upon nature's laws is this marriage of unformed girlhood. We trace in every civilization that has thus ignored the danger-point in womanhood's physical development the same weakness in the race, the same unutterable sadness of premature old age and of widespread disease among the women.

We are not to take credit to ourselves, however, as a civilization humane and wise in this matter. We are doing almost as wicked and wasteful a thing as respects the girlhood of the poorer classes in these United States in the morning of the twentieth century. Read again what we do to our young girls between the ages of fourteen and twenty, when of all the periods of life for women there is most danger of premature death and of wasting and disabling disease.[6] Concerning the two hundred and ninety-five separate employments in which women earn wages and salary, as recorded in the census of 1900, two facts stand out prominently, —namely, the youth of the women and girls, and the low quality and poor pay of the work of the majority among them. Other facts are coming clearly into light, baleful in their significance, as we more closely study conditions. In the canning factories 2,400 rapid and regular motions a day in tin-cutting for the girls employed; girls sixteen to twenty years of age, and speeded to the limit of supreme exhaustion in this race to keep ahead of the other workers. In the confectionery business, 3,000 chocolates "dipped" every day at fever heat of energy. In the cracker-making trade, the girls standing or walking not six feet from the

[6] See Ellen Abbott, *Women in Industry.*

ovens show a white faintness from heat and hurry as they handle a hundred dozen a day; and "can't stand the work long," as even the strongest confess. In the cigar-making industry 1,400 "stogies" a day worked over by girls seventeen to twenty years of age; and not only that but children, boys and girls from five to twelve years old, stripping tobacco as helpers and the whole work so exhausting that even the older girls say they "can't keep the pace more than six years." In the garment trades the sewing machines speeded to almost incredible limits, the unshaded electric bulbs and the swift motion of the needle giving early "eye-blur" and a nerve strain that enables the strongest to earn only five to six dollars a week, while the goal of eight dollars won by a ruinous "spurt" only crowds down the average wage by cutting "piecework" prices. And in this trade "custom-work" brings the unsanitary tenement sweat-shop into union with the best factories, to work the children younger and under worse conditions and leave no rest-time for youth even in the home. In the laundries women are operating machines so heavy that their whole bodies tremble with the strain of their rise; and the muscular system, drawn upon for this "spasmodic effort for an isolated feat," repeated as rapidly as the body can be forced to act, under the spur of a never-ceasing pressure, is often that of young girls, many of them under sixteen years of age. In the metal trades 10,000 "cores" a day turned out after two or three years' apprenticeship, and still the young girl under twenty is most in evidence in the bewilderingly rapid process. In the manufac-

ture of "caskets" and other articles where strong lac-
quer is used, the manufacturer often says he "can't
stand it more than two or three minutes in the room"
where the fumes of the preparation are worst, but his
girls work in it ten hours a day for the pitiful wage
of nine dollars a week, called "good pay for women."
In the soap-making business the girls must wrap 1,100
cakes of soap a day in the bad air and worse smells
of most such places in order to get a decent wage.
The "telephone girl" gets many a harsh criticism; it
might be better if she got a little more attention as
a social factor. Her age is seldom over twenty; seventeen to eighteen years is the average. Physicians tell
us that it is ruinous to the nervous system to do this
exacting work more than five hours a day even with
an hour's rest, complete and in the best possible conditions, between each two and one-half hours of service. But our telephone girls work their five hours in
continuous service and if after four or five years of
such labor they "break down," what then? In mercan-
tile houses the all-day standing which is the rule injures girls so seriously that physicians continually com-
plain about it. The law that requires seats in department stores is so much a dead letter that the girls
laugh bitterly at any question concerning its enforcement. In places where five or six hundred girls are
employed nineteen to thirty seats may be provided;
but to use even these may cost the girl her position.
The hours, from eight to five or from eight to six
o'clock, and the low wage which forbids proper clothing and nourishment if wholly depended upon for self-

support, add to the peril of the shop-girl's condition.
The "moral jeopardy of her position," as Miss Butler[7]
calls it, is also a factor of sinister suggestion, when
we remember that with all their hard and continuous
labor, three-fifths of the shop-girls earn less than seven
dollars a week. The much vaunted "chivalry of men,"
the proudly assumed "reverence for womanhood" pa-
raded in public addresses on the glory and moral excellence of our present civilization, do not work far
down in the social scale. The fact is that because
women are the cheapest of laborers and because young
women must all work for pay between their school
life and their marriage in the case of the poverty-
bound, the poorest-paid and many of the hardest and
most health-destroying of employments are given them
as almost a monopoly. Nature has warned mankind
through unnumbered centuries, since the human intelligence has been able to perceive cause and effect, that
if we wanted strong nations we must have strong
mothers, and if we wanted strong mothers we must
safeguard the girls from overwork and all manner of
economic evils: but we still turn deaf ears to the
warning.

In circles of society less pressed by economic need
we misuse girlhood in many other ways. The pressure
upon the early precocity of the girl in school, the strain
of "society" functions too elaborate and nerve-wearing
for youth, the undercurrent of vulgar and wicked selling of maidenhood in legal but unholy marriage to the
highest bidder in rank and money,—all these things

[7] Elizabeth B. Butler, *Women in the Trades.*

despoil the precious and lovely freedom and joy of the potential mother. Some time we must be wiser and shield and protect, as now even the most careful parent finds it almost impossible to do alone and unaided by social customs and ways of living, what nature has asserted by her most solemn commands to be the first right of human beings of the mother-sex, namely, a happy and natural girlhood. Given that for the majority of the sex, given the right use of the period of marriage and maternity not only as related to the duty to the family but also as that may be a preparation for the best use of the later years, then indeed would the second youth of women show such fruitage in personal values and in social service as the world has not yet seen. Then would it be clearer, even to dull perception, why more women than men live to old age and why more women than men "keep the child-like in the larger mind" and hence may have many a belated spring-time of growth.

The moral of all this must be pressed home to the master forces of vocational direction and control. It must of all things be emphasized that not only is "teaching woman's organic office in the world," but that married women and mothers have done most of the teaching of all the younger children in all the past civilizations, and there are the best of reasons why they should continue to do so. Instead of penalizing the marriage of women teachers the public school management of the United States should offer a premium for the marriage of these women; especially those whose proved fitness for the teacher's office presents the first diploma in the curriculum of successful motherhood. The private schools now utilize such women both as heads of schools and as teachers. The premium that should be offered by the public school system need not and should not be a continuance in the school work under the same exhausting and inexorable demands which are met by the unmarried teacher, who works so well after her many years of experience in "the system" while trying so heroically to change and improve it. The premium given the married woman-teacher, with children or of whom society may expect offspring of a needed kind, should be in freedom of choice of lines of work, in adjustable hours, and in all other details of flexibility of service needed by the housemother. Although compensation should of course be given, the scale of wages of these part-time workers should not disarrange those schedules which secure to unmarried teachers, who give uninterrupted service for a long career and who constitute the permanent staff in every school, their full share of "equal pay for women for equal work with men" in the higher competitions of professional life. Such schedules are a vital need, not only for the sake of justice but for the right use of those exceptional educators among women who, whether married or unmarried, can serve as superintendents and heads of departments in the highest positions. There is nothing more needed in education, however, than a vastly increased teaching force, and a corresponding opportunity to modify and vary the grade system, especially in the elementary schools, to suit the needs of a wider range of child capacity. We ought to have two or three part-time married women teachers to every celibate woman, younger or older, who gives whole service to the public schools. Moreover, the care-taking of the weak and ignorant and undeveloped, the moral protection of children and youth in recreation and in labor, the succor of the needy, and the general expression of social control and social uplift, these are woman's special functions in the social order and have ever been her peculiar responsibility. The vital need in these fields to-day is not alone for a minority of trained workers, such as the Schools for Social Workers are turning out each year, but also for a large majority of citizens devoted to the public weal and able and willing intelligently to carry out and perfect, modify and balance the schemes of the experts and "paid workers" who make "scientific philanthropy" a life work. Women will doubtless always take a larger share in this part-time service in the lines indicated than men can do; and older women, those in the third stage of life, are now entering this field with enthusiasm. As volunteers and as helpers, paid and unpaid, they are doing much of the constructive and ameliorative, the reformatory and the preventive work of social reform. When, however, women enter this field late in life, or after a merely amateur and impulsive response in earlier life to the call of social need, they enter by a vocational leap, as it were, from the inner to the outer circle of human interests. This gives, at the worst, an awkward meddling with established rules of procedure; and at best fails to give highest effectiveness. Women who

have had four years of college and two years of special training in a Teacher's College or School of Philanthropy and then, after two to six years of professional work in their chosen field, marry to take charge
of an individual home, are too valuable assets of educational opportunity to be left without social pressure
and financial incentive to continue that work with the
necessary modifications. The same is true of the minister, the lawyer and above all the doctor and the
nurse, as well as of all other women specialists in professional labor.

The difficulties of the woman-worker who marries
and has children increase as we go down the scale
through commercial, clerical and manual employments;
but they are not insuperable; and the ingenuity of industrial mechanism needed for the higher utilization
of the paid work of women in other than purely private
domestic lines waits for development only for a more
just perception in the common sense regarding women's
work-power. The present pressure upon the wages of
men that makes so many housemothers obliged to add
to the family income at the worst time of their lives for
economic strain, and at any work they can get, however exploited and health-destroying, is no solution of
the problem; it is an aggravation of it dire in social
results. Real solutions of social problems are not
worked out by people wholly "under" their circumstances.

With, however, a true solution of the problems of
womanhood, achieved not by flights of fancy but by
patient infinitesimal efforts of daily living in which no

inherited or present duty is neglected, and no opportunity for shaping toward future conditions is ignored, we shall gain at last for social culture in all lines, and for industry in many forms, a needed class of slowly-trained, slowly-apprenticed workers in every field where women naturally excel; to rise finally at the third period of their lives to positions of command where women are now most needed. This will mean new ways of conserving hitherto exploited capacities and gifts of the mass of mankind. For women of the right sort and the right training, shielded by men's protection and care from the heaviest economic pressure during early life and developed in personality by the special demands upon them in the home, will see to it when they arrive at their rightful place of control that neither professional demand nor the industrial order shall take such a heavy toll from life itself in the effort to make a living!

"Old men for counsel?" Yes, surely, now as of old; and it is well for humanity that it learned this bit of social wisdom so early. Old women for new work for the race? Yes, surely; and well will it be for human progress when mankind learns this new lesson of social wisdom and makes fitting social use of the post-graduate mother, eager and fresh in her second youth, for a new path-finding for the feet of the coming generations before she draws down the curtain and says Good-night.

IX

PROBLEMS OF MARRIAGE AND DIVORCE

A CAPTURED wife or a purchased wife can have little authoritative to say concerning her condition in marriage or the terms of her dismissal or her escape from the marriage bond, provided she may be dismissed or is allowed to escape. A wholly subject woman can have no legal power to determine who shall represent the authority of the family which hands her from one guardian to another. There can be, therefore, no problems of marriage and divorce, in the sense in which we now use the words, until there is a possibility of a marriage contract legally defined and binding alike on husbands and on wives; and there can be no marriage contract until women have at least a few personal rights secured to them by law and custom. The rise of the marriage contract, therefore, with its recognition of some power of personal choice and some right of individual liberty accorded to women, is the suggestive clue to the course of social evolution which in any given era outlines the terms of legal marriage. The rise of the marriage contract is itself, however, simply one element in the slow movement of society toward the recognition of contract powers in general, and the emergence of women from a perpetual legal minority. Problems of marriage and divorce, therefore, are and must be parts of the whole problem of the just and useful position of women in society. This is the reason why ultra opponents of "Women's Rights" always and instinctively relate the greater freedom of women to domestic disaster; and this is also the reason why the ultra proponents of "Women's Rights" as instinctively begin their demand for larger sharing of the powers and obligations of social life by women with some radical attack upon that family order which rests upon the legal despotism of the husband and father.

There is to-day a feeling of almost hysterical alarm regarding the present conditions of family life. The demonstrable and large increase of divorces throughout Christendom, the weakening of family ties by reason of changed economic, educational and social conditions which secure to minor children as well as to wives great freedom of choice and liberty of action, give deep concern to all, and awaken moral terror in many. No one, however, who really believes that we should not return to the absolute control of women by men, and to the harem and the zenana as the ideal home, need be in fear of any unique domestic catastrophe.

Most of us have come to believe that marriage and the family are social institutions, rising in answer to social needs and changing in accordance with general social evolution, and at no time to be studied as isolated facts, but rather always as related parts of the

whole process of social development. All who believe
in this manner should approach the problems of marriage and divorce with clear minds and sunny tempers,
with breadth of vision and with balanced judgment.
Such students at least can remember, and with satisfaction, that the statistics of divorce, which so often
provoke pessimism respecting our American family
life, must be read in connection with other statistics
which prove a progressively higher average of just and
noble family relationship among those who do not become divorced. The facts of scandalous proceedings
in the "smart set" should never blind the judicious to
those other facts which show that the "malefactors of
great wealth" are few, and the favored of fortune
who behave like silly and wicked youth are a small
minority. Admitting, however, the distinct increase in
divorces relative to population, and accepting it as an
evil in that which it indicates as well as in that which it
proves, there must also be confessed a considerable and
regrettable trend of modern life in the direction of the
instability of the family. The love of change and the
impatience of control among our youth; the easy movement of population which makes "home" often but
an attachment to the moving-van; the flexible yet com-
plicated social arrangements which make it easy to
shirk individual responsibility; the economic pressure,
intensified by the desire so painfully common to live
more luxuriously than one can afford; the widespread
results of invention which release many from drudgery
before they are fitted for skilled labor; the free public
education which enables many to appropriate the super-

ficial fruits of culture before they have attained moral discrimination in their efficient use for the higher purposes of life—all these and many more elements of our rapidly changing civilization tend to make the home and all its interests subject to unprecedented disturbance from the many-sided life without. Also we must give serious attention to the fact that in the United States there is great divergence of inherited standards, laws and customs regarding the basis of marriage, the righteousness or wickedness of possible divorce and the propriety or impropriety of remarriage after domestic changes, which confuses the matter. For want of a clear ideal of religious values and social demands involved, the rule of personal desire and individual idiosyncrasy has too great predominance. Here, where ethical doctors disagree and moral teachers widely differ, youth makes its ideal an exaltation of romance in marriage choices; and mature years demands the right of the most extreme individualism. The sense of intellectual freedom to believe what one wishes, and the "will to believe" what is most pleasant and seems most easy to realize in action, often join to make individual preference the only rule of life.

We have in our marriage laws and customs reminiscences in a specific manner of the three main channels of thought and life which make up what we call Christian civilization. We have first the Jewish ideal of marriage, which has come to us with our special religious inheritance. This is an ideal which includes a belief in the rightful and proper subjection of women to men, but exacts of men protection for women.   It

elevates the conception of marriage to a plane of purity
and faithfulness superior alike to celibacy and to un-
chastity; but includes divorce, easy for men to obtain,
difficult for women; yet justifiable for both, provided
the terms of separation and of possible remarriage are
defined by the wisdom of the law as interpreted by
rabbis. We have also a large inherited influence from
the Roman law which has given the legal basis of all
our later statutes and which has modified all tribal customs of the Germanic peoples. In Roman marriage,
the patrician form, religious and indissoluble, and the
plebeian form, secular and legally terminable, but carefully guarded as a legal contract, both hold firmly
respect for family autonomy as well as the subordination of caprice to justice and right. These elements of
the sacred and the secular marriage of Roman law are
retained in some form in our present civilization. We
have inherited also another potent influence upon the
domestic order, one which is in our blood more than
in our religion or our law, namely the Anglo-Saxon love
of personal liberty and sense of individual rights; that
which first gave to women a voice in the disposition of
their own persons, and initiated for our special social
order a proud restraint upon the tendency of the family to sacrifice to its own autonomy the happiness and
well-being of its members. These varied ideals and
elements of custom and law were all incorporated by
Latin Christianity into its control of marriage, although all were modified and changed in emphasis.
The Church adopted the high demand for faithfulness
in the marriage tie, the subordination of woman to

man in the domestic life, and the ethical significance of the family order which the Jewish religion inculcated. It rejected Jewish divorce and lowered the rank of marital virtue by placing celibacy above it in the scale of spiritual excellence. The Church accepted as its own standard the patrician form of Roman marriage as a religious sacrament, indissoluble save by death, and making second marriages even after such bereavement rather shameful concessions to human weakness. A large trace, however, of the plebeian form of secular regulation is to be found in the history of all Christian nations; and Protestant Christianity restored the State to its superior control over marriage. The trend of all laws, customs and moral reforms in Christendom, especially in Protestant Christendom, has been toward a wider and deeper realization of the Germanic respect for womanhood and the Anglo-Saxon forms of marriage, after the right of contract was recognized and the social value of the wife in part estimated. Especially has Christian civilization appropriated the Germanic idea that a woman has some right to refuse to marry a hated or disliked man, and that youth has a right to selective love and its fruitage in a chosen union of the sexes.

To-day these varied reminiscences of our past mixed inheritance give us disagreements even in the fundamentals of ethical ideals in marriage; and often the friction that we develop in discussion dates back to our composite union of national ideals in the melting pot of early Christianity.

Wherever and whenever the rights of women are

recognized as those belonging to all human beings alike, there and then arise problems of marriage and divorce. For there and then marriage becomes a *contract,* and a contract can be broken for the same reasons that a contract may be made, namely, the good of the parties involved. The difficulties inhering in the adjustment of the domestic order to—

> "Two heads in council,
> Two beside the hearth,
> Two in the tangled business of the world" [1]

are identical with the difficulties that inhere in democracy as a general social movement. Despotism is easy if you can secure a despot capable of holding his place. All else is a matter of adjustment to justice and right; and all such adjustment is difficult. In the midst of the confusion of ideal and action one thing is sure; namely, that women in the new freedom that has come to them in the last hundred years of Christian civilization will not longer endure the unspeakable indignities and the hopeless suffering which many of them have been compelled to endure in the past. That last outrage upon a chaste wife and a faithful mother, enforced physical union with a husband and father whose touch is pollution and whose heritage to his children is disease and death, will less and less be tolerated by individual or by social morality. In so far as greater freedom in divorce is one effect of the refusal of women to sustain marital relations with unfit men —and it is very largely that to-day—it is a movement

[1] Alfred Tennyson, *The Princess.*

for the benefit and not for the injury of the family. Permanent and legal separation in such cases is now seen by most enlightened people to be both individually just and socially necessary. Whether such separation shall include remarriage of either or both parties is still a moot question in morals. The tendency, however, in all fields of ethical thought is away from "eternal punishment" and in the direction of self-recovery and of trying life experiments over again in the hope of a better outcome. It is likely that marriage and divorce will prove no exception to this hopeful tendency. Moreover, so far as the testimony of actual life is valid as against theories only, the countries where no re-marriage is allowed show a lower standard of marital faithfulness, of child-care and of true culture of the moral nature in the relationship of the family group, than is shown in those countries that grant for serious causes absolute divorce with full freedom for re-marriage.

That all divorces now obtained are for serious reasons, however, no one dare affirm. The most harmful element in the problem both in its personal and in its social aspects is the fact that selfishness, superficial and trivial causes of pique, of wounded vanity, of rash and childish whim, of even the mere suggestive power of newspaper scandals, may lead to a hasty and unnecessary termination of that most important of all human relationships, the marriage upon which the home is builded. The special need, however, even at this danger-point, is not to focus attention, as is usually done, upon evils to be avoided in divorce laws and their operation. What is needed most is studious and practical devotion to constructive social measures that may be adopted for aid to those in marital difficulty, and for the prevention of those social and personal conditions which lead to marital difficulty. It is high time we began to work for the lessening of *causes of divorce,* for relief in family distress and misery, for helpful measures of discipline through recognized and adequate agencies for all who need an external conscience and an outside judgment to make a success of their married life. Not only is it true that an ounce of prevention is worth a pound of cure, but it is also equally true that a pound of help at the right time and in the right way to weak and ignorant and wayward people is worth a ton of prohibition. What many people need most is not to be forbidden a divorce, but to be helped radically in their lives and in their circumstances to a position where they will not want a divorce.

In this connection we must consider the fact that our own is the first form of civilization that has tried in any large way the experiment of placing the entire burden of securing the success of marriage and the family life upon the characters and capacities of two persons. In primitive social orders, and in the older civilizations, each married pair and their children were sustained and disciplined and in greater or less degree controlled by the collective family order in which they lived. Now, we trust two people in early youth, undisciplined, undeveloped, perhaps deficient in mental, moral, physical or economic power, to marry as they will; bear children or not without let or hindrance; take care of their children or not as seems desirable or possible to them; separate with ease, with or without legal procedure—and the burden of all the failures in marriage, parenthood and the family relationship is placed upon society as a whole. The consequences of the many failures that thus result have brought all thoughtful persons to the point where they see clearly that society, which in its social service is called upon to take care of failures, must assume a social control and discipline that will reduce those failures to the minimum. This means that we must come to an agreement about the method and extent of such social control of the present individualistic marriage as shall be just to persons and helpful to the social order.

The first question to be raised and answered in the effort to reach such an agreement is this: What force in modern society is adequate and suitable as the agency of such social control of the individualistic marriage in the interests of social welfare? The answer seems clear to many of us. The modern State is the only adequate and suitable agency for efficient social control of marriage. The old tyranny of tribal custom is gone; it will not return. The unquestioned despotism of the patriarchate is no more—and where is the sane person who would desire its revival? The family bond of blood relationship, which used to place all domestic responsibility in a "family council" with an acknowledged head, is already stretched to cover so wide an area of personal choice that it cannot hold firm against unsafe or unwise choices; and the tendency is toward more and more democracy in the family life. The accepted rule of rabbi and priest no longer exists, and he would be rash indeed who should urge its reinstatement with the support of the strong arm of the law. The modern State, however, has absorbed within itself the "mother-right" and the "father-rule"; the Church control and the educational standard; and the law, as the expression of its own will and not as the temporal enforcement of spiritual canons. The modern State is the final appeal in individual need and the ultimate authority in social conduct. Of all modern institutions, therefore, the State alone is powerful enough, definite enough, and united enough in its ethical demand, to accept and efficiently exercise for all mankind the responsibility of the care, the control and the development of individual life in all group relationships. It is, consequently, the only fit agency by which social control of individualistic marriage, in the interest of social well-being, may be assumed and maintained.

The most important first step, therefore, in efforts of constructive work toward securing the stability of the family is insistence upon a uniform civil marriage service. The civil authority over marriage needs no demonstration to any form of Protestant Christian faith; for it is wrought into the history of the more democratic forms of Church administration.[2] The early settlers of the United States preserved clear traces of Cromwell's assertion of State control over marriage

[2] See G. E. Howard, Ph.D., *History of Matrimonial Institutions*, chapters *Rise of Civil Marriage* and *Obligatory Civil Marriage in the New England Colonies*.

and family order in the requirement, universal in the colonies of New England and the Eastern Coast, that a magistrate alone should have power to legalize marriage. A "minister might be present" and "make a short exhortation," but he must "not preach a sermon" on such occasions, lest he thereby detract from the dignity of the civil officer. We have not kept that jealous regard for the civil marriage, since we now allow ministers of different faiths to legalize the relation between the sexes. But we do recognize that when the minister of any religion is allowed to legalize the marriage bond he does it with delegated power; for he has always to say, "By the power vested in me by the State I pronounce you husband and wife." It is clear to many of us that we should return, and at once, to the early New England requirement for a civil marriage as the true and only legalization, whatever additional religious service may be desired as satisfying the religious sentiment.

This required civil marriage should be limited in form to such words as persons of all religious faiths could conscientiously use; it should be performed in such place as would safeguard privacy and protect from all trivial and coarse associations; it should be performed only by special magistrates set apart for this important function, and capable of properly representing the dignity and power of the State in this most vital public and private concern. The beautiful "Halls of Marriage" of some European Guild buildings might well be reproduced in the United States. Justices of distinction and high character, who were no longer physically equal to the hardest work of the courts, might well be set aside for this task as a crowning honor and service. Women judges, also, when we have them, could serve well in this duty of ushering a new family group into existence.

If we could once establish the State in its rightful place of social control of marriage, we could then move on to the logical next step in securing greater stability and efficiency in the family order—namely, the protection of the family against the marriage of the unfit. The most radical and vital treatment of pathological conditions in the modern family is not to tinker with divorce, which at worst is only a symptom of deeper social disease, but to take measures to prevent so many people from marrying who are not physically, mentally, morally or economically able to make marriage a social advantage. The stability of the modern family, that is to say, the stability of the family under gradually extending democratic conditions, depends not alone or chiefly upon keeping people together who have once married, and that without regard to their worth or their happiness; but rather in removing from the currents of family descent the poisonous elements of human degeneracy which always make for social disorder and disintegration. Experience has proved beyond the shadow of a doubt that the largest producing cause of human misery and social retardation is the marriage and child-bearing of the feeble-minded, the epileptic, the victims of diseases induced by vicious habits, and of all those of degenerative psychosis tending toward insanity, crime or help-

lessness. [3]   We have a larger number of these degenerates, in relation to our population, than ever burdened preceding civilizations.   That is because modern
charity keeps such degenerates alive and safe where
under harsher social conditions nature would kill them
off early.   We are, therefore, under bonds to future
generations, if we would not make our very growth in
social tenderness a means of social degeneration, to
make it impossible for the markedly unfit to bring
forth seed after their kind.   When the State assumes
its rightful control over marriage, the legal family can
be wholly protected against this evil; and sexual relationships of an irregular sort can be made innocuous,
to the future at least, by means of various forms of
human "sterilization" already understood and to some
extent practised.   That "God gives children" who
should never be born is a superstition that must be
outgrown, if social progress is to be made in conditions
where nature's hand is stayed in her useful destruction
of the worse than useless human failures.   The twin
superstition that the sexual instinct is too personal and
private a possession to be rightly governed by public
laws must also be outgrown.   Many States are trying
experiments like those of Indiana along the line of
such social control both of legal marriage and of sex-
associations not legalized, as shall protect society
against its worst foe, which is the hopeless incom-
petency to social demands of any considerable class
of the population.[4]

[3] See S. A. K. Strahan, *Marriage and Disease.*
[4] Amos G. Warner, *American Charities,* chapter *Causes of Degeneration.*

Next in importance to preventing marriages which should not be allowed, is to help in making more permanent and successful those that society has permitted. Here again it is not the effort to make "uniform divorce laws," of whatever sort, which is the vital thing —certainly not the effort to secure such uniform laws as will forbid all escape from the marriage bond even when it has become intolerable; nor is it the settlement of the vexed question of re-marriage after divorce. The vital thing is to secure such social agencies as may urge deliberation, offer wise counsel, and provide needed aid to ignorance and waywardness and wilful selfishness when difficulties appear in the family life. The vital need is for the State, aided by volunteer helpers, to place at the service of the foolish and the confused, the distressed and angry, a truly parental aid in "patching things up" and "trying to go on" even when the family outlook is dark and threatening. The new Domestic Relations Courts, one of which has been established in New York City, and one in Chicago, are a promising beginning of what is most needed. The Children's Court, with its probation system applied first to children only and now to delinquent parents with their children, has shown us the way. The number of grown-up children, people with adult bodies but childish minds and babyish tempers, is appalling. They need as careful and ingenious discipline as do minors, when they come to grief through faults and misfortunes. A set of magistrates, chosen for special qualities of mind and heart; a private hearing, where the interview may have the sacredness of the confessional; a probation system, made so flexible and all-embracing that it may worthily take the place of the old "family council" of an earlier type of domestic order; a rigid law, compelling a pause of some proper and specified time before the most rebellious couples are able to escape from their assumed obligations to each other; a needed relief from constant irritation of each other's presence while this pause exacts deliberation before final decisions; a tendency, strongly and consciously established by the Court of Domestic Relations, in favor of the rehabilitation of the family and against all separation or divorce not found to be necessary as a release from unbearable conditions— these are the vital needs to-day. To secure them, two things are absolutely essential; first, *the abolition by State laws, rigidly enforced, of all commercial trafficking in divorce by any lawyer of any grade or sort;* and, second, a turning of the forces that make for moral guidance in the community from the negative to the positive, from the prohibitive to the constructive, in dealing with the problems of marriage and divorce. So long as any class of people in the community can make money by breaking up families, families will be broken up that might be held together. So long as the moral sense of the churches and of social workers is engaged chiefly in trying to get laws about divorce fixed in certain directions, rather than in trying to help people not to want to get divorced, there will be so heavy a responsibility laid upon the weak and undeveloped that they cannot measure up to its demands. We must make the family life more stable;

that everyone admits. We can only make it more stable in a democratic society by working from within outward; from character and social condition toward law; not solely or chiefly by changes in statutes and by penalties for disobedience to laws made for the most part by people who are so wisely and happily married that they are wholly content!

What if, after all has been done that can be done to keep married couples together and to secure a permanent father and mother for each child of such married couples, some people demand entire separation, legal divorce, and the privilege to remarry? Then it seems that in a democratic order, where the right of an individual to determine the main essentials of his life to his utmost power is guaranteed, society may not say nay to this demand. It is a tragedy if a marriage has proved so bad a mistake that death is preferable, as in many cases it is, to continued union. But the mistake itself is the tragedy, not the outward expression of it in legal divorce. It has been shown again and again that it is usually after the marriage has been really given up as impossible, and the couple have been definitely separated, however privately, for a considerable period, that the legal divorce is sought: that is to say, legal divorce is most often merely a public recognition of a private fact. As such it seems justified by social justice. There is no power that can make, through the law, a dead relationship live again. There is no possible miracle by which statutes can make love out of hatred, happiness out of misery, faith out of distrust, a home out of a prison from which a man and woman long only to escape. Nor can any law forbidding either separation or divorce make that a suitable place in which to bring up children which has become not a home, but such a prison. The State, however, when it assumes its rightful and needed control of marriage and family life, will make the children's welfare a chief consideration in settling vexed questions of giving or refusing divorce. Here again the present tendency to deal with such unfortunate children from a repressive and prohibitory point of view as related to their parents, must change to a positive and conscious tendency to minimize for the children themselves the misfortune incident to their parents' mistake or wrong-doing.

Far too little care is now exercised in regard to the conditions of life, moral and social, which surround the children of divorced parents. Where there has been such separation of fathers and mothers for causes which will not admit of palliative treatment such as has been suggested through a properly organized and administered Domestic Relations Court, the children of divorced parents should be held as wards of these Domestic Relations Courts during their minority. That provision in itself would act as an automatic check on haste and selfishness in seeking a divorce in the case of all parents who love their children. As wards of the Domestic Relations Court the children of divorced parents should have some special person, preferably not a relative of either parent and not a partisan friend of either, appointed by the court as a special guardian to look out for their interests solely.

Perhaps the worst thing that can be done with such
unfortunate children of divorced parents is the usual
placing of them in a divided care: one part of each
year with the father and his family, who "know the
mother was seriously at fault whatever he might have
done"; another portion of the year with the mother
and her family, who are "morally certain that she
was wholly in the right and the father wholly wrong."
The conflicting atmosphere of two such homes, even
in cases where each family life is restrained and careful in expressions before the child, is a bad surrounding for any young person. And where there are vulgar
passion and unreasoning prejudice in full display before the bewildered loyalty of the child to both parents,
the situation is cruel and hurtful in the highest degree.
If a man and woman have made shipwreck of their
married life and have brought children into the world,
those children must be looked out for by some power
above and beyond even parental love, in the interest
of their own development and of the social good. In
this world we pay for mistakes a penalty as great,
save in the inner consciousness of rectitude of purpose,
as for crimes. One of the penalties for mistakes in
marriage is, or should be, this submission to the strong
arm of the law in a disposition of the lives of the
children involved that transcends parental control.
There is no way in which the asset of parenthood can
be divided when the marriage bond is broken. Therefore neither parent has exclusive right, even the
"good" parent as against the "bad" one. The trick
of the voice, the turn of the hand, the color of the

eye, the shape of the head, the mental gift, the moral
taint or cleanness, the very life and being of the child,
partake of both parents. "Not even the power of
Omnipotence," says the ancient poet, "can make that
which has been as if it were not." Out of the wrong
or the error of the union of these twain, this child has
come into life. No decree of judge or jury can make
it the child of but one parent. All that society can do,
and that society should do, is to declare that this fruit
of a broken promise shall have its own life as unshaded and as fair for growth as it can be made. To
force both parents to live together in a horrible trav-
esty of home cannot give those defrauded children
their rights. To hand them over first to one, and then
to the other parent, in a mixed and conflicting influence
and devotion, cannot make good the lack of the united
care of two people who love them and love each óther.
To give them wholly to the one parent thought most
fit for their care is still to leave them orphaned and
desolate; for some very poor specimens of mankind
have a charm that children love and miss, even though
the remaining caretaker has all the virtues! Nothing
can make up to children for the death of their parents
or for the loss from the living of the true feeling and
united service of those between whom they seldom wish
to "choose," but from both of whom they instinctively
claim the best that can be given. The least that society can do for these children whom divorce of parents
has thus afflicted is to assume a superior position of
guardianship that shall minimize the evils of the situation and preserve as far as may be the feeling of

loyalty to both parents until reason and judgment shall guide affection to a true understanding of the sad condition.

The greatest of all needs in this whole realm of obligation toward children is for more and more effective ethical training; suited to present and not to past social conditions. We cannot longer make people cower before "that hangman's whip, the fear of hell." We cannot longer make the majority of instructed people accept as final authority, and obey as a supreme command, the canons of any church. We cannot longer secure in sufficient degree the higher ideals, and self-control in their realization now required, solely by the ancient appeal to filial feeling. That appeal to filial feeling rested for its greatest leverage upon a reverence for the superior wisdom of the old which is now endangered, if not destroyed, by the constant appeal to do new things to make the oncoming generation wiser and better than the last. All the movements of modern thought and life are against the old forms of social control which made for family stability and the sacrifice of personal desire for the welfare of offspring. We must translate our ethical teaching and our spiritual approach into new terms suited to the new idealism of the new social order. This is not hard to do, since social science, as truly as religion and family autonomy, makes the primal object of the family the well-being, the nurture, the training and the happiness of offspring. Social science makes it incumbent upon the man who would be a good citizen, and the woman who would make just return for social expenditure on her behalf, to place the interests of their children in marriage above all small demands of their own desires. No sociologist accepts Milton's idea of marriage as "an arrangement solely for the happiness" of individual men and women. Marriage is indeed the highest means society affords for securing the happiness of the majority of human beings, Marriage is also the finest and most effective moral discipline of both men and women who love each other and wish to, and do, call out the best in each other's nature. But if there are children born of the union, and marriage can hardly be fully complete either as joy or as discipline without children, then the social duty to make that marriage successful in the highest sense as a foundation for family life must be accepted as binding.

The deepest and most compelling need is, therefore, to reincarnate the old sanctities of the domestic order in new forms. Marriage must still, and more than of old, be considered a Sacrament. Not in the sense that elevates one church ceremony above all other rituals, and denies to adult human beings the right to free themselves from intolerable conditions provided certain formulæ have once been pronounced. But a Sacrament in the sense that makes marriage a spiritual as well as a physical bond, that makes it the outward symbol of the inner unity of the race.

Marriage, again, must be held, as our Anglo-Saxon ancestors made it appear, as a free contract between those who choose each the other. Not in the sense of that selfish individualism that makes freedom synonymous with a choice that regards only the passion of the heart, and that ends its obligation when its preference ceases. Not that—on peril of the loss of social order itself; but a free contract "on the soul's Rialto" in the sense of an inviolable right of selective love to guide the path to the altar of a pledged devotion.

Marriage, again, must be held more consciously than it is now as a social arrangement for the benefit of society as a whole. Not in the sense of a mechanical control, that tries stupendous or even ludicrous experiments in artificial production of supermen and superwomen; but marriage as a social arrangement for the benefit of the social whole in the sense that subordinates even love itself, even the passionate longing of the lonely heart, to the higher interests of humanity and to the imperious demands of the social conscience.

To help thus in even the smallest degree to reincarnate the old sanctities of the family bond in new forms is a far better service at this time of unrest than, on the one side, to exalt freedom as an end in itself; or, on the other side, to try to revive obsolete forms of subjection of the individual to the domestic autonomy. Above all things socially futile and morally insolent is the attitude of men who attempt to solve alone, without either the judgment or the authority of women, the problems of marriage and divorce! There is nothing which so betrays and emphasizes the evil effect upon the spiritual nature of men of the long subjection of women to masculine control, as the findings of church councils and court decisions and academic discussions, in which men alone participate, as these

are related to family life. The monstrous assumption
that men can know better than women what women
want, or ought to want, or really need, in that marriage relation which means to human beings of the
mother-sex a tax upon the whole nature such as men
cannot experience, would be impossible to decent and
intelligent men were it not for the extreme egotism
engendered in all human beings by the possession of
unjust power over others.

On the other hand, nothing is more mischievous in
a period like our own, when our ideals of democracy
have run ahead of our social technique in their administration, than to ignore the claims of society to set
metes and bounds by law to the relation of the sexes.
To exaggerate the demands of romantic love as above
those of the social good, is a mistake of the utmost
danger. To assume the anarchistic attitude toward
marriage, and to believe that that relationship between
men and women which is free of courts and statutes is
equal or superior to that which is entered upon soberly
and publicly under legal bonds to definitely defined obligations, is a mistake that implies a fatal lack of moral
balance. "He is not free who can do what he wills,"
says St. Augustine. He only is free who can will what
he ought, responds our modern thought. The marriage law may be faulty; it may be one-sided; it may
be in some particulars a dead record of ancient and
outworn ideals; it may contain things that the moral
sense and legal practice should get rid of at once—
but the conviction that law and not personal caprice
should rule the most vital of human relationships is

vastly more important than any manifestation of that law and should be held inviolate at all times. As Milton himself says, to "let upstart passions catch the government from reason" is but to confuse moral issues; and the reason of the race has always embodied itself in laws to which individual wishes should be subordinate.

New thoughts for the new time we need most surely in the realm of law as applied to the family order. To let what Channing called "that bondage to habit which lives on its old virtues" enslave us is foolish indeed. New thoughts and new works for the new days; but above all, in respect to the home which is the central socializing force in human society, a new consecration to the utmost reach of social wisdom and to the most faithful obedience to the social demand upon the personal life.

X

WOMAN AND THE STATE

WHAT is the State? "The State? I am the State,"
declares the political despot. A few women have been
despots and successfully proved that sex is not an absolute disqualification for an absolute monarchy. "The
State? We are the State," declared the reigning families of Feudalism; and women were heads of these
great families in the absence of the lord of the manor;
and when widowed, or unmarried, solely represented
the family power. Hence, sex has been proved in
many civilizations and in many eras of our own civilization no practical disqualification for aristocratic
leadership in the State.

"The State? We are the State," said, for ages,
the owners of landed property; and the "freehold
vote," the "property vote" has often included women.
Hence, sex has been proved no positive disqualification in a political order based upon lands and dollars.
The State has passed or is rapidly passing from despotism, from aristocracy resting on militarism, from the
control of landed proprietors and the owners of large
estates, to what we call democracy, based on manhood

suffrage. In this process, women have lost for a while their footing in the political arena. If the rule of the State goes by blood of one reigning family, then it has proved easy to escape a Salic law and, for the sake of holding a dynasty secure, make a woman queen in default of a male heir. If the rule of the State goes by blood of several reigning families who hold the fighting strength of the people at their disposal, then it is easy to ordain that those great houses shall be represented in the councils of the nobles and have their soldiers on the fields of battle which determine the history of the State, even if a woman's hand sends the troops and wields the political power. If the rule of the State goes by rent rolls, broad acres, and chests of gold, then it is easy to see that "the dollar should vote," no matter whether man or woman holds it, and that the land should speak, even if a spinster or a widow is its sole heir. We call the modern State democratic. Hélie defines the State as "the people organized into a political body." [1] He declares it "becomes a free people, organized into a democratic State, when all the citizens can participate in the direction and examination of public affairs." As regards men, our civilization has moved rapidly in the last two hundred years toward such a State of "one man, one vote." At first white men only were full citizens, now men of all colors may be, racial distinctions tending rapidly to disappear as qualification or disqualification for the electorate. As Renan, speaking of race mixtures in government, says wisely, "Ethnography is a science of

[1] Faustin Hélie, Institute of France.

rare interest, but to be free it should be without political application."

The subject of still greater interest, the subject of
sex, is not yet freed from political application even in
the minds of most leaders of thought.   When Bluntschli [2] says, the "State as a manlike, composite person, produced by the union of men, is not merely a
civil person but a moral civil person," he means only a
moral civil person composed of the masculine sex alone.
And when Maurice Block [3] declares that the "Principle
of nationalities is legitimate when it tends to unite in
a compact whole the scattered groups of the population, and illegitimate when it tends to divide them,"
he seems not to consider women as a group of human
beings who should become conscious parts of that compact whole.   Indeed, Paul Janet "distinguishes the family from the State," in that "the State is composed of
men free and equal, but the family rests upon in-
equality";[4] from which it seems that in his view even
adult women never emerge to a free and equal position.   If Janet's theory were true, that would, of
course, mean a perpetual guardianship and control of
all women by all men and especially of all wives by
all husbands, and yet no political expert now clearly
preaches that logical outcome of the theory.   In point
of fact, while blood and land and money were the basis
of governmental rule, widows and spinsters were often
counted in as a part of the body politic.   Aristotle,
who defended slavery, found some trouble in defend-

[2] J. C. Bluntschli, Editor *Staatswörterbuch.*
[3] Maurice Block, *Principle of Nationalities.*
[4] Paul Janet, Institute of France, *Political Science.*

ing the perpetual legal minority of even married women, and, to quote Janet again, it was indeed a "delicate achievement of Aristotle when he distinguished conjugal from paternal power, calling the first a republican and the second a royal power." If, however, "the family is the social unit" in the literal meaning of those words, and the phrase "universal suffrage" as the basis of a democratic State includes only men, then the head of the family, the man, does and must exercise "royal power" not only over his children but over his wife, for he speaks for the whole family when he votes. This might pass without much question while democratic States were demonstrating merely a new mechanism of political order; but when the democratic State becomes consciously moved by social sentiment, the submergence of one-half of the race in the family order becomes a source of uneasiness, both moral and intellectual.

To go no further back than our own United States history, the first legislative body in America, inaugurated at Jamestown, Virginia, in 1619, was elected by all the male inhabitants. Monarchy, nobility, landed estates and money had suddenly ceased to be a basis of the suffrage. A common manhood was fallen back upon as the one great reason for equality of rights in government. But women, at that period, were not considered human in the same sense that men were. They owned no property if married, their husbands possessed all they inherited or earned. They could not exercise the slightest contract power. They were unable to act as legal guardians for their youngest children; they had no power to protect their persons against their husbands, even in gross misuse; they must live where and how their husbands determined. Legally, they were perpetual minors. We must remember that at this period women were still under the common law in which an ancient enactment thus outlines a husband's duty: "He shall treat and govern the aforesaid A." (meaning his wife) "well and decently and shall not inflict nor cause to be inflicted any injury upon the aforesaid A., except in so far as he may lawfully and reasonably do so in accordance with the right of a husband to correct and chastise his wife." Said Blackstone in 1763, "as the husband is to answer for her misbehavior, the law thought it reasonable to intrust him with the power of restraining his wife by domestic chastisement in the same moderation that a man is allowed to correct his apprentices and his children for whom the master and the parent is also liable in some cases to answer." The Civil Law as well as the Common Law gave the husband the right of corporal punishment of the wife, "a severe beating with whips or clubs for some misdemeanors; for others only a moderate correction." The husband who killed his wife committed murder, but a wife who killed her husband was believed to commit "petty treason" and could be punished in the most cruel manner as a rebel against duly constituted authority as well as a common criminal.

This family subordination, as John Stuart Mill so clearly showed, was the basis of political nonentity for women, when equality of rights for men was first insisted upon.[5]   In the year 1797 Charles Fox said: "It has never been suggested in all the theories of the most absurd speculation that it would be advisable to extend the elective franchise to the female sex."   Five years before that, however, Mary Wollstonecraft published her *Vindication of the Rights of Women,* but doubtless Charles Fox had not heard of it; or, if he had, imagined it the ravings of a lunatic.   It could hardly be otherwise when almost all women were wives and wives were without any legal standing as human beings under the law.   The effect of this condition upon their economic status is well illustrated by a true story related in 1856 in *The Westminster Review,* as follows: "A lady whose husband had been unsuccessful in business, established herself as a milliner in Manchester.   After some years of toil, she realized sufficient for the family to live upon comfortably, the husband doing nothing meanwhile.   They lived for a time in easy circumstances after she gave up business; and the husband died, bequeathing all his wife's earnings to his illegitimate children.   At the age of 62 she was compelled, in order to gain her bread, to return to business."   The effect of this condition of wives upon the moral nature of men can be best understood by a pretended "chivalry" which left the "age of consent" of little girls from 7 to 10 years, and claimed for men as their right every immoral indulgence denied to women. In England no woman protested publicly against her husband's infidelity until 1801, and not until 1857 was a special court for divorce established; all relief from

[5] John Stuart Mill, *The Subjection of Women.*

the most intolerable marital conditions being, previous
to that date, a luxury for the rich only.   The full and
logical outcome of this family tutelage was given by
the Rev. John Knox-Little in Philadelphia as late as
1880 when he declared "Wifehood is the crowning
glory of Womanhood, in it she is bound for all time.
To her husband she owes the duty of unqualified obedience.   There is no wrong which a man can do which
justifies his wife for leaving him.   It is her duty to
subject herself to him always and no crime that he
can commit can justify her lack of obedience."

As in Feudalism "Every man must have his Lord"
or drop into abject poverty without place or lot in
life, so of old every woman, as an inferior sort of
human being, must have her husband or be cast adrift
to hopeless disaster.   The present happy time of usefulness, honor and well-paid work of the successful
spinster shows clearly how far we have come from that
day when, without a husband, a woman was nothing,
and, having one, she had nothing else of her own!   It
was at first natural and inevitable, therefore, that such
views of womanhood, commonly held, should forbid
their sharing in a suffrage based on humanity alone.

Says Woodrow Wilson in his useful textbook on
The State: "From the ancient State, the despotic, the
military, has emerged the economic, and last the democratic order, when human quality is declared the just
basis of political equality."   This is a fine statement
of the woman suffrage position, although not fully
applied.

"The Western township," to quote Woodrow Wil-

son again, "sprang out of the school as the New England township sprang out of the church." Women as
parts of the school and the church were in these germ
centres of the modern State which produced our American Republic. The only difficulty was that men were
so busy getting themselves all counted that they did
not remember to apply their own principles to women.
And women in the pioneer days of both East and
West were so overburdened with drudgery at home
and in the fields and with spinning, weaving and the
rest, that they could not think of anything but the day's
work. Besides, they were then so left out of educational currents of thought and information that they
could not "sense" their own rights and duties in the
larger life. No one can affirm that this is now the
case of women in general; and exceptional women were
able and brave to apply democracy to themselves long
ago.

Jamestown in 1670 restricted its suffrage to "free-
holders and housekeepers," granting a "voyce only to
such men as by their estates, real and personal, have
interest enough to tye them to the endeavor of the
publique good." This showed that full manhood suffrage was only allowed when no one as yet owned
large estates; thus indicating the persistent "economic
element" in political concerns. In the Plymouth Colony
in 1620 all male inhabitants voted, all being alike
"poor emigrants"; but in 1630 it was declared "that
no man shall be admitted to this body politic but such
as are members of some of the churches within the
same. This showed that although all the first Pilgrims

came "for freedom to worship God" in their own way, very soon other motives increased the population of the colony. This religious exclusiveness kept disfranchised for thirty years about three-fourths of the male population. It would probably disfranchise a much larger proportion if enforced at the present time. New Haven Colony had the same church-member clause very definitely stated, restricting "free burgesses" to church-members, who alone had the "power of transacting all public civil affairs." From 1634 onward none could vote in the Colony of Massachusetts who were not "freemen"; and the value of this freehold estate, which was the necessary basis of suffrage, was duly defined in dollars and cents in the Massachusetts charter of 1691. The electorate, therefore, had both a money basis and a church-member basis in all our Colonial life.* The last survival of the religious restriction is found in the Constitution of South Carolina, which, as late as 1790, allowed only "free, white men who acknowledged the being of God and believed in a future state of rewards and punishments" to vote.

The distinct qualification of sex was, however, not found in the earlier charters; and doubtless if the Pilgrim Mothers had not been so overworked and under-educated they might have taken advantage of that fact and "got in on the ground floor" of the American Republic. Indeed, in New Jersey the law defining the basis of the electorate read "all inhabitants" and directions were given for those "worth fifty pounds clear estate" to deposit "his" or "her" vote and from 1691 to 1780 women in Massachusetts Colony

voted under the Old Charter for all elective offices.
When, in 1784, "manhood suffrage" in New Jersey
took the place of "freehold suffrage" the women lost
their vote and the Massachusetts Constitution disfranchised them, thus giving another historical proof of
the wavering and illogical nature of social reforms.
It may be that the New Jersey and Massachusetts
women were remiss in not insisting upon being retained as eligible to vote when the property qualification was given up; but the political and social changes
incident to outgrowing that property qualification were
so numerous and so absorbing that women doubtless
forgot themselves as truly as the men forgot them.

Some women were alert, however, and tried to secure their own citizenship in very early Colonial times
when the ownership of estates was a necessary qualification of suffrage.   Mistress Margaret Brent, in
1647, as attorney for Lord Baltimore's brother, asked
for "playce and voyse" in the legislature, on the ground
of her property rights, but she was denied; we must
infer in fear of establishing a bad precedent.   Mrs.
Corbin also, a sister of Robert H. Lee, sent in her sole
petition for a vote in Virginia elections in 1778.   Yet
although Condorcet, on July 3, 1790, appealed for
equal citizenship for French women, they were for the
most part forgotten entirely in the great eighteenth
century struggle for the "rights of man."   Not only
in America, but wherever the demand for the rights
of man as against the rights of property stirred the
people and secured enlargement of the basis of the
suffrage for men, the women were either designedly or

unconsciously left out of the count. The chief reason for this inconsistency was, of course, the fact that they were not at the time considered human beings as needing or of right possessed of the same relationship as men to the body politic.

The first voting privileges given to women as human beings and on the democratic suffrage basis was, as was natural, in matters connected with education, and to those women who "had no man to represent them"; as when in Kentucky in 1838 "widows with children" were given a voice in "school suffrage." This limited franchise in educational matters was extended to all women in Kansas in 1861 and later to the women of many other States. Tax and Bond Suffrage has been given in several States and the women of New Orleans, Louisiana, made splendid use of it to make their city healthy in a notable struggle for drainage and sanitary measures of various sorts. Kansas, now in a campaign for full suffrage, has had municipal suffrage for women since 1887, and many women have served as high officers of municipalities in that State, among them several women mayors. Full suffrage has been used by women in Wyoming since 1869 without causing the social fabric of the American Republic to dissolve into chaos, and with such dignity and usefulness that the following resolution was passed in 1893: "Be it resolved by the Second Legislature of the State of Wyoming: That the possession and exercise of suffrage by the women of Wyoming for the past quarter of a century has wrought no harm, and has done great good in many ways; that it has largely aided in banishing crime, pauperism, and vice from this State and that without any violent and oppressive legislation."

It is common knowledge that six sovereign States of our Union now have women voters on the same terms as men; and that five others are at present engaged in active campaigns to wipe out sex-discrimination at the ballot box; and that in every State there is going on an agitation for equality of political rights between men and women unparalleled by any other movement for a social change. It is also known, if not often remembered by the politicians, that the largest petitions ever presented to the National Congress or to the several State legislatures have been those by women for their political enfranchisement. These petitions have been headed by the most distinguished women of the country, not alone noted, like Lucy Stone and Mrs. Cady Stanton, for their interest in this matter, but for their devotion to other concerns of the public weal: such women as Clara Barton, the heroine of the Red Cross work; as Julia Ward Howe, who at her death was pronounced the "leading lady of the land"; as Lydia Maria Child and Harriet Beecher Stowe, known the world around for their services to humanity through the pen; as Frances Willard, best beloved of women leaders in the great organization of the Woman's Christian Temperance Union; as the Doctors Blackwell, who opened the medical profession to women; and, in more recent days, Jane Addams of Hull House, and Mary McDowell of University Settlement; Mrs. Raymond Robbins, leader of the Women's Trade Union movement; President Woolley

and many other college women of distinction; and a
host of social workers and writers and professional
women of every sort. It is also in evidence in the
public press, the magazine and book world, that this
movement for the enfranchisement of women encircles
the globe.[6] Mrs. Carrie Chapman Catt, the world
leader of the movement, as president of the Inter-
national Woman Suffrage Alliance, is going around the
world to meet and help the women of every nation,
even the peoples of the Orient, in this new effort to
"free" sex, "like ethnography, from political application." It is too late in the day, therefore, for any
student of social or political science to ignore the matter; and too late in the day for women who prefer a
"lord" of their own to the justice of the body politic,
and special class privileges to the social conscience, to
stem the tide of this increasing humanizing of government.

In 1821 a "Lady of Distinction," writing to a "Relation shortly after Marriage," urges upon her to
"have the most perfect and implicit faith in the superiority of her husband's judgment and the most absolute obedience to his desires, as giving the greatest
success and most entire satisfaction in her wedded
life," and also "relieving her from a weight of thought
that would be very painful and in no way profitable."
Now, at this late date, we have the Anti-Suffragists de-
siring to be relieved of the political "weight of thought

    [6] See *The Modern Woman's Rights Movement,* Dr. Kaettie Schir-
macher, trans. by C. C. Echhardt, Ph.D.; also, Eugene A. Hecker,
A Short History of Woman's Rights, and Alice Zimmern, *Women's
Suffrage in Many Lands.*

most painful and not profitable." A new proof, if one were needed, of the cramping effect of the past subjection of women. The chief argument of the Anti-Suffragists is that "Government is force" and women neither can nor should have force or exercise it. Let us quote Woodrow Wilson again: "The force which the democratic States embody is not the direct force of a dominant dynasty, nor of a prevalent minority, but the force of an agreeing majority." That force of an agreeing majority when in execution is always delegated force, representatively embodied in chosen agents. It wipes out of existence all actual basing of the suffrage upon physical force. It makes its fundamental appeal to public opinion. It is easily expressed by the choice of men alone, by the choice of women alone, or by the choice of men and women. Whatever class most embodies and best expresses the major opinion of society can fitly choose its agents. The mechanism of the vote is devised expressly for the purpose of enabling "an agreeing majority" to execute its decisions without an appeal to force, physical or military. That women cannot fight, therefore, or should not do so, is, it is obvious, no more a proper disqualification for the suffrage than would be a rule that men over a certain age or under a certain standard of physical strength should be deprived of their vote. By proxy, and by substitute, and by representative, and by chosen officers, the forceful business of the State is now carried on. Some time, if war is not outlawed for good and all, the nations will be wise and humane enough to

choose one pugilist to settle disputes instead of bearing
the economic burden of standing armies, great navies
and millions of idle men! Some such course will have
to be pursued if the common people persist in their
aversion to serving as food for cannon or to support-
ing men who stand idly ready to be such food in case
of war. Sensible people cannot much longer mistake
the true nature of the actual "force" of the modern
democratic State.

The significance of the woman suffrage movement is
twofold: it is a response to the general movement of
democracy toward the individuation of all members
of all previously subjected or submerged classes of society; and it is also a social response to the new demands of citizenship which have followed inevitably
the new and varied increase in the functions of government.

The response to the general movement toward democracy has in less than one hundred years changed
the condition of woman in the chief centres of so-called
Christian civilization from that of "status" to that of
"contract"; from that condition in which the married
woman while her husband lived could not hold property, make a business contract, receive wages in her
own right for her own work even outside the home,
acquire legal power over her own children, act as
guardian for a minor child, her own or another's, or
in any manner acquire the rights of an adult individual
under the law. During her marriage she was, as a
perpetual minor, protected in some manner against
"abuse" (of which in quantity and in quality men and

not women were the judges), but in no sense invested with the rights of an independent adult person.

It was, of course, inevitable that the doctrine of the rights of man should come at last to include the rights of woman, just as it was inevitable that the rights of white men should come at last to include the rights of black and yellow and brown men. The great eighteenth century struggle in human progress was for the recognition of what Charles Sumner called "That equality of rights which is the first of rights." It was for a scheme and practice of political organization which should deny special privileges to any, which should secure fuller liberty and greater justice in all the relations of life to all the different classes of men than had before been known. Although the winning of such measure of democracy in government as we have attained does not bring in the millennium, and has not yet been applied perfectly enough even to men to fully measure its influence for good, any student of history can challenge the most pessimistic observer of American life to furnish an example of any more aristocratic form of government which has resulted in as high an average of physical, mental and moral well-being for the majority of the people as even such a partial democracy as our own. Since Abigail Adams demanded of the framers of the Constitution some recognition of the rights of women in their deliberations, many have seen that there is no argument that can be framed for equality before the law for all classes of men that does not also apply with equal force to both sexes. The woman suffrage movement, however, is only as old as the immortal Seneca Falls meeting of 1848. That was a "Woman's Rights Meeting," and only incidentally and with hesitation pledged to a demand for the ballot; its chief stress being laid upon higher education for women, better industrial conditions, more just professional opportunity for qualified women, and larger social freedom; together with a strong appeal for the legal right of adult women to have and to hold property and to secure that "contract power" that marks the dividing line between a responsible person and a child or an imbecile.[7]

There are two arguments, and only two, that can possibly be brought against the application of the general principles of democracy to law-abiding and mentally competent women: one is that women are not human beings; the other that they are a kind of human being so different from men that general principles of right and wrong proved expedient as a basis of action in the development of men do not apply to them.

Few now subscribe to the ancient belief that "women have neither souls nor minds," but are a "delusion and a snare," invented for practical purposes of life, but not to be counted in when the real life of humanity is under consideration. Are then women of such a different sort of humanity that they do not need individual protection of the law, do not require the mental and moral discipline of freedom and personal responsibility for the development of character, are justly

---

[7] See *Declaration of Rights* of this meeting in *The History of Woman Suffrage*, by Susan B. Anthony and Ida Husted Harper.

and fully provided for through the political arrangements of men, by men and for men, and therefore should be forcibly restrained from complete citizenship? Some, many, seem thus to believe.

The fact that women as a sex, not the favored few of a privileged class but women as a sex, have suffered every form of exploitation at the hands of men and without redress until very recently (an incontestable and easily demonstrated fact, attested by every law book of all Christendom) is sufficient answer to that. The further fact that until women initiated and carried through a great struggle, which although bloodless and pacific on their part, lacked no element of martyrdom, no woman could learn anything but the most elementary scraps of knowledge or develop her vocational power or attain industrial opportunity of any sort commensurate with her needs, is a further proof that women's interests are not fully cared for by men. Women are not so different from men that they can be educated without a chance to go to school, be able to protect themselves against prostitution or ignoble dependence through self-support without the legal right to earn their own living or the legal right to hold and manage their property. Women are not so different from men as to become strong in character without having the discipline of moral responsibility or to become broad-minded and socially serviceable without the opportunity to "learn by doing" the duty of a citizen. Men and women are different, but not so unlike that they can become fully developed human beings in circumstances totally different.

The political democracy fought for in the eighteenth century, and partially obtained, led inevitably to the educational democracy struggled for and partially obtained in the nineteenth century, and most strikingly illustrated in the American public school. The industrial democracy now striving toward realization must follow the sharing of political rights and duties and the educational preparation for good and wise citizenship which we have in such large measure already atttained. The democratizing of the family and of the social life is an inevitable and more and more conscious demand in order that we may have a home in which real and not sham, full-orbed and not partial, democracy may be nurtured and developed. Unless women are made a vital and a responsible part of democracy in education, and democracy in political service, and democracy in industrial organization, they cannot bear and rear fit citizens for a genuine and a matured democratic State. Therefore, unless you repudiate democracy, you must finally include in its range all classes and both sexes.

The second element in the significance in the woman suffrage movement is the social response to the new demands of citizenship made by the new type of State which has been developed in this latter stage of human progress. The family and the Church used to take care of education; industry used to be a personal concern of domestic handicraft. Now all the functions of social order have been differentiated and started on separate and inter-related careers. The Church is not now a legal power; the school has become a function of the State; the new industrial order has necessitated legal protection of the weak and ignorant against the strong and shrewd. The State has gradually, and in these later days with astonishing celerity, taken over not only education, but charity and constructive social effort toward the common welfare. A thousand details of truly spiritual activity, which once were held solely within the sphere of domestic and religious life, are now concerns of government. Government has ceased to be military and static, it has already become social and dynamic. As Woodrow Wilson says, it has large "ministrant as well as constituent functions."

What are the great functions of social service for which "human beings of the mother sex" have been held chiefly responsible since society began? The care, the nurture, the development of child life; the care of the sick, the aged and the infirm; the relief of the unfortunate; the protection and care of the defective; the general ministry of strength to weakness. These are the functions that the modern State has taken over from the home and from the Church. These are the functions the modern State *cannot perform without the direct and varied aid of women.* These are the modern State activities that make the largest army of public employees the teachers, of which ninety per cent. are women; and the next largest army, the caretakers of the sick and insane and unfortunate of every kind, of which at least three-fourths are women. "Yes," the anti-suffragist says, "women should work for society as subordinates through State employment, but they should not become a part of the political power of control and supervision." Then, if that be so, women are degraded from their ancient position in the office of personal ministry; for women, under the old régime of education, had command of the training of all the girls and all the little boys; and, under the old régime in charity, not only did the work, but determined what the work should be.

Now, at last, struck with this fact, the anti-suffragist has taken the monstrously grotesque position that women should fill *"appointive"* positions of supervision and even of control in education and philanthropy, but should never be voted for and vote even in connection with these functions. An office, however, like that of judge or overseer of the poor, which in one State is "appointive," may be in another State "elective." The constant tendency in the United States is for private initiative to create models in the educational and in the philanthropic field; for the appointive powers of executive officers and legislative bodies of a few States to adopt these new models as a part of the State provisions through specially appointed commissioners or boards; and for other States finally to copy the new idea through the regular channels of elective procedure. In private education and philanthropy women are expected to bear more than their full share in support, control and activity. When the State takes over tentatively, as an experiment, some private enterprise, they say, even some of the most conservative anti-suffragists, a governor or mayor might properly take over also a selected woman or two to manage the interest of education and charity thus absorbed.

When, however, the people take over the school for the blind, the custodial home for the idiot, the asylum for the insane, the children's home, the care of the poor, the establishment of the city playground, the manifold enlargements of the public school provision for our cosmopolitan population, at what point does it become unwomanly for women to retain charge of their own special and inherited business? Where does it become improper or useless or unnecessary for women to protect children and youth, and to determine the conditions surrounding their sister women in reformatories and prisons, and to secure right care for the aged and infirm and unfortunate? No living human being can find that point. Thousands of the students of the modern social order and its historical bases in more primitive social organization can prove to any unprejudiced mind that social harm has resulted whenever and wherever these new functions of charity, of education, of social control, of public amusement, and of social effort toward personal welfare, have been taken over by the State from the home and the Church and the domestic shop and factory, without taking over also some recognized power of control by expert women as well as the subordinate service of women in general.

If, then, women are human beings and not so unlike men as to render all human experience useless in the matter of their character development, they, too, as well as men, must be sent to school to political duty and responsibility if they are to serve rightly as mothers and teachers of potential citizens of democratic States.

If, then, the State, as can be easily proved, has taken on in modern times functions of social influence and social service in education, in charity, in protection and development of the personal life, thus undertaking the things which, from the foundation of society, have been peculiarly "woman's sphere," it is as absurd as it is unwise and socially harmful to deprive the State of the service of women in all capacities of both subordinate activity and of trained supervision and control.

This all means on both these grounds that women must be given the duty and the responsibility, as well as the protection and the power of the ballot, in order that there may be established a free, recognized and obvious channel by which the value of women's contribution to the State may be conserved and effectively applied to social welfare.

President Taft's wise appointment of an expert and noble woman as head of the National Children's Bureau is a prophecy as well as a fine accomplishment.

Colby says: "Suffrage means a vote or a participation in government and, specifically, the privilege of voting under a representative Government upon the choice of officers and upon the adoption of fundamental laws." [8] To rank women in general with children, aliens, defectives, and inferior races in defining the terms of suffrage, while yet women are already

---

[8] James F. Colby, *Suffrage*, in Lalor's Political Encyclopædia.

concerned so vitally, so obviously, and in so welcome a manner, in the formation of that public opinion which determines the choice of officers and the adoption of laws, preserves a monstrous anachronism, absurd, if it were not morally injurious to both men and women.

The "moral unity" of the nation is secured, we are told by high authority, when "certain ideas, beliefs and feelings are held by all the members of a given society." Can this moral unity express itself by the suffrage of only one-half the race, only one-half the adult, responsible, law-abiding and intelligent human beings?

As Henri Baudillart well says, "Political societies in so far as they are collective beings, reflect and reproduce everything to be found in the nature of the individuals who compose them. Respect for every right, the practice of every duty, the cultivation of every faculty, the development of human nature, such is the object of society." If this be so, and if the State is the organ by which society controls, disciplines, educates and protects human beings in behalf of these vital social interests, we cannot leave women out of the electorate without social harm.

ANALYSIS OF CONTENTS

I

THE PRIMITIVE WORKING-WOMAN

II

THE ANCIENT AND THE MODERN LADY

V

PATHOLOGY OF WOMEN'S WORK

VII

THE SCHOOL AND THE FEMININE IDEAL

VIII

THE SOCIAL USE OF THE POST-GRADUATE MOTHER

IX

PROBLEMS OF MARRIAGE AND DIVORCE

American Women: Images and Realities
An Arno Press Collection

[Adams, Charles F., editor]. **Correspondence between John Adams and Mercy Warren Relating to Her "History of the American Revolution," July-August, 1807.** With a new appendix of specimen pages from the "History." 1878.

[Arling], Emanie Sachs. **"The Terrible Siren": Victoria Woodhull, (1838-1927).** 1928.

Beard, Mary Ritter. **Woman's Work in Municipalities.** 1915.

Blanc, Madame [Marie Therese de Solms]. **The Condition of Woman in the United States.** 1895.

Bradford, Gamaliel. **Wives.** 1925.

Branagan, Thomas. **The Excellency of the Female Character Vindicated.** 1808.

Breckinridge, Sophonisba P. **Women in the Twentieth Century.** 1933.

Campbell, Helen. **Women Wage-Earners.** 1893.

Coolidge, Mary Roberts. **Why Women Are So.** 1912.

Dall, Caroline H. **The College, the Market, and the Court.** 1867.

[D'Arusmont], Frances Wright. **Life, Letters and Lectures: 1834, 1844.** 1972.

Davis, Almond H. **The Female Preacher, or Memoir of Salome Lincoln.** 1843.

Ellington, George. **The Women of New York.** 1869.

Farnham, Eliza W[oodson]. **Life in Prairie Land.** 1846.

Gage, Matilda Joslyn. **Woman, Church and State.** [1900].

Gilman, Charlotte Perkins. **The Living of Charlotte Perkins Gilman.** 1935.

Groves, Ernest R. **The American Woman.** 1944.

Hale, [Sarah J.] **Manners; or, Happy Homes and Good Society All the Year Round.** 1868.

Higginson, Thomas Wentworth. **Women and the Alphabet.** 1900.

Howe, Julia Ward, editor. **Sex and Education.** 1874.

La Follette, Suzanne. **Concerning Women.** 1926.

Leslie, Eliza . **Miss Leslie's Behaviour Book: A Guide and Manual for Ladies.** 1859.

Livermore, Mary A. **My Story of the War.** 1889.

Logan, Mrs. John A. (Mary S.) **The Part Taken By Women in American History.** 1912.

McGuire, Judith W. (A Lady of Virginia). **Diary of a Southern Refugee, During the War.** 1867.

Mann, Herman . **The Female Review: Life of Deborah Sampson.** 1866.

Meyer, Annie Nathan, editor.**Woman's Work in America.** 1891.

Myerson, Abraham. **The Nervous Housewife.** 1927.

Parsons, Elsie Clews. **The Old-Fashioned Woman.** 1913.

Porter, Sarah Harvey. **The Life and Times of Anne Royall.** 1909.

Pruette, Lorine. **Women and Leisure: A Study of Social Waste.** 1924.

Salmon, Lucy Maynard. **Domestic Service.** 1897.

Sanger, William W. **The History of Prostitution.** 1859.

Smith, Julia E. **Abby Smith and Her Cows.** 1877.

Spencer, Anna Garlin. **Woman's Share in Social Culture.** 1913.

Sprague, William Forrest. **Women and the West.** 1940.

Stanton, Elizabeth Cady. **The Woman's Bible** Parts I and II. 1895/1898.

Stewart, Mrs. Eliza Daniel . **Memories of the Crusade.** 1889.

Todd, John. **Woman's Rights.** 1867. [Dodge, Mary A.] (Gail Hamilton, pseud.) **Woman's Wrongs.** 1868.

Van Rensselaer, Mrs. John King. **The Goede Vrouw of Mana-ha-ta.** 1898.

Velazquez, Loreta Janeta. **The Woman in Battle.** 1876.

Vietor, Agnes C., editor. **A Woman's Quest: The Life of Marie E. Zakrzew-ska, M.D.** 1924.

Woodbury , Helen L. Sumner. **Equal Suffrage.** 1909.

Young, Ann Eliza. **Wife No. 19.** 1875.